# Early Charlie Chaplin

## The Artist as Apprentice at Keystone Studios

James L. Neibaur

THE SCARECROW PRESS, INC.
Lanham • Toronto • Plymouth, UK
2012

Published by Scarecrow Press, Inc.
A wholly owned subsidiary of The Rowman & Littlefield Publishing Group, Inc.
4501 Forbes Boulevard, Suite 200, Lanham, Maryland 20706
http://www.scarecrowpress.com

Estover Road, Plymouth PL6 7PY, United Kingdom

British Library Cataloguing in Publication Information Available

**Library of Congress Cataloging-in-Publication Data**

Neibaur, James L., 1958–
   Early Charlie Chaplin : the artist as apprentice at Keystone Studios / James L. Neibaur.
      p. cm.
   Includes bibliographical references and index.
   ISBN 978-0-8108-8242-3 (hardback : alk. paper) — ISBN 978-0-8108-8243-0 (ebook)
   1.  Chaplin, Charlie, 1889-1977—Criticism and interpretation. 2. Keystone Film Company.  I. Title.
   PN2287.C5N455 2012
   791.4302'8092—dc23                                                       2011041145

∞™ The paper used in this publication meets the minimum requirements of American National Standard for Information Sciences—Permanence of Paper for Printed Library Materials, ANSI/NISO Z39.48-1992.

Printed in the United States of America

For Terri Carpenter's second-grade class during the 2010–2011 school year
at St. Joseph's school in Racine, Wisconsin,
who learned about Charlie Chaplin while I was writing this book
and helped inspire the process.

# Contents

# Acknowledgments

Thanks to the following people for helping with this project. Phil Posner, Doug Sulpy, Ted Okuda, Terri Niemi, Rob Farr, Brent Walker, Ali and Dave Stevenson, Jerry Lewis, the late John McCabe, *Cineaste*, Kino on Video, Looser Than Loose Video, Milestone Film and Video, Blackhawk Films, Wisconsin Center for Film and Theater Research, Senses of Cinema, *Film Quarterly*, *Films in Review*, *Classic Images*, Racine Public Library, SilentComedians.com.

# Introduction

A tremendous amount has been written on the life, art, and career of Charlie Chaplin, and nearly all of his screen work has enjoyed thorough analysis and discussion. However, one area of Chaplin's career that has consistently received little attention and limited appreciation is his tenure at Mack Sennett's Keystone Studios. Chaplin spent his first year in films at Keystone, learning how to translate his established stage act for the intimate movie camera as well as beginning to understand the rudiments of film direction. He appeared in 36 films, nearly half of his 81-film career output. This experience was his apprenticeship, and for all the crudity of the films themselves, especially the earlier ones, the Keystone productions deserve far better assessment than they have heretofore been given.

The limited coverage of Chaplin's Keystone period can be forgiven, at least partially, as the condition of the existing films has often been the roadblock that kept writers from offering as thorough an appreciation as they deserved. Chaplin's stardom rose very rapidly upon the release of his first few Keystone films, he left the studio after only one year, and his stardom continued to increase. His earlier films became even more marketable than before. In an effort to capitalize on the movies he'd made at Keystone, the productions were recut, retitled, and rereleased fairly regularly throughout the silent era (which ran roughly 15 more years). Over time, the endless screenings caused the master prints of these films to wither from overuse. What eventually existed, especially by the dawn of the twenty-first century, was a collection of grainy, flickering images, making an honest critical approach to the work nearly impossible.

The Keystone films are also not under copyright. Thus, they can be freely copied and offered on any home video format with attractive low prices because it is nearly all profit for the distributor. As a result, casual consumers have purchased low-cost Chaplin collections with an interest in seeing what the purported greatest comedian in movie history had to offer. When confronted by the grainy, often imperceptible picture quality, and soundtracks that are hastily added by the distributor, whether or not they match the action, mainstream buyers will dismiss Chaplin, and silent movies in general, as archaic and worthless. In order for Chaplin's Keystone period to enjoy any real appreciation, a complete restoration of the films would be necessary.

Various Chaplin studies have valiantly tried to examine the Keystone era using the available shoddy prints as sources. Gerald McDonald, Michael Conway, and Mark Ricci attempted the first broad filmographic overview with their book *The Films of Charlie Chaplin*. Much later, Ted Okuda and David Maska's *Chaplin at Keystone and Essanay* did a reasonably good job of reviewing these films with acknowledgment to the source material and its limitations. As the latter authors state, a Keystone one-reeler like *The Face on the Bar Room Floor*, for instance, could not have been properly assessed previously because not only were existing prints incomplete, but the scenes were in the incorrect order of sequence.

In late 2010, the British Film Institute completed a years-long restoration process of Chaplin's Keystone productions. It was a daunting process, with several different prints often needed to restore just one 10-minute film. The results, however, were excellent, offering clean, clear images for films that had heretofore not been of particularly good quality since the early twentieth century. DVD distributor Flicker Alley soon made the restored films readily available for purchase in the United States. Thus, it is now time for an accurate assessment and a revisionist approach to the work.

Movies were quite young in 1914, and audiences were thrilled by the idea of a picture that moved. Directors like Edwin S. Porter and D. W. Griffith had already begun making great strides in using editing and different camera angles to propel a narrative. Immigrant audiences, many still limited to the language of their birth country, could enjoy such films as Porter's *The Great Train Robbery* (1903) or Griffith's *Musketeers of Pig Alley* (1911) and respond to the excitement of Porter's crosscutting or Griffith's use of close-ups to define character.

Mack Sennett had worked at Biograph with Griffith before setting up his own studio in 1912 to make comedies. His vision was one of constant frenetic movement, and Sennett often joked that if the films moved quickly enough, nobody would know if they were good or bad. Studies of Chaplin's career may downplay the films he made at Keystone simply because of their basic style. The Keystone films are certainly crude slapstick comedies, but they are also brilliantly executed examples of early motion picture comedy, concentrating on sheer movement within the frame, stunts, and editing techniques to present a rapid rhythm that audiences of the time found exciting. Perhaps audiences could not specifically identify these aspects of production as reasons why the films were so effective, but they realized their own emotional reaction to the productions.

When Chaplin added subtler nuance to his character within the framework of the knockabout Keystone style, it separated his character from the others. It added depth to the simple slapstick gags. Something about him reached across the screen and into the hearts of the audience. He rapidly became the company's biggest star.

Chaplin's Keystone films have often been dismissed in studies as merely a primitive buildup to much greater accomplishment. The frenetic activity and raucous slapstick are sometimes off-putting to those who appreciate the more refined feature-length efforts Chaplin would make years later. Of course a film as deep and fulfilling as *The Circus* (United Artists, 1928) is superior to a one-reeler like *Caught in the Rain*, but to dismiss these important earlier comedies in so cavalier a manner is shortsighted.

During only one year, Charlie Chaplin's talents as a comedian and film-maker grew rapidly, as did his popularity with movie audiences. By the time he left Keystone at the end of 1914, he commanded an enormous salary and complete creative control at the Essanay studios. The concept of the movie star had been defined.

Using the restored Keystone films, this study will examine Chaplin's first 36 screen appearances, arguing with the established idea that they are merely a rough draft for Chaplin's later work. These films represent Chaplin without frills, at his grittiest and most uncompromising. He is completely at the level of his early twentieth-century audiences, especially immigrant audiences. Moviegoers cheered with delight as they watched Charlie respond to authority with a kick in the backside and approach women with a flirtatious tip of his hat. Often feeling repressed in a new land, immigrant audiences saw one of their own defying all structure and brashly going his own way on his own terms. It caused them to laugh and rejoice. Along with all of this, Chaplin's character depth and use of subtle nuance effectively reinvented the way acting in movies was presented. And he did it all in the course of only one year.

# CHAPTER 1

# Charlie Chaplin's Early Years

Before embarking on a film career that helped define the language of motion picture comedy, Charlie Chaplin was already a formidable name in England's music halls as a member of Fred Karno's acting troupe.

Charles Spencer Chaplin was always said to have been born in London, England, on April 16, 1889. However, as recently as 2011, a letter Chaplin had received in the 1970s was discovered which indicated that he was actually born in a gypsy caravan at Black Patch Park in Smethwick, Staffordshire. His father, Charles Spencer Chaplin Sr., and his mother, Hannah, were both singers. His mother, whose stage name was Lily Harley, was known for light opera. His father was an amusing performer of novelty songs. Charlie's parents separated when he was three years old. His father was an alcoholic who died from cirrhosis of the liver when Charlie was 11, and his mother suffered from a series of mental and emotional problems that required frequent stays in an asylum. Charlie and his older half-brother, Sydney, had to fend for themselves as children on the streets of London. Each inherited natural talents from their parents and soon became involved in stage productions as singers and dancers.

After a successful engagement in the legitimate theater, Charlie Chaplin joined the Karno troupe in 1908, quickly becoming its most popular performer. The Karno troupe toured the United States during 1910–1912. Chaplin's most popular act was *A Night in an English Music Hall*, featuring him as a drunken lout in the audience, interrupting the other acts and causing a comic ruckus (Chaplin would later reinvent this act on film with *A Night in the Show*, Essanay, 1916). An immediate hit with American audiences, Chaplin returned to England for only five months and was back in America again in 1912, when he was offered a motion picture contract. Movie producer Mack Sennett was in the audience for one of the Karno troupe's performances and thought Chaplin would

1

*Charles Chaplin, sans makeup.*

be a good fit at his newly established Keystone Studios, where they specialized in the sort of roughhouse slapstick Chaplin performed on stage.

Chaplin had seen motion pictures, and while he was intrigued with the idea of preserving comedy on film, he never entertained a serious interest in doing so. But now, confronted with an offer by the head of a studio that specialized in comedy film production, Chaplin felt the opportunity was worth exploring. He agreed to begin making films for Sennett upon completing his stage commitments in November 1913. Some of the incentive was the doubling of his current pay. His initial salary would be $150 per week, which would increase to $175 as his popularity grew, and would include a $25 bonus once he began directing his own films.

Neither Sennett nor Chaplin was quite prepared for how quickly his star would rise, how popular he would become with period moviegoers, and the higher level at which his comedies would be applauded over other stars. It could not be perceived that the comedies he was about to make at Keystone would be the catalyst for a significant motion picture career, or that a character he would create and begin to develop at the studio would become among the most iconic images in the history of entertainment.

Sennett could certainly see that Chaplin was creative and skilled, that he could command an audience, and that he was funny in the sort of knockabout manner that befit Sennett's own comic vision. Chaplin was perhaps more in the dark as to how things would progress in films. He could not pass up the money, and he was fascinated by the idea of filming his performances. A young man filled with comic ideas, Chaplin was also unaware of the set way in which things were done at Keystone, and that deviating from this method could cause some friction. Unaware of how films were made, Chaplin could not have realized that someone else would be directing how he would perform.

Karno encouraged creativity. So did Sennett. But in film production, repeated takes cost money, eating into the budget, and Sennett could not allow his comedians to hamper profits in such a manner. Chaplin would be forced to learn on the job how to be creative within the parameters of filming at Keystone. Despite some dustups along the way, within the course of a year, Chaplin established his stardom, his screen character, and his prowess as a director to a level unseen in the new film medium.

# CHAPTER 2

# Mack Sennett and the Keystone Studios

Mack Sennett was originally a stage actor, migrating to the new medium of film shortly after the turn of the century. Employed at the Biograph studios, Sennett had a knack for comedy, but oddly enough, his mentor was David Wark (D.W.) Griffith, whose specialty was melodrama. Griffith would very quickly become one of the most significant pioneer filmmakers, using such cinematic techniques as crosscut editing and close-ups to propel the narrative and enhance the performances. Later achievements by Griffith, including the feature-length epics *The Birth of a Nation* (1915) and *Intolerance* (1916), would be responsible for enormous advances in cinematic art. Sennett learned a great deal from Griffith, especially in regard to movement within the frame and creating a discernible rhythm with editing. Fascinated by basic plot structures and the possibility to use frenetic activity and broad gestures to burlesque standard situations, Sennett eventually investigated comedy film direction's possibilities.

In 1912, Mack Sennett received financial backing from Adam Kessel and Charles Bauman of the New York Motion Picture Company to start his own Keystone Studios. With an eye for establishing his first productions with proven talent, Sennett hired directors Henry Lehrman and George Nichols from Biograph, along with actors Ford Sterling and Mabel Normand. Fred Mace, another early Keystone performer, would join them when the studio relocated from Fort Lee, New Jersey, to Edendale, California, in August 1912.

Sennett's ideas for comedy were chiefly centered around raucous slapstick, and he specifically hired performers who could perform according to his vision. Some of Sennett's farces are based on some of the Biograph melodramas he'd witnessed being filmed. Mabel Normand was very attractive, and in one of her earliest Keystone films, *The Water Nymph* (1912), she appears as a diver in a bathing suit. While a one-piece suit exposing the arms and legs seems quite conservative in the twenty-first century, it was considered daring and suggestive during the early part of the twentieth century, only increasing the film's popularity. Sennett, who directed as well as acted in this film, noticed the reaction Mabel in a swimsuit received from moviegoers, and he eventually put together a group of attractive women known as the Mack Sennett Bathing Beauties. Sennett also put together a group of bumbling policemen, known as the Keystone Cops, beginning with the film *Hoffmeyer's Legacy* (1912).

By 1913, the Keystone films were already quite popular with moviegoing audiences. Unlike the legitimate theater, motion pictures were considered

*Mack Sennett.*

entertainment for the lower classes. Most of the moviegoing audiences were immigrants, and they responded merrily to, say, Ford Sterling's stereotyped Dutch or German characterizations. Often confronted by authority in their daily lives, these moviegoers laughed and cheered at the bumbling nature of the Keystone Cops, which reduced law enforcement to a series of wild pratfalls.

When Mack Sennett hired Charlie Chaplin at the end of 1913, he didn't have any specific plans for the English stage comedian. He just realized, based on having seen his act, that Chaplin had the talent for knockabout comedy, and the enthusiasm to perform it well. However, Sennett did not have a set character for Chaplin to play. When assessing what Sennett was doing at Keystone at the time he hired Chaplin, it is difficult to imagine that this English newcomer would revolutionize the studio's method and eventually the entire concept of comedy in cinema.

This is not to dismiss what Sennett had already established prior to Chaplin's arrival at the studio. There is a real brilliance to the way Sennett could create a veritable alternate universe with his comedies, filled with grotesque characters, bewildered innocents, bumbling authority figures, and any number of ethnic or physical stereotypes (Roscoe Arbuckle, for instance, was dubbed Fatty by Sennett; it is a nickname the actor despised for the rest of his life). There is equal brilliance to the way the Keystone comedies seemed wild and uncontrolled when, in fact, the fast pace and quick edits created a discernible rhythm. Audiences would laugh and cheer loudly throughout each production, making Sennett's comedies the most popular of their time. There were no cast lists in the credits of these films, nor were any actor names mentioned in newspaper ads. Occasionally actor or character names were part of the title, such as *Mabel's Lovers* (1912) or *Fatty's Day Off* (1913), but generally audiences were unaware of such names as Ford Sterling or Fred Mace, despite being quite familiar with their work.

The Keystone films were immediately popular and increased in popularity very rapidly. When a Keystone comedy was advertised at a local theater, moviegoers would sometimes attend the show to see the one-reel production and leave before the feature attraction unspooled. Sennett's very special universe proved to be a fun, raucous place where the lower classes could escape from the doldrums of everyday life.

By the end of 1913, when Sennett saw Chaplin perform on stage, the Keystone studios were looking for new talent. Fred Mace had left the studio, replaced by stage comic Roscoe Arbuckle. Arbuckle's boyish innocence within the requisite slapstick situations added another dimension to the comedies that had been relying solely on the broadest gestures and more blatant facial expressions. There was also a rumor that Sennett's biggest star, Ford Sterling, was seeking employment elsewhere. Sennett hoped that Chaplin might be an effective replacement for Sterling.

*Ford Sterling was Keystone's first big star.*

Upon accepting Sennett's proposal to appear in movies, Chaplin had no aspirations other than satisfying his own curiosity. He did not initially want to direct films and wasn't prepared with a specific character to play. Sennett felt that simply placing the newcomer in a typical slapstick one-reeler would be sufficient. Of course this did not always work well with stage-trained actors. Arbuckle, for instance, had a habit of looking at Sennett as he shouted instructions from the director chair, costing the budget-minded Sennett more production money. Arbuckle was nearly fired, but Mabel Normand intervened and insisted Sennett keep him.

Chaplin's instincts kept him from making the same mistake as Arbuckle when he began his first film, *Making a Living* (1914), which was being directed by Henry Lehrman. However, Chaplin was a man of ideas and used to having creative control, so he made suggestions to Lehrman for gags and business that might enhance the production. He still did not imagine himself as a director but thought that, as the film's star, he had the right to improvise, and even to suggest bits of business to enhance the performance of his supporting players. This made Lehrman particularly suspicious of the English newcomer, despite his popularity overseas. Years later, in a 1923 interview in Samuel Goldwyn's *Behind the Screen*, Mabel Normand would recall that she was frequently approached on the set by other actors asking, "Do you find that Chaplin fellow funny?" Chaplin's introduction to the medium he was about to redefine was quite inauspicious.

In many of his earlier films, Chaplin would be expected to simply extend his noted drunk act from the Karno troupe, Sennett believing that this was the comedian's established character and that he'd be most comfortable within its parameters. While Chaplin comfortably accepted whatever role he was expected to play in these earlier Keystone productions, he did not respond like a novice, despite his lack of cinematic experience. Years of headlining in a popular acting troupe caused Chaplin to have some self-respect for his own accomplishments, even though directors like Lehrman and George Nichols, another Biograph veteran, dismissed this experience as without any connection to movie acting. Chaplin, in what he believed was an effort to make a better overall picture, would offer suggestions to the director and to supporting players, while adding gags and ideas not already in the scenario outline. While most Keystone comics were prone to such improvisation, Chaplin's ideas were more intricate and took up more time to execute. Since Sennett was extremely budget minded, his closest directorial associates such as Lehrman and Nichols would insist Chaplin's ideas took up too much time, and both complained to Sennett that Chaplin was difficult. His popularity was enormous, however, and Chaplin soon realized his worth to the studio. Eventually, he began directing his own films, and his supervisory power increased to full creative control by the end of his Keystone tenure.

However, despite this opportunity, Chaplin needed more time to experiment with his headier ideas. Sennett did not approve of the need for several retakes (a big expense for the studio), while Chaplin was a perfectionist who never felt the scene was worth printing after only one or two takes. It is chiefly for this reason that Chaplin only lasted at Keystone for a year.

But as we look over the level at which Chaplin's comedies began at the studio, and their aesthetic superiority by the time he left (less than a year later), it is impressive how much Chaplin learned about the filmmaking process, and how important this period was to all of his later classics.

There is nothing wrong with simply being funny. And the Keystone lot was filled with people who had oddly shaped bodies or elastic faces, were capable of applying garish makeup for effect, and could mug, grimace, flip, and tumble in a manner that offered a visceral delight for uncritical audiences. Beneath all of this, there is a real structure and perspective to the films, with topical parody, satire, and many groundbreaking discoveries as to how the primitive technology of cinema in the 1910s could exhibit fantasy and surrealism. But at the very moment he stepped onto a movie screen, Charlie Chaplin had that clichéd "certain something" quality that attracted him to audiences at a higher, or perhaps deeper, level than even such popular Keystone stars as Ford Sterling, Roscoe Arbuckle, and Mabel Normand. His first film for Sennett was not a particularly good movie by Keystone's own standards, important only as being Charlie Chaplin's movie debut. But even in an unsuitable role and a weak movie, Chaplin somehow stood out. Even the critics noticed immediately.

There was a great deal of kismet in how Chaplin came to Keystone, how he ended up with the Little Tramp character, and how he was able to exhibit the sort of character that captured audiences in a way that remains as baffling as it is impressive today in the twenty-first century.

# CHAPTER 3

# Chaplin's Keystone Films

Biographies and studies of Chaplin films have been a standard part of literature on cinema since the comedian's initial popularity. Because of poor quality film prints and no cast listings, it has been difficult to cite complete credits for Chaplin's films. Online sources, such as the Internet Movie Database, often repeat errors from other books. The clarity of the recent Keystone restorations has now allowed for the informed viewer to recognize uncredited performers. Brent Walker's exhaustive, thorough book on Mack Sennett's films, *Mack Sennett's Fun Factory*, offers the most complete list of credits for all of the Sennett productions, correcting the errors of previous filmographies.

It should be noted that in most Keystone comedies, actors with smaller roles will often play more than one part. Hence, one will sometimes see cast and character identification such as "Chester Conklin (Policeman, Bum)," as found in the entry for *Making a Living*.

Along with accurate credits, the subsequent chapters on Chaplin's Keystone films will assess each entry as to its significance in the development of his work as a comedian and filmmaker. In some cases, the Keystone films were released in the order that they were made. However in the case of *Mabel's Strange Predicament* and *Kid Auto Races at Venice, Cal.*, the films were released in reverse order (some say *Kid Auto Races* was shot during a break in filming *Mabel's Strange Predicament*). Due to this case in particular, each film is assessed in the order of release. *Kid Auto Races* was moviegoers' first look at Chaplin's tramp, one of the chief reasons for that film's importance.

One of the last of these Chaplin films is the feature *Tillie's Punctured Romance*, which was released in December 1914 but filmed much earlier (Chaplin produced several short films while in production on *Tillie*, as did other actors appearing in this ambitious project). The final Charlie Chaplin short comedy produced at Keystone, *Getting Acquainted*, was not the last to be released. The

*The Keystone Studios.*

last Chaplin Keystone release was the two-reeler *His Prehistoric Past*. In fact, some newspaper ads for this final Chaplin Keystone used a publicity photo of Chaplin that was clearly marked as having come from the Essanay studios where Chaplin was employed upon leaving Keystone.

While the usual approach is to assess the films in order of production, the method of listing and assessing the Chaplin Keystones in order of release allows for the most accurate representation of Chaplin's growth and development as a comedian and filmmaker.

# CHAPTER 4

# *Making a Living*

**Alternate titles:** *A Busted Johnny; Troubles; Doing His Best; Take My Picture*

Running time: One Reel
Filmed December 17, 1913–January 9, 1914
Released February 2, 1914

**Credits**
Directed by Henry Lehrman
Produced by Mack Sennett
Written by Reed Heustis
Cinematography by Enrique Juan Vallejo

**Cast**
Charlie Chaplin (Would-Be Reporter), Virginia Kirtley (Daughter), Alice Davenport (Mother), Henry Lehrman (Reporter), Minta Durfee (Woman), Chester Conklin (Policeman, Bum), Emma Clifton (Jealous Husband's Wife), Billy Gilbert (Jealous Husband), Charles Inslee (Newspaper Editor), Eddie Nolan (Cop at Apartment Steps), Beverly Griffith (Seated Man Talking to Editor), Grover Ligon (Seated Bald Man in Newspaper Back Office), Edgar Kennedy (Car Wreck Bystander in Striped Shirt)

The fact that *Making a Living* represents Charlie Chaplin's first appearance in a motion picture automatically makes it a movie milestone. However, unlike the debut of Buster Keaton, whose first screen appearance was a triumphantly hilarious turn in Roscoe Arbuckle's *The Butcher Boy* (1917), Chaplin's film debut is more of a curiosity.

*Making a Living* features Charlie as a fast-talking street sharp man. He is bedecked in a frock coat and sports a monocle and a drooping mustache. A top hat rests on his head. He does have a cane. Charlie's initial appearance shows him attempting to con money out of a passerby (Henry Lehrman), who turns out to be a newspaper reporter. However, when he starts to flirt with the reporter's girl (Virginia Kirtley), a brawl ensues. Later, when the reporter takes a photo of

*Chaplin as a wily city slicker in his film debut.*

a car crash, Charlie steals the camera, runs to the newspaper office, and claims the shot as his own.

*Making a Living* is a typically fast-paced Keystone comedy, and despite appearing in his first film with a character unlike that which he'd later establish, Chaplin's performance does stand out. Other studies have opined that the lack of charisma from Lehrman, Kirtley, and others in the cast is what causes Chaplin to be so noticeable. However, much of the cast is composed of the same Keystone stalwarts who appear in Chaplin's later efforts at the studio. Viewing a film like *Making a Living* with an understanding of what Chaplin would later accomplish may sometimes influence attempts to appreciate the film. If our perspective is altered to match one seeing the comedian for the first time, we may have a greater appreciation for what he accomplished in his screen debut.

While engaging in the florid gestures that were a natural part of the Keystone comedies (and probably necessary on stage, where broader movement was needed for the audience in the back row), Chaplin appears to already understand the intimacy of performing for the movie camera. In his first encounter with the reporter, Charlie is smiling, his eyes are twinkling, and his right hand is resting in his pocket as his left hand jauntily twirls a cane. Charlie appears confident and relaxed. He cleverly opens the conversation by merrily admiring the reporter's ring, and then deftly segues into an ersatz tale of woe, having warmed up his victim. No longer relaxed, Charlie now tightens his stance, rests his hand on his cheek, ventures forward as he speaks as if sharing something embarrassing. As his listener takes his eyes off Charlie, turning to ponder what is being said, Charlie's expression changes. He looks askance at the reporter, wondering whether he is indeed falling for the ruse. Pulling out all the stops, Charlie then rests his hands on his stomach, pulls the inside of the fabric from his pants pocket to reveal it being empty. He is broke, and he is hungry.

If we compare Charlie's pantomime with the reporter's reaction, it is clear that Chaplin is a better performer than Lehrman. While Lehrman does little more than listen, without altering his steady reaction, Chaplin expresses a series of subtle mannerisms that not only effectively convey what he is saying but also make him oddly likable. He is a sharp-dressed con man, but to audiences of 1914, he is fiendishly clever and audacious. And his ruse nets the desired re-

*The city slicker has a way with the ladies, Virginia Kirtley (left) and Alice Davenport.*

sponse. This sort of subtle acting was not usually a general part of the Keystone method.

When flirting with the girl, Charlie engages in the blatantly coy, grinning, hat-tipping, hand-kissing gestures for which Keystone comedians were noted. Charlie takes it one step further by not only flirting with the girl, but also her mother (Alice Davenport), endearing himself more solidly. When the reporter comes by, the girl expresses no interest in the bouquet he is holding. When he and Charlie see each other, a slapstick brawl ensues. As Lehrman and Chaplin perform a slapstick battle, the diversity in styles is evident. Lehrman employs over-the-top Keystone gags like walloping Charlie with his own cane. Chaplin has Charlie use the cane to fend off his adversary by deftly poking it into his stomach and keeping him at length.

After the brawl, the spurned reporter wanders off and witnesses the car crash. In a funny dig at newspaper reporters being more interested in the story than the circumstance, he crouches down and interviews the victim before offering to help free him from the wreckage.

Despite his tenure under D. W. Griffith, Mack Sennett did little in the way of directing a film. Where Griffith liked to experiment with angles, close-ups, and other methods that would define his vision, Sennett invariably allowed the action within the frame to be the absolute focal point. Henry Lehrman's approach is in this same manner, as Sennett's directorial perspective would

*A neat tracking shot shows the city slicker on the run.*

essentially permeate most standard Keystone productions. Lehrman would eventually do more as a director; however, *Making a Living* is, like most Keystone productions, interesting due to the movement within the frame. The car crash is rather spectacular, with an automobile seen flipping down a mountain until it lands in a shambles. Once Charlie steals the reporter's camera, planning to take credit for the pics, the shot of him running down the street is perhaps the best framed one in the picture. Charlie runs toward a camera in a tracking shot that reveals people and cable-car tracks in the background. With this shot, Lehrman displays an understanding of mise-en-scène, as his subsequent shot of himself running in pursuit of Charlie is also enhanced by the business in the background (a bigger crowd milling about, and some automobiles). That the film concludes when Charlie and the reporter end up on the front grill of an oncoming cable car is a fitting conclusion.

In an era when so little of silent cinema survives, it is gratifying that a milestone like *Making a Living* is readily accessible. It may be confusing for some who are familiar with Chaplin's later classics and cannot warm up to this very different character in a much cruder production. However, this film's significance as Charlie Chaplin's first screen appearance cannot be overstated. There are other factors that make this curious film interesting. The shots of the reporter's job site, with typesetting and printing presses active and visible on screen, for instance, make the film's status as a cultural artifact more substantial.

When placed in the context of its own time, *Making a Living* would seem to be a run-of-the-mill Keystone product, as period viewers would not realize the central comedian in the picture would eventually be noted as the single most important figure in comedy movies. However, the February 1914 issue of *The Moving Picture World* stated in a review:

> The clever player who takes the role of the nervy and very nifty sharper in this picture is a comedian of the first water, who acts like one of Nature's own naturals. It is so full of action that it is indescribable, but so much of it is fresh and unexpected fun that a laugh will be going all the time almost. It is foolish-funny stuff that will make even the sober-minded laugh, but people out for an evening's good time will howl.

Hence, Chaplin's inauspicious debut was still effective enough to cause notice among period critics. The "certain something" was already evident.

Chaplin himself was quite dissatisfied with this film, and he remained bitter as late as when he penned his autobiography 50 years later. In *My Autobiography*, he recalled having improvised many funny bits of business that ended up being edited from the final print. Apparently director Lehrman, already a veteran of the fledgling movie industry, found the newcomer's suggestions off-putting.

Reportedly dismissive of Chaplin's status as a stage comedian, Lehrman would have assumed an auteurist's level of control. Chaplin may not yet have had a cinematic vision, but he did understand improvisational comedy, and it is unfortunate whatever business he improvised was jettisoned and no longer survives.

Lehrman and Chaplin played adversaries on screen, and after this project they were not at all fond of each other in real life either. Chaplin considered himself a veteran of comedy performance and Lehrman merely someone who had begun working in a new medium a few short years earlier. Lehrman thought of himself as a veteran of motion pictures and Chaplin as a newcomer. The idea that someone from England could come to America and begin making suggestions in his very first film to a director who had been helming movies for years was something the egotistical Lehrman found repugnant.

Chaplin realized with this first film that in order to be more than just a cog in a very large moviemaking machine, he would have to establish a more absolute central character in his next film. Always extremely serious about his work, Chaplin pondered the various possibilities he could use in an effort to do work with which he could be proud and not ruffle too many feathers. Chagrined at having to take direction from one who did not appreciate the sort of comedy ideas that made him successful on the London stage, Chaplin knew that in order to continue enjoying the salary that was at a higher level than anything he'd encountered previously (unlike the experience of Buster Keaton, who actually took a severe cut in pay to go from stage to films), he would have to get his ideas used without much conflict. Having received reports from one of his veteran directors that the newcomer was "difficult," Sennett had his eye on the Englishman.

# CHAPTER 5

# *Kid Auto Races at Venice, Cal.*

**Alternate titles:** *The Pest; Kid Auto Races*

Running Time: Split Reel (half of one reel, approximately six minutes)
Included on the same reel as the film *Olives and Their Oil*
Filmed January 1, 1914
Released February 7, 1914

**Credits**
Directed by Henry Lehrman
Screenplay by Reed Heustis
Cinematography by Frank D. Williams

**Cast**
Charlie Chaplin (Tramp), Henry Lehrman (Director)

*Kid Auto Races at Venice, Cal.* is an excellent example of Mack Sennett's penchant for sending a film crew to an actual event and using it as a backdrop for an improvised comedy film. When one sees Chaplin's Little Tramp enter the scene, one can imagine how galvanizing this image must have been for audiences of 1914. As an actual soapbox race takes place, and onlookers are enjoying the event, the tramp waddles in and out of the camera range of newsreel photographers. The newsreel director (Henry Lehrman) shoves him out of the way, but the tramp continues to walk in front of the lens and stand in different poses. Movie audiences of the time likely reacted in the same manner as those in the auto race audience. First they are confused, then bemused, then soon giggling and laughing at the silly man's antics. With the recent British Film Institute restoration, *Kid Auto Races at Venice, Cal.* allows us to clearly see the faces of the onlookers in the background. We can actually witness an audience seeing Charlie Chaplin for the first time and gauge their reactions.

The Little Tramp character was Chaplin's own creation. He recalled that, in his effort to develop a substantial character that would stand out beyond the eye-bulging, arm-flailing performances on the Keystone lot, he searched the costume department to put together a costume of conflicting pieces. The hat and coat are too small, the pants and shoes are too big, the mustache is trimmed down to accent rather than obscure his facial expressions. Once he donned the entire outfit and makeup, he worked on the character's mannerisms and nuance.

This character was first explored in *Mabel's Strange Predicament*, which began filming prior to *Kid Auto Races* but was released afterward. After years of investigation by various film scholars, the best determination is that a break in filming *Mabel's Strange Predicament* resulted in Chaplin working on *Kid Auto Races* in the interim. Thus *Mabel's Strange Predicament* began filming, *Kid Auto Races* was shot during a brief hiatus during that production, and *Mabel's Strange Predicament* then finished production upon completion of the auto race comedy. Hence, it was *Kid Auto Races* that introduced the iconic Little Tramp character to audiences.

Charlie's initial appearance is at the center of the frame, facing the camera filming him, and responding as though the cameraman is pointing out that he is in the way of the action. He appears to be fascinated by the concept of being filmed (it is probably a natural reaction among the mainstream during the early days of moving pictures), and from that point attempts to insert himself into every shot.

*Cinematographer Frank D. Williams and director Henry Lehrman flank Chaplin's Little Tramp.*

As the camera pans the audience, it finds Charlie, who gets up and moves along with the panning camera in order to keep himself within the frame. When it reaches the point where the camera has returned to the action on the track, the newsreel director shoves him away. As Charlie continues to find his way on camera, the newsreel director shoves him more forcefully, often knocking him down (due to his slapstick stage background, Chaplin could already take an effective Keystone pratfall).

With no real plot structure to follow, Lehrman has no choice but to allow Chaplin to improvise. So we have Charlie gaily strutting about, striking a statuesque pose, making faces, twirling his cane, even standing idly as if watching the action without realizing the camera is nearby. And yet despite this redundant approach, the various methods that Charlie uses to get on camera are just different enough to make the film consistently amusing, even today.

For audiences of 1914, there was a headier reason for the positive response. Charlie the tramp was similar to the early twentieth-century Americans, many of them immigrants, that made up the majority of theater audiences: curious, attempting to find a way into the action, and curtly shoved aside. He remains undaunted throughout the very short film, and his cleverness in finding various ways to get in front of the action and be noticed is its greatest point. Audiences saw someone to whom they could relate, someone continuing to confront authority and keep at the center of attention. It is a small-scale, but nevertheless triumphant exercise in the underdog overpowering the overlord. This would be the basis of many subsequent Chaplin films, so it is interesting to find that its genesis appears in his third movie.

It is also worth noting that Henry Lehrman's direction of this brief, split-reel film seems to explore various shots more so than in the longer and more elaborate *Making a Living*. Chaplin is seen in long and medium shots, entering from either side of the frame. It is also interesting that Lehrman, playing the newsreel director, is sometimes seen on camera with a cameraman, sometimes not. Charlie will react to the camera on screen or, at times, will react directly toward the camera filming this production, facing the viewing audience. It is an interesting correlation of cinematographic ideas and likely made the film that much more effective with period moviegoers, and it offers another good example of Lehrman's directorial vision.

Despite being filmed after Chaplin had already shot the initial scenes for *Mabel's Strange Predicament*, *Kid Auto Races* is really little more than an extended screen test. However, unlike his debut *Making a Living*, this film effectively sets the tone for what is to come.

The February 1914 issue of *The Cinema* praised the six-minute subject: "*Kid Auto Races* struck us as about the funniest film we have ever seen. Chaplin is a born screen comedian; he does things we have never seen on a screen before."

# CHAPTER 6

# Mabel's Strange Predicament

**Alternate title: *A Hotel Mixup***

Running Time: One Reel
Filmed January 6, 1914–January 12, 1914
Released February 9, 1914

**Credits**
Directed by Mabel Normand
Screenplay by Reed Heustis
Cinematography by H. F. Koenekamp

**Cast**
Mabel Normand (Mabel), Charlie Chaplin (Drunk), Chester Conklin (Husband), Alice Davenport (Wife), Harry McCoy (Mabel's Admirer), Al St. John, Billy Gilbert (Bellhops), Bill Hauber (Clean Shaven Man in Lobby, Mustachioed Guest in Pajamas), Frank Cooley (Hotel Manager)

Begun after *Making a Living* but released after *Kid Auto Races at Venice, Cal.*, *Mabel's Strange Predicament* is a typical Keystone bedroom farce that is important in Chaplin's initial development. It is the first film in which Chaplin acted in his tramp costume. It is also his first time being directed by Mabel Normand, with whom he would eventually clash on creative ideas, but of whom he would remain fond until her early death. (For more information on Normand or any of the other players in the Keystone films, refer to appendix A.)

One of the important factors regarding *Mabel's Strange Predicament* is how Normand allowed Chaplin enough creative freedom to establish his presence. He chose to use elements of the drunken lout he played in his music hall days and incorporate them into the new character he was developing for cinema. Chaplin devised his own makeup and costume for this character, and as he states in *My Autobiography*: "I had no idea of the character. But the moment I was dressed, the clothes and the makeup made me feel the person he was. I began to know him, and by the time I walked on to the stage, he was fully born."

The obligatory fast and frenetic pacing of the comedy does not obliterate Chaplin's subtle nuance. Within the structure of Normand's film, Chaplin is clearly investigating possibilities for his own character's dominance, and Normand appears to be allowing the scene stealing with full awareness.

*Mabel's Strange Predicament* features Charlie as an annoying drunk who aggressively flirts with women in a hotel lobby. One of these women is Mabel, who rebuffs the drunken Charlie's advances with greater passion than any of the others. This only increases Charlie's interest. Later, when a pajama-clad Mabel is locked out of her room, she hides in the room across the hall, where Chester (Chester Conklin) lives. Mabel is eventually discovered under Chester's bed by her boyfriend (Harry McCoy) and by Chester's wife (Alice Davenport). And while Charlie does not figure specifically in the central plot of the film, cutaways to his exploits in the lobby and his being brought into the action upstairs (even if only peripherally) cause him to stand out.

It is interesting to see how the opening scenes in *Mabel's Strange Predicament* allow Charlie to evolve into his drunken character. His flirtations are initially more tentative, and the subsequent rejections leave him a bit forlorn. However, once he takes a few swigs from a bottle concealed on his person, he becomes more aggressive. While Normand's direction allows for some cutaways to her story (she is, after all, the top-billed star), the camera lingers for some time on Charlie in the lobby, getting drunker and more aggressive. Soon he is sloppy, staggering, and belligerent. When a pretty young woman turns up her nose, he slides off his chair and falls to the floor, sticking his foot in a nearby spittoon.

Despite having less directorial experience than Henry Lehrman, Mabel Normand sets up her shots more cleverly. Her cutaway from herself playing ball with the dog in her room to the drunkenly amorous Charlie following a woman up the stairs from the lobby is a perfect transition for Charlie to find Mabel, in pajamas, trying to get back into her room. She ends up in Chester's apartment across the hall while trying to avoid Charlie's aggressive advances. Undaunted, Charlie brazenly enters Chester's room and starts looking for Mabel, who is hiding under the bed. Chester looks on with bemusement as this stranger searches through his bureau drawers and other such ridiculous places in an effort to find Mabel.

Eventually Chester's wife and Mabel's boyfriend are in the same room. Cutting from a medium shot of Chester, his wife, and Mabel's boyfriend to a close-up of Mabel under the bed, fidgeting with a wide-eyed expression of innocence and embarrassment, Normand uses crosscut editing to further establish a greater understanding of cinematic presentation than Lehrman does. Despite Chaplin's peripheral status in the plot, she also allows him to remain a focal

*Charlie intrudes upon Mabel Normand.*

point throughout the reel. The ending is a typically convenient Keystone wrap-up. Mabel and her boyfriend make up at the end, but poor Chester, who is completely innocent in all matters, gets a barrage of slaps from his unforgiving wife. Charlie, meanwhile, leaves the scene completely, staggering away once he realizes Mabel is quite firmly in a relationship.

Normand's allowing Chaplin to improvise freely does a great deal for her film, which rises above its standard bedroom farce trappings and offers another element to the comedy. In fact, the veteran Keystone players in the cast, including the popular Normand, are given less attention in the period criticism. The February issue of *Exhibitor's Mail* stated:

> The Keystone Company never made a better contract than when they signed on Chas. Chaplin, the Karno performer. It is not every variety artiste who possesses the ability to act for the camera. Chaplin not only shows that talent; he shows it to a degree which raises him at once to the status of a star performer. We do not often indulge in prophecy, but we do not think we are taking a great risk in prophesying that in six months Chaplin will rank as one of the most popular screen comedians in the world.

Mabel Normand's charm and charisma are quite evident in this film as much as in any of her other performances. But Chaplin's drunk act is the axis of the film. It remains in the center, the funniest and most interesting portion of the picture. There has been some discussion in other studies that Chaplin may have been placed in this film as an afterthought to punch it up with gags. As a result, Sennett allowed him to create his own costume and character, while Normand granted him free rein to improvise. Chaplin's drunk, a character at which he specialized, was a safe choice that works effectively. Searching through bureau drawers in Chester's room, leaning against a woman's derriere as she stands near where he is seated, evolving into the drunken character with gradually more forceful behavior, Chaplin is certainly given far greater opportunity to improvise than Lehrman allowed him on *Making a Living*. Even Sennett, in later years, stated that he found the scenes in the lobby very funny, and that Chaplin's comic abilities were fully realized with this film.

Chaplin recalled in his autobiography:

> The secret of Mack Sennett's success was his enthusiasm. He was a great audience and laughed genuinely at what he thought funny. He stood and giggled until his body began to shake. This encouraged me and I began to explain the character: You know this fellow is many-sided; a tramp, a gentleman, a poet, a dreamer, a lonely fellow, always hopeful of romance and adventure. He would have you believe he is a scientist, a musician, a duke, a polo player. However, he is not above picking up cigarette butts or robbing a baby of its candy. And, of course, if the occasion warrants it, he will kick a lady in the rear—but only in extreme anger.

Chaplin and Normand would later clash on another film, then connect as friends thereafter. In *Mabel's Strange Predicament*, Chaplin's first film with Normand, they share little screen time together, but the introduction to these two brilliant comic minds is the portent of work they would do in later films like *Caught in a Cabaret* (under Normand's direction) and *His Trysting Places* (under Chaplin's) that would allow each to fully realize the creative ideas of the other. Normand would become far more benevolent, allowing Chaplin more creative input than the comedian would often allow on his own films, but their subsequent work together would generate a strong cinematic relationship that would echo throughout Chaplin's career.

However, now that he had established a screen character that he felt would fit in nicely with the Keystone product but would also allow his creative ideas to flourish, Chaplin was eager to experiment further.

# CHAPTER 7

# *A Thief Catcher*

**Alternate title:** ***His Regular Job***

Running Time: One Reel
Filmed January 5, 1914–January 26, 1914
Released February 19, 1914

**Credits**
Directed by Ford Sterling

**Cast**
Ford Sterling, Mack Swain, Edgar Kennedy, William Hauber, Rube Miller, George Jeske, Charlie Chaplin

For years in various interviews, Chaplin would recall having appeared as a Keystone Cop during the early portion of his Keystone tenure. Since no filmed evidence existed of this having happened, Chaplin's memory was dismissed as faulty. But there are indeed some lost Keystone films, and the Ford Sterling comedy *A Thief Catcher* had been among them (the supposition that Henry Lehrman directed this film is incorrect). The circumstances of this film being discovered again as late as 2010 are nothing short of remarkable.

Film historian and archivist Paul Gierucki discovered some reels of 16mm films at a thrift sale. One was labeled Keystone Film, with no other information. Gierucki bought it. Months later, when he had time to screen the film, he was shocked to discover that it was not only a lost Ford Sterling Keystone comedy, but that in one scene, Charlie Chaplin portrays a cop. The plot has Sterling unwittingly discovering a robbery in progress and being captured by the crooks. His dog goes for the police, and they come to the rescue. One of the cops is Chaplin. Chaplin is on screen only briefly, and this film has really very little to do with his Keystone development.

*Charlie appears as a Keystone Cop.*

On his Mack Sennett blog, macksennett.blogspot.com, Sennett historian and expert Brent Walker offered a description of the film, following a 2010 festival screening:

> *A Thief Catcher*, first and foremost, is a showcase for its star Ford Sterling, who is a gifted and under-appreciated comedian. Sterling's flourishes in the film—which include at one point getting his own fingers inextricably entwined as though they were imaginary "Chinese handcuffs"—had the audience howling. In the film, Sterling is a rural sheriff (or at least is wearing a sheriff's badge—some subtitles may have been deleted from the reissue print that would explain his precise status) who ends up being held captive in a shack by a trio of what are described in the title as "yeggmen" (an old phrase for safecrackers  or burglars). When Charlie Chaplin arrives onscreen, there is very little doubt that it is indeed the famous graduate of Fred Karno's music hall troupe. Wearing a slightly oversized policeman's coat and a flat (rather than tall) hat, and wielding a billy club, Chaplin's appearance and body movement are unmistakably unique to anyone having even the passing familiarity with his work.

Chaplin begins a series of "Chaplin-esque" gestures: first stopping to hoist his belt, then putting his left hand up to the other cop to mime "I'll handle this," then shifting his billy club from his right hand to his left and using it to poke Swain in the stomach to get his attention. When Kennedy exits the shack to join his partner, Chaplin pushes Swain out of the way with his right hand to get to Kennedy, then punches Kennedy lightly on the shoulder with the right hand while going into the familiar crouch and stances (neck tilted slightly forward, legs apart) Chaplin assumed whenever he "meant business."

Had the film always been accessible, this appearance would likely have been of little consequence. However, because of its having been lost, and the unusual circumstances upon rediscovery, *A Thief Catcher* has its own significance. Perhaps the story regarding its discovery by Gierucki is a better story than the film's merit would suggest, but since Chaplin's stature in cinema is so gigantic, any unknown footage in which he appeared would be a certifiable "event" for anyone with a serious appreciation of film's rich history. Thus, this ordinary Ford Sterling Keystone comedy will always stand out as special, despite its aesthetic limitations.

# CHAPTER 8

# *Between Showers*

**Alternate titles:** *A Rainy Day; The Flirts; In Wrong; Charlie and the Umbrella; Thunder and Lightning; Roaming Romeo; Stolen Umbrella*

Running Time: One Reel
Filmed January 27, 1914–January 31, 1914
Released February 28, 1914

**Credits**
Directed by Henry Lehrman

**Cast**
Charlie Chaplin (Masher), Ford Sterling (Masher), Chester Conklin (Cop), Emma Clifton (Girl), Eddie Nolan (Cop)

Of all the Keystone comedies in which Charlie Chaplin appeared, *Between Showers* is most representative of the studio's noted method of presentation. Many Keystone productions take place in a park, where conflicts are resolved with butt kicking and brick throwing. The typically simple plot of *Between Showers* has Charlie and Ford Sterling both accosting the same young woman (Emma Clifton) after a rainstorm. When she is hesitant about crossing a puddle in the street, Sterling hands the woman his newly stolen umbrella and goes off to find some discarded wood as a bridge across the puddle. Charlie happens along and gets the same idea. As both he and Sterling clamor for the best possible bridge material, a benevolent cop comes along and lifts her over the puddle. Sterling returns to reclaim his umbrella, but the woman believes it to be a gift and insists on keeping it. Sterling reacts violently, and Charlie comes to the rescue. The film concludes in typical Keystone manner, with flying bricks, before the fadeout.

Coming this early in his tenure in Mack Sennett's productions, this film reveals more of the Keystone spirit in Chaplin's performance, but it is even more interesting to compare him to Ford Sterling, who is cast here as a fellow masher.

Sterling was the first comedian to join Keystone, leaving Biograph with Mack Sennett in 1912 when Sennett decided to start his own production company. Sterling quickly rose to the level of star comic on the lot, but his blatant gestures and overplayed mannerisms, although very funny in their own right, represented a style that was on the way out. The difference in styles between the two comedians is quite severe. Where Sterling was prone to florid gestures, Chaplin's were more refined. Chaplin was redefining comedy in cinema, and Sterling's method would soon be archaic.

Ford Sterling opens the film by holding a tattered umbrella in the rain. He sees a cop (Chester Conklin) holding a new umbrella and, as the officer is preoccupied with a female friend, replaces that umbrella with his own. Sterling goes through all manner of gestures and facial expressions. There is even a shot of just his hand reaching into the frame where the cop and the girl are talking. His hand points to the cop's umbrella and makes a motion as to his plans to take it. When Sterling tries to retrieve his stolen umbrella from the woman later on, he puts his hands around her neck and starts shaking her. She responds by punching and kicking him as Charlie watches and laughs. When she shoves Sterling and he knocks into Charlie, the two of them brawl.

This is all very primitive, of course, but this sort of knockabout slapstick was Keystone's forte. Comedians and directors like Mabel Normand, Roscoe

*Chester Conklin sneaks off with Emma Clifton while Charlie and Ford Sterling stand nose to nose.*

Arbuckle, and Chaplin himself were slowly beginning to refine this style, but *Between Showers* is a good example of the studio's most basic and essential method of presenting comedy. These films were quite popular with movie audiences, which were essentially composed of the middle and lower classes. This primary level of physical humor was applauded for the very reasons we today dismiss it as crude and unrefined. Audiences laughed at the audacity of Sterling shaking a woman by the neck, at the woman retaliating, at Charlie getting involved, and at ending the whole battle by hurling bricks. Even period film critics responded favorably. In the March 1914 issue of *The Cinema*, the film was called "a screamingly funny comedy."

Henry Lehrman's direction and the haphazard structure of *Between Showers* separate his style completely from the tighter framework and better timing of Mabel Normand's method for *Mabel's Strange Predicament. Between Showers* is really just a series of crude slapstick gags hanging on the most basic of plots. Perhaps the shot of Sterling's hand creeping into the frame during the film's opening scene might be defined as some level of Lehrman's directorial cleverness, but overall *Between Showers* exhibits a style that was more in line with Mack Sennett's own rudimentary approach to film direction. This style would soon be honed by other Keystone directors like Normand and later Chaplin himself, each of whom possessed a greater cinematic vision.

This would be the last time Chaplin and Lehrman would work together. Chaplin would later dismiss him as a director with a supreme lack of cinematic ambition, preferring to rely on easy setups and simply get the job done. In his autobiography, Chaplin would recall:

> I still had abundant suggestions. . . . He would listen and smile but would not accept any of them. "That may be funny in the theater," he would say, "but in pictures we have no time for it. We must be on the go—comedy is an excuse for a chase." All the action had to be fast. . . . In spite of his comedy theories, I happened to get in one or two bits of individual funny business, but, as before, he managed to have them mutilated in the cutting room. I do not think Lehrman gave a very promising report to Sennett about me.

Others, however, remembered Lehrman differently. Film historian Joan Myers said of Lehrman:

> When I asked (Keystone child actor) Coy Watson Jr. about the experience of being directed by Lehrman, he responded, "He was a very sensitive man. And my father thought he was one of the best directors working in Hollywood."

At about the time he filmed *Between Showers*, Sterling had decided to take a job with Carl Laemmle at Universal to start a series of his own. He was taking Henry Lehrman with him. It was a decision that involved more money and, Sterling believed, greater prestige. Chaplin was actually being groomed as a possible replacement. Sterling's tenure at Universal would be short lived. He returned to Sennett after only one year. By that time, Chaplin had left Keystone for a more lucrative contract at the Essanay studios. Lehrman would go on to produce his own Lehrman Knock Out (LKO) comedies.

As Chaplin refined the Keystone gestures, the comedian did not eschew the studio's established style completely. Chaplin is clearly adapting the standard Keystone mannerisms into his character in *Between Showers*. He has the gestures and expressions already working effectively, but coupled with his own hat-tipping, eyebrow-raising nuances that gave his character more complexity than the more superficial comedians surrounding him. He also exhibits his prowess at doing a pratfall, kicking his heels up and landing firmly on his back. Chaplin had definitely arrived.

However, with each new film appearance, Chaplin became more inspired to attempt some of his own ideas. He realized that more and different gags would

*Charlie chortles at Ford Sterling's predicament.*

be possible with the greater intimacy of the motion picture camera, and his fertile imagination was constantly active. Having enjoyed some level of notoriety in the British music halls, as well as a discernible amount of creative control over his work, Chaplin considered himself established enough to exert at least some of that control in his film projects. With each film, Chaplin tried to contribute more than merely acting according to another's comic vision.

Looking at this early Keystone period in retrospect, often viewers have little patience for the wild slapstick and the frenetic activity, already realizing that Chaplin's talent was far better than what was then on display. But *Between Showers* in its own right, and within its proper context, remains an important Keystone comedy in that it continues Chaplin's creative progress and connection to period audiences. As he continued to appear in movies, Chaplin gained further knowledge about the craft of motion pictures.

# CHAPTER 9

# *A Film Johnnie*

**Alternate titles: The Movie Nut; His Million Dollar Job; Film Johnny; Charlie the Actor**

Running Time: One Reel
Filmed February 1, 1914–February 6, 1914
Released March 2, 1914

**Credits**
Directed by George Nichols
Screenplay by Craig Hutchinson

**Cast**
Charlie Chaplin (Gate-Crashing Movie Fan), Peggy Pearce (Actress), Edgar Kennedy (Director), Hampton Del Ruth (Leading Man), Roscoe Arbuckle, Ford Sterling, Henry Lehrman (Themselves), Minta Durfee (Herself, Woman in Theater Audience), Hank Mann, George Jeske (Stagehands), Billy Gilbert (Usher), Harry McCoy (Audience Member Who Fights with Charlie, Fireman), Frank Opperman (Man with Mustache), Bill Hauber (Man in Theater Knocked Over by Charlie), George Nichols (Older Actor on Screen), Bert Hunn, Dan Albert, Walter Wright (Men in Theater Audience)

A real improvement among Charlie Chaplin's first few films at Keystone, *A Film Johnnie* looks satirically at the fledgling movie industry and the effect films already had on the public. Crammed together in abandoned storefronts with poor temperature control, films remained a product for the lower and middle classes, while the highbrows preferred legitimate theater. *A Film Johnnie* casts Charlie as one of those moviegoers, and it derives humor from his response to the beauty of a movie star.

In the opening scene, Charlie is shown outside a storefront, which is doubling as a makeshift movie house (quite common in the days of the nickelodeon). He reacts with delighted affection toward a poster of an actress in the current film, played by Peggy Pearce (not Virginia Kirtley, as has been reported elsewhere). In his autobiography, Chaplin fondly recalled Pearce:

> Peggy Pearce, an exceptionally beautiful girl with delicately chiseled features, a beautiful white neck, and a ravishing figure, was my first heart-throb. She did not make her appearance until my third week at Keystone, having been ill with the flu. But the moment we met we ignited; it was mutual, and my heart sang. How romantic were those mornings, turning up for work with the anticipation of seeing her each day.

Chaplin would also note that this romance was fleeting. Pearce would again appear with Chaplin in *His Favorite Pastime* but would leave Keystone soon afterward, only to return about a year later. (For more information on Pearce, see appendix A.)

In *A Film Johnnie*, Charlie pantomimes about her beauty by pointing to the picture and twirling his forefinger around his own face. He reaches deep into a sock and finds a nickel. Entering the theater, he attempts to take his place among the moviegoers. The scene of the audience watching the movie is very nicely filmed by director George Nichols, a Keystone old-timer who was working with Chaplin for the first time. Nichols trains his camera on the audience, filming their reaction to the movie they are seeing, and crosscutting to what is happening on the screen.

Charlie immediately bothers the already seated audience members, stepping on toes and sitting on laps until he takes his seat in the front row. Once the actress appears on screen, Charlie applauds wildly. When she blows a kiss to the leading man, Charlie reacts with fluttering eyes. In a later scene, when she is accosted by a larger man, Charlie rises from his seat and yells at the screen. When other members of the audience approach him, he starts a fight and is tossed out of the screening by an usher.

Along with being an amusing parody of how the first movie audiences were already reacting to cinema during its infancy, this opening sequence also presents Chaplin extending his *Kid Auto Races at Venice, Cal.* character. However, unlike the earlier film, Charlie's intention is not to get in the way or create a disturbance. He is simply reacting honestly to what is occurring on the screen, and that causes the disruption.

In the early days of film, moviegoers often believed the actors were the characters they were noted for portraying. They would be surprised to discover that an actor who frequently played a villain would be friendly and benevolent in real life, or that a beloved comic might be sullen or withdrawn when not performing. Even today, some obsessed fans truly believe the actors are the characters they portray, but during the early motion picture era this reaction was more common. *A Film Johnnie* effectively uses this for comedy.

After causing a disturbance in the movie theater with his antics and being tossed out into the street by an usher, Charlie decides to actually meet the cinematic object of his affection. He journeys to Keystone Studios and stands on the sidewalk in front of the studio as actors and directors arrive. He first approaches Roscoe Arbuckle and playfully tells him, through laughter, how much he enjoys his work. The benevolent actor hands the tramp some change. He is then met by Ford Sterling, sans makeup. Charlie responds to him in the same manner as he had Arbuckle, including placing his fist under his own chin to mime the comic goatee Sterling is noted for wearing in his films. Because he often plays comic villains, Sterling does not give the tramp a handout but instead steals the change he received from Arbuckle!

Most of the film features Charlie wreaking havoc on the movie set. There are many opportunities for gags, and Chaplin's fertile comic mind allegedly came up with several possible comic sequences but, as with Henry Lehrman, director George Nichols summarily dismissed the comedian's suggestions. Wanting to shoot quickly and remain on schedule, Nichols, according to Chaplin in later interviews, would insist there was not enough time to work out new ideas that had not already been included as part of the scenario.

While much of his direction is concerned with keeping the frenetic activity in the frame, the most basic and oft-used method of any Keystone director, some of Nichols's directorial choices deserve notice. One particularly impressive scene has Charlie in the foreground, standing amidst a set being built. After initially getting in the way, Charlie then watches in amazement as the crew quickly erects the set for a scene about to be filmed. Nichols shoots Charlie, center frame, in the foreground, with the fast-paced set-building activity furiously swirling about him. As he waits, the object of his affection arrives. Nichols shoots this by having the actress suddenly appear in the frame, alongside Charlie, as she talks to someone off screen. Charlie notices and is dumbstruck by being in her presence. She does not notice him at all. Movies were young, and movie stardom was even younger, so this presentation of the initial reaction to motion picture celebrity is particularly interesting. Charlie is paralyzed by actually seeing her in person. His eyes cross, his body stiffens, and once she ventures on, he begins slapping his own face in disbelief.

As Charlie later watches a scene being filmed where the actress is being accosted by an actor playing a villain, he runs into the scene to rescue the startled woman. When the director interferes, Charlie kicks him and he goes flying into some props. Charlie then starts shooting a prop pistol all over the set as the actors and workers flee. Walking around the set victoriously, Charlie then lights his cigarette by firing the gun at it.

Another particularly interesting sequence features the company rushing to an actual fire, filming its actors in and around the area of the blaze. The Keystone company frequently filmed at actual events (Chaplin's *Kid Auto Races* is a perfect example). Charlie runs down the street to follow the cast and crew (in a neat tracking shot by Nichols) and, upon arriving, once again sees the actress accosted by a villain and spoils the scene being filmed. This causes more frenetic slapstick around the fire, with the camera being knocked over and the firefighters eventually spraying down the brawlers. The drenched actress grabs Charlie by the neck and begins shaking him, snapping him out of his fantasy. The film ends with a close-up of the waterlogged Charlie twisting his ear and spitting out water—a gag he would continue to use throughout his film career.

Although it is a bit disjointed, *A Film Johnnie* is still generally good with some clever ideas and amusing sequences. While director Nichols may have been reticent about allowing Chaplin the time to work out his improvised comic ideas, he does allow Charlie to be the focal character in the comedy, even to the point of concluding the film with a close-up. In all of his previous Keystone efforts, Charlie was decidedly peripheral to the action, an addition to the central portion of the film. Even in *Kid Auto Races*, Charlie is an intrusive outsider. He plays essentially the same role in *A Film Johnnie*, but the film is about him and his exploits, not about the event and his reaction to it.

Chaplin was enjoying the challenge of moviemaking on several levels. He enjoyed the constant activity, the idea of performing in a new scenario every few days, working with an ensemble, and honing his mannerisms to respond more effectively to the intimacy of the movie camera. He did not, however, like that his ideas were being overlooked in so cavalier a manner, especially by those who had spent less time in movies than he had on stage.

His stage success may not have impressed the Keystone filmmakers, but they did receive some mention in reviews of his films. *The Cinema* stated: "The sensation of the year is the success of Chas. Chaplin, whom trade reviewers declare far funnier in Keystones than even in (his stage success) *Mumming Birds*. One of these films is *A Film Johnnie*. . . . All the Keystone heads are in this and it is packed with indescribably funny incidents." However, some of the film periodicals were unaware of Chaplin's name (Keystone films began with a title card featuring the Keystone logo, but no cast list). A review in the *Motion Picture World* referred to him as Edgar English!

Chaplin did not read these reviews. He may have been unaware that movies received any critical press at all. And Keystone films were produced and released so frequently, an actor would be on his fifth film by the time his first was in distribution. Chaplin's growing stardom was not on his mind, but being allowed more of the creativity he'd enjoyed on stage was something he was thinking about with every project.

# CHAPTER 10

# *Tango Tangles*

**Alternate titles:** *Charlie's Recreation; Music Hall; Tango Tangle*

Running Time: Three-Quarter Reel
Filmed February 4, 1914–February 10, 1914.
Released March 9, 1914.

**Credits**
Directed by Mack Sennett

**Cast**
Charlie Chaplin (Drunk), Ford Sterling (Bandleader), Roscoe Arbuckle (Clarinetist), Edgar Kennedy (Dance Hall Manager), Chester Conklin (Cop), Frank Opperman (Patron, Clarinetist), Charles Avery (Straw-Hatted Man Lifted by Arbuckle), Al St. John (Guest in Convict Outfit), Bill Hauber (Flautist), Glen Cavender (Drummer, Dancer in Pointed Hat), Eva Nelson (Dancing Partner), Hank Mann (Dancer in White Overalls), Alice Davenport (Dancing Partner), Rube Miller (Man Pushed Away from Hatcheck Girl), George Jeske (Cornet Player, Dancer), Harry McCoy (Piano Player), Minta Durfee, Peggy Pearce, Bert Hunn (Dancers). (Some sources erroneously identify Minta Durfee as playing the hatcheck girl.)

It was standard practice at Keystone for Mack Sennett to have an idea and use an appropriate location to film the comedy. This time, the location was the Venice Dance Hall on Abbott Kinney Pier in Venice, California. *Tango Tangles* is another of the most rudimentary Keystone one-reelers, relying on slapstick situations with no discernible plot. It is also one of the most interesting of Chaplin's early vehicles.

Sennett's approach as a director was the point-and-shoot method. But his attempt to keep the action in the frame was somewhat more concentrated, because the activity in his films was far more volatile. As the film was helmed by Sennett himself, the reactions in *Tango Tangles* are especially broad, the pratfalls are more spectacular, and the movement is rapid and constant. The fact that the film's premise is no more than several people causing havoc at a dance hall makes it one of the most typically simple of the Keystone films in which Chaplin appears.

*Tango Tangles* is also a rather ingenious example of fast-paced slapstick mayhem. A series of superficial conflicts all hang on the film's thin premise, so the entire eight-minute picture (it runs just under a reel) is completely reliant on gags and characters.

The actors are without their trademark outfits. Roscoe Arbuckle comes off as closest to his usual screen character: his cherubic face was never obscured by garish makeup, mustaches, or beards. Ford Sterling is without his trademark goatee. Chaplin is nattily dressed and sans mustache. He once again plays a drunk, though, causing us to conclude that Sennett felt it would be most comfortable to keep the relative newcomer fairly close to the character he'd played in the music halls for years.

Sterling is the bandleader, Arbuckle is a musician in the band, and Chaplin is merely an obnoxious drunken patron of the dance hall. Sterling and Arbuckle fight over a young woman. One of the first and most outrageous physical gags in the film has an angry Arbuckle grabbing a diminutive man standing innocently nearby and raising him in the air as a weapon to hit Sterling.

Once the band starts playing, both men are preoccupied, and Charlie starts dancing with the object of their shared affection. He is apparently perceived as no competition by Sterling, who flirts from the bandstand, offering winks and other such gestures, carefully standing in front of Arbuckle as he does so. However when Charlie appears to be getting a bit too familiar with the young woman, Sterling feigns illness, asks Arbuckle to get him some water, and sneaks out onto the dance floor to confront Charlie.

The confrontation between the two men is a wonderfully funny fight, where each combatant bobs and dances about, flinging straight arm fists that connect as slaps if at all. At one point, Sterling removes his coat, takes his shirt out of his pants, approaches Charlie as if to engage in some concentrated pugilism, and then grabs his face and bites his nose. It is all perfectly crude and absurd, but expertly staged by the two comedians.

Arbuckle returns with the water, discovers Sterling is out on the dance floor, and prepares to confront him. Just as Sterling states, via title card, that he will fight anyone who dances with his girl, the much larger Arbuckle tosses him aside. Sterling and Charlie once again battle, but finally each tells the other that they've lost interest in the woman altogether as the picture fades.

Keystone comedies directed by Sennett are perhaps the best examples of the studio's true vision. *Tango Tangles* is particularly boorish and violent, while the characters are merely one-dimensional caricatures. Oddly enough, this is precisely the brilliance behind many of the best Keystone comedies. Sennett appears to leave the characters to find themselves within the context of their adversarial situations. Chaplin offers a lot more nuance while dancing, flirting, or fighting than he had been allowed to do in previous efforts. It seems as though Sennett is leaving him to his own comic devices. Same goes for Sterling and Arbuckle. Arbuckle remains the solid, surefooted character he'd always played, but Sterling appears to be toning down his more florid gestures. With none of his trademark garish makeup to accent his blatant expressions, Sterling proves his true comic prowess as an integral part of this film's ensemble.

The only real preparation for a film like *Tango Tangles* is that Mack Sennett came up with an idea to overtake an actual dance hall by filming his actors cutting up among the actual dancers. He keeps the comedy violent and fast paced while hanging as many gags as possible on the thin premise. After three-quarters of a reel, the film stops. This crude structure, with its equally crude comedy, is quintessential Keystone, but it is not quintessential Chaplin. As a result, studies of Chaplin have either dismissed or panned this film, once again approaching it from the learned perspective of having already seen later classics like *The Gold Rush* and *City Lights*. However, a more reasoned approach would be to accept the Keystone trappings as being typical for the studio and this era, and realize that Chaplin, this early in his career, was not exploring anything more than

*Charlie Chaplin, sans mustache, and Roscoe Arbuckle.*

the possibility of adding subtle nuance to his established Karno-period drunk character.

There is also the period in which the film was made, a period in which moviegoing audiences welcomed the boorishness of the Sennett slapstick. Arbuckle throwing a man across the room, Charlie swinging back to slap Sterling with full force, the woman over whom they are fighting acting detached and bemused by each man's antics—all would be met by gales of laughter from period audiences. According to *The Cinema*, "The ballroom is soon converted into a battlefield, which results in this Keystone being a real scream."

It appears that Chaplin was concentrating on making his drunk character more audacious, even less sympathetic. Moviegoers were responding favorably to his audacity and forgiving his bad behavior because of his drunkenness. This was evident as early as *Mabel's Strange Predicament* and *Kid Auto Races at Venice, Cal.* and would serve Chaplin well for the remainder of his Keystone tenure. It is not the lovable tramp from later films, but an early, confrontational version, and the very character that initially made Charlie Chaplin a star.

# CHAPTER 11

# *His Favorite Pastime*

**Alternate titles:** *The Bonehead; His Reckless Fling*

Running Time: Two Reels
Filmed February 11–17, 1914

**Credits**
Directed by George Nichols
Screenplay by Craig Hutchinson

**Cast**
Charlie Chaplin (Drunk), Roscoe Arbuckle (Drunk), Peggy Pearce (Wife), Frank Opperman (Husband), Edgar Kennedy (Bully), Harry McCoy (Bar Patron), Bill Hauber (Shoeshine Customer, Butler), Billy Gilbert (Shoeshine Boy), Rube Miller (Bar Patron), Bert Hunn (Bartender), George Jeske (Servant), Hampton Del Ruth (Bar Patron)

For the elitist upper class in 1914 society, movies were lowbrow entertainment. Comedy, especially Keystone comedy, was singled out as particularly vulgar and tasteless. A film like *His Favorite Pastime* is a good representation of just why some levels of society reacted to movies in such a manner. In this film, Charlie is a nasty drunk, prone to a level of violence and boorish behavior exceeding that in his previous screen performances.

In recent studies of Chaplin's films, much has been made of Charlie's behavior during the Keystone period. Students of cinema looking for the warm, lovable Charlie from *The Kid* could not reconcile their understanding of his character with this earlier incarnation. Audiences of 1914, however, were approaching these films without the knowledge of Chaplin's later productions. They are not making mental comparisons to the Charlie we see in *The Kid* or *City Lights*. To the general movie patron in 1914, Charlie Chaplin played a character whose drunken audacity was appealing and inspiring. If we approach the film objectively, with its historical context in mind, *His Favorite Pastime* effectively continues Chaplin's development as a motion picture performer.

Chaplin looks further into possibilities with his drunk character from the stage in *His Favorite Pastime*. The comedian's drunk act enjoyed some notoriety on stage, so it was natural for Mack Sennett to capitalize on it in films. Chaplin understood the character well enough to augment it for each plot situation, and he had already proven himself adept at the necessary slapstick. However, *His Favorite Pastime* is far more character driven than any previous Chaplin film, and despite his reluctance to take time for more thought-out gags, the director does seem to allow Chaplin to explore all of his character's possibilities.

The film opens with Charlie and Roscoe Arbuckle among those drinking at a neighborhood tavern. Arbuckle is a particularly unkempt sort and attempts to subtly steal Charlie's drink, casually stretching and reaching for the glass. He then tries to cadge money off of Charlie by explaining, with hand gestures indicating different sizes, that he has many children. Charlie's response is to spit in his face. This act of vulgarity is how Charlie will be represented throughout the remainder of the film.

Charlie drunkenly flirts with another man's wife, is shoved around by the neighborhood bully, kicks another patron through the restroom's swinging doors, flicks ashes in a shoeshine boy's hand as he gestures for a tip, and slaps a man in the rear with his cane as the man is hunched over the sink washing up. When the man wants to wipe the soap from his eyes, Charlie hands him the shoeshine towel, which blackens his face.

To someone well versed in Chaplin's later, more refined films, this all seems too one dimensional and nasty. To audiences of 1914, it represented the sort of drunken audacity that moviegoers found hilarious. With unmitigated gall, Charlie follows home the woman with whom he had been flirting and gets in a fight with her husband and coterie of servants. After Charlie escapes the home, director George Nichols ends *His Favorite Pastime* the same way he ended *A Film Johnnie*, with a close-up of his star.

Throughout the nasty behavior and typical Keystone gags, Charlie adds nuance to his character's boorish exploits. Subtle bits like catching his cane on a chair as he walks past, and tumbling over a stair rail and landing comfortably seated in a chair, are used to augment his character. A nice piece where his drunkenness prevents him from being able to leave through the swinging doors appears to indicate that director Nichols allowed Chaplin at least some room for creative inspiration. As Charlie pushes on the doors and they swing back and hit him, his drunken state will not allow him to comprehend why. He eventually solves the problem pragmatically by climbing under the doors to escape.

The sequence with the doors is discussed in Gerald Mast's study *The Comic Mind*:

*Charlie's favorite pastime is at the local watering hole.*

The saloon door is the ancestor of every inanimate thing that Charlie later succeeded in bringing to life; he turns a piece of wood into a living opponent. He succeeds in treating one kind of object as if it were a different kind of being. Although historians usually refer to this technique as Chaplin's "transposition of objects," "metamorphosis" would be a much more accurate term, for the object is not instantaneously transposed into something else, but undergoes the complete transformation process before our eyes.

*His Favorite Pastime* is also another good example of typical Keystone structure. It is a series of improvised gags with no real plot. It is character driven with Charlie as the focal point. He is not responding to the other characters; they are responding to him. Except for some extras in the background during the bar scenes, Charlie dominates the foreground with his various reactions to different characters and events. While he spits at Arbuckle the bum, when the bully (Edgar Kennedy) knocks him down with a friendly slap, the adversarial Charlie backs down and offers to buy him a drink. Some level of improvisation is evident as Charlie attempts to light a frankfurter taken from the lunch table and wipes his hand with lettuce leaves.

While Chaplin recounts in his autobiography that he had the same trouble with Nichols as he'd had with Lehrman regarding attempts to inject bits of comedy business, there seems to be more opportunity in the Nichols-helmed projects. Nichols keeps him in the foreground, concentrating on his antics, and using the patrons in the background to project minimal movement and almost no reaction to what is happening nearby.

But it is the occasional bits of nuance that separate Chaplin from his Keystone comic brethren. Period reviews responded to this. *Kinematograph Weekly* stated:

> Chaplin has created an entirely new variety of screen comedian—a weird figure in whom one may recognize elements of the dude, the tramp, the acrobat, and, flavoring all, the "silly ass" of whom the drunken swell in (stage success) *Mumming Birds* was so perfect a type. This extraordinary character wanders through the recent Keystone releases—there is no other word to describe the Chaplin touch—and indulges in escapades which are side-splitting in their weird absurdity and their amazing suddenness.

Reviews such as this point out how Chaplin's raw, unpretentious Keystone comedies were almost immediately embraced by critics and moviegoers as something much different than they'd been presented with thus far, even from the same studio. *Motion Picture News* raved: "It is absolutely the funniest thing the Keystone company has ever put out, and this is not written by a press agent."

Of course Chaplin's screen career was still very much in its infancy. He had yet to direct a film, and he was chiefly investigating ways to make his performances stand out. Judging by the critical reaction to *His Favorite Pastime*, Chaplin was succeeding at least at a marginal level with each new venture. The films were being produced roughly twice per month, so change would often be minimal. Chaplin's gradual development, his continued way of incorporating his own ideas, even sneaking them in, was enhancing the overall product and further endearing his already popular screen character with the 1914 moviegoing audience. With more journeyman exploits ahead, Chaplin would soon hit his stride and be allowed greater creative and supervisory control. These earlier films show the development toward that culmination, and each is more fascinating than the other.

# CHAPTER 12

# *Cruel, Cruel Love*

**Alternate title: *Lord Help Us***

Running Time: One Reel
Filmed February 21–27, 1914
Released March 26, 1914

**Credits**
Directed by George Nichols
Screenplay by Craig Hutchinson

**Cast**
Charlie Chaplin (Mr. Dovey), Minta Durfee (Minta), Edgar Kennedy (Butler), Eva Nelson (Maid), Bill Hauber (Gardner), Glen Cavendar (Bearded Doctor), Harry Russell (Bald Doctor), Billy Gilbert (Short Ambulance Attendant), Bert Hunn (Tall Ambulance Attendant). (Alice Davenport is erroneously identified in some studies as playing the maid.)

*Cruel, Cruel Love* is one of the best of Chaplin's early Keystone efforts, along with being one of the most misunderstood. Some studies of Chaplin's films dismiss the Keystones as being of a primitive nature, believing that Chaplin refined his presentation tremendously as his career progressed. While Chaplin certainly did hone his character, this process started at Keystone. Yet Keystone allowed for some versatility along the way. In *Cruel, Cruel Love*, Chaplin eschews the tramp character and dives head first into writer Craig Hutchinson's outrageous parody of old-fashioned melodrama.

Having a far more consistent narrative than any of Charlie's other Keystone one-reelers, the story has Charlie assisting a pretty maid (Eva Nelson) who has twisted her ankle. He is caught by his fiancée (Minta Durfee), who gets the wrong idea and abruptly gives back his engagement ring, never wanting to see him again. Charlie tries to explain, but to no avail, so he returns home. Despondent, he decides to commit suicide by taking poison. The butler (Edgar

45

Kennedy), looking on, realizes his foolish employer has simply consumed water and laughs uproariously from another room while Charlie writhes in agony, believing he has poisoned himself. Meanwhile, the maid's boyfriend, the gardener (Bill Hauber), explains to the fiancée that Charlie was innocent, and she has him deliver a note of forgiveness. Charlie, upon receiving the note, tells the boyfriend it is too late, so he runs to get the fiancée.

Believing he now has only seconds to live, Charlie summons an ambulance to aid in possibly getting the poison out of his system. When the medics arrive, the butler confides in them, so they go along with the joke and have some fun with the frightened Charlie. The fiancée arrives, believing she is running to her lover's deathbed, but she is also told by the butler that Charlie is in no danger. She runs in and tells Charlie, who responds by beating up the butler and the medics in a wild slapstick battle. Charlie and his fiancée then embrace as the picture fades.

While the body of this film is its parody of vintage melodrama, the opening of *Cruel, Cruel Love* nicely displays Chaplin's continued development of subtle character nuance. When Charlie slips an engagement ring on Minta's finger, his giddy gestures are effectively understated. When he is distracted to the point where he misses a chair as he sits and plops to the ground, it is natural and not

*Minta Durfee is Charlie's fiancée.*

forced. While this sequence is typical Keystone fare, Chaplin plays it in a manner that is more refined.

However, aside from continuing to augment the expected Keystone histrionics with his own, more intimate style, Chaplin appears to be having the most fun once he takes what he believes is poison and begins reacting wildly to its psychological effect. The florid gestures employed here are not simply the stuff of standard Keystone comedy. Chaplin goes even further over the top, engaging in the sort of behavior that extends upon early melodrama's full-body movement to display every possible emotion.

Director George Nichols mostly keeps Charlie in the foreground. Essentially resting on the usual Keystone practice of concentrating on medium shots to contain the action, he closes in on Charlie frequently to show his more garish facial expressions. Nichols's process of alternating between long and medium shots to contain the frenetic action, a standard directorial method at Keystone, is especially interesting here. The lengthy scene in which Nichols focuses on Charlie, alone in his room, writhing and flipping about the floor with the belief that the poison is immediately consuming his body, is an action of just one figure. Usually Keystone comedies had action among several characters; free-for-all slapstick skirmishes were the norm. Nichols's using the same filming method for an individual concentrates as much on the character as the action. The mise-en-scène has Charlie surrounded by negative space. Nichols's shots give him room to move, and Chaplin has a field day chewing the scenery and expressing himself in a most uninhibited manner.

Perhaps the most interesting directorial idea has Charlie envisioning his ultimate end once he's taken the poison. The pictures fades to a brief cutaway of Charlie in hell being taunted by pitchfork-wielding demons. It is only seconds long, and it would have taken Nichols longer to film than for the scene to be executed. Despite this being cinema's infancy, the special effect works smoothly.

Charlie's reaction is even more violent upon receiving the message indicating he has been forgiven. Now he has to deal not only with the poison that is killing him, but also with the belief that he is dying for naught. The savvy butler never tells Charlie that he is in no danger, and instead just lets him flip and bounce about the room, believing he has only minutes to live. In an attempt at an antidote, while waiting for the arrival of the ambulance he's called, Charlie holds his nose and starts guzzling milk. His face reacts more negatively to its taste than when he had taken the poison.

Nichols then effectively channels Edwin S. Porter's crosscut method of editing to show several things happening simultaneously. The director crosses back and forth from the doctors hurrying to the scene in a horse-drawn carriage, to the maid's boyfriend running to summon Durfee, to Charlie's writhing in his room. The edits are made with a perfectly effective rhythm. Every shot shows a different kind of movement, all of them frenetic, and while Nichols keeps each scene moving, he also paces them against each other, never holding a shot of one sequence longer than another. It is a very impressive buildup toward the standard free-for-all conclusion.

By the time the doctors arrive and the butler is cluing them in on the true lack of danger, Charlie is on his knees praying frantically. The doctors are amused, making sport of Charlie. Their more staid reaction versus Charlie's violent outbursts and the butler's uproarious laughter are another nice set of contrasts. Once Durfee arrives, finds that Charlie is safe, and informs her beau that he drank only water, the picture shifts into ordinary Keystone mode. Charlie attacks the butler and doctor, effectively beating away all those who allowed him to suffer with the idea that he was dying. His embrace of Durfee in the end is shown in close-up, which is how Nichols liked to conclude his Chaplin pictures.

*Cruel, Cruel Love* offsets its delightfully crude comedy with a strong performance by Chaplin in the center of the film and its satirical intent. The rhythm of Charlie's writhing is shot in long takes, only interrupted by occasional cutaways to the laughing butler. Grabbing at the window drapes and throwing them over his body, grimacing for the camera, falling back into a chair from a close-up, Chaplin embraces his opportunity to discard all inhibition, and Nichols appears to be letting him improvise freely. He uses objects quite sparingly, almost not at all. It is mostly Charlie, as a person, and his own agonized reaction to what he believes is a truly fatal mistake.

*Cruel, Cruel Love* is most effective in its parody and its presentation. Chaplin's earliest films do not always have a steady, linear development of his tramp (the majority of the character's recognizable personality traits did not appear until he'd left Keystone). As a result, an aberration like *Cruel, Cruel Love*, in which Chaplin essays a completely different character, is considered a step back (reminding latter-day viewers of his debut role in *Making a Living*) or a holding pattern. In fact, these offbeat Chaplin Keystones include some of Chaplin's best work as an actor, especially when, as in *Cruel, Cruel Love*, he is given much freedom. Chaplin is allowed to stretch beyond the parameters of the character he'd been cultivating.

Chaplin would play characters other than his noted tramp throughout his Keystone tenure, right up until his final films for the studio, as such versatility was a fairly standard practice at the studio. While he continued to hone a consistent character, one that would eventually reach an iconic status bestowed on a very few, Chaplin's rare excursions into other territories as an actor were nevertheless a valid extension of his growth as a performer. There are several later Chaplin films made after he had achieved his greatest level of creative control in which he ventures outside of his tramp character, including *Burlesque on Carmen* (Essanay, 1916) and *The Idle Class* (First National, 1919).

*Movie ad for* Cruel, Cruel Love. *Actors' names are not advertised.*

As an accurate parody of melodrama, *Cruel, Cruel Love* stands out as being much different from any other Chaplin Keystone film, and its very uniqueness makes it among the most interesting comedies of his early career. If one compares it to the Sennett-directed *Tango Tangles*, which was almost completely devoid of any narrative, *Cruel, Cruel Love* comes off as especially tight in story structure. Nichols also enhances the film with a shot composition that frames the action nicely, uses crosscut editing to add even further excitement, and allows Chaplin to completely disarm himself with his passionate performance. It is a most satisfying production, especially for coming so early in Chaplin's career.

Some studies reason that Chaplin may not have been sold on the Little Tramp character this early in his career. In the Karno troupe, he was used to essaying a variety of different comedy roles while specializing in a few that he would revisit more frequently. Perhaps this might have been his initial plan for films. In any case, history now lets us realize that he firmly established himself as the Little Tramp character after a few films and continued to hone this characterization for the remainder of his career.

While *Cruel, Cruel Love* was a success at every level, Chaplin remained unhappy. He wanted to contribute beyond the trappings of another director's vision. Nichols, a talented director who had been around since the dawn of cinema, had his own methods and continued to dismiss Chaplin's attempts to offer suggestions as intrusive and too time consuming. Chaplin was continuing to do great work in movies but was becoming increasingly frustrated by being limited to acting. It would still be a few films before he was able to branch out into other creative avenues.

# CHAPTER 13

# *The Star Boarder*

**Alternate titles:** *The Landlady's Pet; The Has House Hero; The Fatal Lantern; In Love with His Landlady*

Running Time: One Reel
Filmed March 2–9, 1914
Released April 4, 1914

**Credits**
Directed by George Nichols
Screenplay by Craig Hutchinson

**Cast**
Charlie Chaplin (Boarder), Minta Durfee (Landlady), Edgar Kennedy (Landlord), Gordon Griffith (Son) , Harry McCoy (Boarder Piano Player), William Nigh, Alice Davenport, Billy Gilbert, Rube Miller, Al St. John (Boarders)

Despite having the same director and screenwriter as the offbeat and superior *Cruel, Cruel Love*, *The Star Boarder* is a much more typical Keystone, as well as one of Chaplin's least interesting early films. Charlie, in the title role of the favored boarder in a rooming house, enjoys special privileges from his smitten landlady. This is, quite obviously, due to a mutual attraction. His dalliances with the landlady are nothing more than silly flirtations but still raise the jealous ire of her husband, who is carrying on with one of the lady boarders. Meanwhile, their young son is taking photos of the various goings-on, and when he presents them via a magic lantern show, the boarders and management are equally embarrassed. The concluding result is a typical Keystone free-for-all. For his part, the youngster receives a spanking.

While the premise is interesting, and the flirtatious dalliances and free-for-all conclusion are prime Keystone ingredients, *The Star Boarder* falls flat. The comedy is a bit too perfunctory, relying on predictable gags and situations. Even

Chaplin's usual attempt at nuance and a couple of interesting solo spots do not add enough interest.

The opening sequence establishes the landlady's favoritism toward Charlie by showing him taking his time getting out of bed for breakfast while the other boarders sit impatiently in the dining room, waiting to be served. The landlady refuses to serve the others until Charlie comes down to the table. He rises from his bed, and rather than answer the handbell for breakfast and come immediately to the table like the others, Charlie spends some time primping in front of his bureau mirror.

George Nichols is once again at the helm, and his composition of shots and placement of objects in the frame are the most interesting aspects of this scene. Nichols shoots Charlie's room with the bed barely inside the frame at the left and the bureau stationed just as far to the right. It is a clever arrangement with much negative space in the middle, giving the illusion that Charlie likely has the biggest room in the boardinghouse. Also impressive is Nichols's composition showing the other boarders seated at the table. Men and women are seated on either side, while at the head of the table, facing the camera, sits a large, imposing man. The large man anchors the shot perfectly, so when Charlie joins the group and sits closer to the foreground, we can see how he is being served first and given larger portions.

*Charlie is landlady Minta Durfee's favorite.*

Chaplin considered Nichols a by-the-numbers director who would not listen to suggestions, but it is obvious in each of his films with Nichols that the director is clearly willing to spotlight his star. His ideas and his vision, such as the way in which Charlie's room is framed, attest to the film's benefiting from Nichols's veteran status. While Nichols eschews close-ups in *The Star Boarder*, he allows two different set pieces where Charlie is either the only individual on camera, or accompanying figures are so far into the background, they're barely discernible.

In the first, Charlie attempts to play a game of tennis (a game that Chaplin himself was quite good at playing). Nichols steps back and allows Charlie some comic business with the racket and tennis ball. Charlie bounces the ball and it hits him in the face, knocking him backward. He winds up and hits the ball with his racket, and it sails far enough to become lost. Nichols frames these shots with Chaplin well in the foreground. The other tennis players are too far back to allow any distraction for viewers.

In the next scene where Charlie is spotlighted, Nichols places him alone in the kitchen area. The camera has the entire kitchen area in the shot, with Charlie moving from the background to the side foreground as he raids the icebox of its liquor. After a brief cutaway to the action outside, Charlie is shown alone in the pantry, staggeringly drunk, with bottles strewn about. It was likely no more than a reason for Chaplin to once again fall back on his established drunk act. Nichols centers the camera with Charlie sitting off to the side, and the empty bottles are placed in front of him, strewn about at mid-frame. Charlie completely commands the frame, with nothing but negative space around him.

Despite these minor yet interesting highlights, *The Star Boarder* never amounts to anything above average. Chaplin's amusing set pieces are the only indication of his trying to do more with the material. Even the free-for-all at the end, after the youngster exposes the dalliances with his magic lantern show, is less amusing than, say, the similar ending to *His Favorite Pastime*, mostly because it seems, this time, simply a pat conclusion without any real resolution. Even a purely raucous piece like *Tango Tangles* has much more of a point to its slapstick mayhem.

Chaplin took some advantage of his opportunities here, but a potentially funny scene where he and the landlady wander off to find the errant tennis ball, flirting and tickling once they're out of sight, is interrupted too quickly by the presence of the landlord, who points out that the missing ball is right in front of them. The potential of the scene is thwarted by ending so abruptly.

This would be Chaplin's final film with George Nichols, who was soon to leave the studio. While Chaplin would later recall him negatively, some of Nichols's own ideas enhanced a lot of the scenes in his films, and one can assume that Chaplin learned more about object placement and shot composition from Nichols than he would later admit. Nichols did have his own vision, and a great deal of solid experience, so newcomer Chaplin's constant suggestions and changes seemed insulting. In fact, Nichols complained to Sennett, which made Chaplin angry with the director and, later, caused him to have nothing positive to say about his experience working with him. Chaplin would also note, however, that others in the Keystone company would admonish him for confronting Nichols on the set, reminding Chaplin of the director's veteran status.

Despite his worthy skills, Nichols was not one to redefine cinema or to help create its language. However, his shot composition was often much better than could usually be found in one-reel comedies as far back as 1914. *The Star Boarder* is just not one of the better efforts from its director or its star.

# CHAPTER 14

# *Mabel at the Wheel*

**Alternate titles: *His Daredevil Queen; A Hot Finish***

Running Time: Two Reels
Filmed February 26 and March 16, 1914
Released April 18, 1914

**Credits**
Directed by Mabel Normand, Mack Sennett

**Cast**
Mabel Normand (Mabel), Charlie Chaplin (Villain), Harry McCoy (Boyfriend), Chester Conklin (Father), Mack Sennett (Spectator, Newsreel Director), Edgar Kennedy, Mack Swain (Spectators), Bill Hauber (Mechanic), Grover Ligon, Dave "Any" Anderson (Villain's Henchman), Minta Durfee, Alice Davenport (Women in Stands), Charles Avery (Man in Grandstand), Fred J. Wagner (Race Starter), Dan Albert, Charles Lakin (Men in Crowd), Eddie Nolan (Spectator), Dave Lewis (Man Pushing Motorcycle)

The first two-reel comedy in which Chaplin appears, *Mabel at the Wheel*, is another offbeat, rather curious effort. Chaplin, sporting a top hat and a goatee, appears to be aping Ford Sterling, erstwhile Keystone star who had recently left the studio. There has been some speculation that perhaps this role was originally slated for Sterling. Even if such a case were true, the idea that Chaplin would be asked to act in the same manner as Sterling rather than revamp the role for his own character seems a bit odd.

Due to this curiosity, *Mabel at the Wheel* is another Chaplin Keystone that is often summarily dismissed as an offbeat throwaway. Actually, Chaplin takes real advantage of his opportunity to engage in a character that had been established by another comedian. The direction is interesting in how it works within the parameters of the established Keystone structure, stretched to two reels, and how the directors choose to present Charlie within the context of a Mabel Normand starring vehicle. While he is clearly a supporting player here, his screen time makes him something of a focal point, even thought he is cast as the adversary to the principals.

During the filming, a tiff between Chaplin and Normand escalated to the point where she was in tears and he was nearly discharged, another fact that makes *Mabel at the Wheel* something of a milestone. Due to this circumstance, Chaplin was soon allowed to write and direct his own films, a freedom that few Keystone performers enjoyed (Normand and Roscoe Arbuckle being the most noted).

The friction that occurred between Normand and Chaplin was another situation where the comedian was attempting to engage in creative endeavors that distracted the director. Being rebuffed by veterans like Henry Lehrman, Mack Sennett, and George Nichols was inconvenient, but Chaplin took special umbrage when a 21-year-old female novice dismissed his ideas as intrusive. Normand was usually quite benevolent and welcoming to suggestions. She liked Chaplin and admired his talent. But she was helming a two-reel comedy with limited experience and needed to focus without being distracted by one of the actors wanting to add different ideas. Chaplin argued, she argued back, and Chaplin walked over to a curb, sat down, and refused to work. Mabel was in tears. Since she was the darling of the Keystone lot, many thuggish extras were ready to fight the diminutive Chaplin. Normand was also Mack Sennett's girl-friend at the time, so Chaplin figured he would probably be fired.

Upon hearing about the situation, the budget-minded Sennett was chiefly concerned about the time being lost. He was not going to fire Chaplin. Normand indicated she did not want him fired, and Sennett was getting reports from theater owners on the first few Chaplin films that were now in release. The comedian caught on immediately, and theaters were clamoring for more films "with that little tramp fellow." Sennett needed Chaplin and wanted him to complete more films quickly to satisfy the demand. Thus, he took over direction on *Mabel at the Wheel*. Mabel Normand and Charlie Chaplin would soon get over their disagreement and remained friends thereafter. Chaplin would remember her fondly in later interviews, even when recalling this particular incident.

The plot of *Mabel at the Wheel* is quintessential Keystone, but with more opportunity for a director to open it up, and not confine it to, say, a park setting. Dealing with auto racing, there is the necessity to bring the action out onto the road and onto the track, providing the film with a larger framework.

Charlie is the Sterling-esque villain with designs on Mabel, but she is smitten with a race car driver. In an effort to be noticed, Charlie kidnaps the driver before the big race, so Mabel takes his place at the wheel. Angry, Charlie and his cronies do all they can to sabotage her efforts, including hurling bombs at the drivers. Mabel ends up winning the race and being celebrated, while Charlie is attacked by his own henchmen.

*Mabel Normand and Harry McCoy.*

Within this simple Keystone-worthy premise, a comedian like Ford Sterling would have stood out significantly as the villain. That was the character for which he was best known (that and as the police chief of the popular Keystone Cops). Chaplin, in a role allegedly designed for Sterling, decides to explore it thoroughly rather than reassess it according to his own style. It is his job to stand out as Sterling might have. As a result, Chaplin employs gestures and facial expressions that are pure Sterling, and very funny in their own right. It is not a parody like Will Rogers would do in *Big Moments from Little Pictures* (1924, Roy Clements). Chaplin plays the villain in a manner that can be considered a straight-up Sterling imitation. Some studies have called this a real step down, believing Chaplin's comedic superiority to Sterling would define this as slumming. Actually, Chaplin is once again tapping into resources he didn't always use as an actor, and his observation of Sterling is funny and central to the theme of this film.

It is not possible to tell exactly what scenes in *Mabel at the Wheel* were directed by Sennett and which were helmed by Normand. There is a nice tracking shot of Charlie riding his motorbike toward the camera as his character is introduced. When he leaves the scene with Mabel seated on the back of the bike, the gag with him going over a bump and Mabel flying off into a mud puddle is in a medium shot from the back. She returns to Harry and his race car, while Chaplin, still on his bike, reaches back and finds that Mabel is missing.

While the gag is clearly a director's gag (and could have been helmed by either Sennett or Normand), its movement is not simply that which exists within the frame. These sequences are shot somewhat more elaborately, with a camera stationed in a moving vehicle either in front of, in back of, or alongside that which is on screen. While later comedy compilations, chiefly *The Golden Age of Comedy* (1958, Robert Youngson), would make reference to revolving stages on the Sennett lot, where the background moved to give the illusion of a fast car, for example, these are clearly tracking shots. At one point, when Chaplin stops his bike, the truck with the camera shooting from alongside apparently keeps going, as the comedian is briefly out of the frame.

While aping Sterling's style so completely, Chaplin zeroes in on that actor's quirks and rarely adds his own brand of subtlety. However, in the scene of him reaching behind and discovering the jettisoned Mabel is no longer riding on the back of his motorbike, Charlie reacts in a much more measured fashion, without being blatant. He is suddenly Charlie doing Charlie, not Charlie doing Sterling.

*Charlie drives off with Mabel Normand.*

The racing footage is shot at an actual event, something Keystone would frequently do, and the intercutting between footage of the race being held and the exploits of the comedians is effectively done. Meanwhile, Chaplin's imitation of Sterling continues to include all of the facial twitches, flailing arms, and staggering reactions that the other actor had established as veritable trademarks. When Charlie attempts to sabotage a tire by piercing it with a pin, he does so casually while looking around, and he ends up poking a pit crew member in the derriere. Later when he takes a seat in the bleachers next to Mabel, he tries to get her attention by poking her in the leg with the same pin. The pin becomes a weapon, with Charlie poking all those around him at different times, as he believes necessary. These bits are pure Sterling, even down to the sly, fiendish facial expressions Charlie employs as he uses the pin for various methods of sabotage.

Director Mack Sennett shows up on camera in two roles, as a newsreel cameraman and a member of the audience. He is especially interesting as a boorish fan whose imposing presence takes up a little too much room and obstructs the other viewers, while also flirting with a few of the ladies seated nearby. Sennett

An ad for Mabel at the Wheel *gives this short film billing over the feature.*

appears to enjoy placing himself at center frame, as a character who also seems to take up a significant amount of room within the shot. Not that Sennett is a particularly large man, but seated next to the diminutive Chester Conklin, he appears to be an intrusive lummox.

As the race commences with Mabel taking control of the wheel, the cross-cutting goes from the race to the audience to Charlie's attempts to halt the proceedings. There are some nice aerial shots of an actual race, and the seamless cutaways to the people in the stands add some excitement. Their reactions are cohesive with the action, and when the first portion of the race concludes, the audience is shown collapsing in their seats with relief. The scene will also frequently cut to Charlie, armed with bombs, throwing them at the track in an attempt to stop the race. Undaunted, the drivers plow right through the explosions and smoke.

*Mabel at the Wheel* is a funny and successful Mabel Normand film, with Chaplin merely a supporting player doing a dead-on imitation in a Ford Sterling role. But while this performance shows Chaplin's talent for imitation, there really is no need for a comedian of his ability to be imitating anyone. While he longed to emerge past the level of being just another comical cog in the vast Keystone machine, Chaplin nevertheless agreed to continue taking on roles that did not develop his established screen persona, perhaps because they challenged other areas of his acting prowess.

Chaplin scholar Doug Sulpy has some misgivings as to Mabel Normand being credited with the direction of this film: "Mabel was either very skilled, or someone else directed this film (throwing the whole 'conflict' story into question). An analysis of *MATW* shows it's very tightly edited, with almost as many shots as the feature-length *Tillie's Punctured Romance*." However, Keystone expert Brent Walker's research, as included in *Mack Sennett's Fun Factory,* indicates Mabel Normand did direct this film, with Sennett contributing only marginally.

While doing what he was told and to the best of his abilities in *Mabel at the Wheel,* it was greater creative control that Chaplin desired. As he became more aware of how successful his first few films were at the box office, he pressured Sennett for more creative input. He wanted to contribute beyond merely performing, and he desired no more dustups with Normand or anyone else. Sennett was not immediately ready to let this newcomer direct a film but realized he needed to keep one of his most popular stars happy, as the Chaplin films in release were enjoying real box office success.

In retrospect, it seems odd that Sennett would have misgivings about Chaplin's potential as a film director, and it may cause one to wonder how many gifted comedians on the Keystone lot might have done well as comedy directors if Sennett had allowed them the chance. Not completely opposed to the idea, Sennett was not interested in allowing Chaplin to direct until he could be sure that his most popular star would helm a releasable film.

*Harry McCoy angrily looks on as Mabel Normand scolds Charlie.*

For his next couple of movies, one directed by Joseph Maddern, who had never yet helmed a Chaplin film, and another two-reeler supervised by Mabel Normand, Chaplin's suggestions were accepted more readily. Maddern was simply told by Sennett to indulge the comedian's ideas, while Normand was quite prepared to allow her co-star to help enhance her project, their friendship having survived the brief conflict in *Mabel at the Wheel*. Now that Chaplin had firmly established his stardom and offered several portents to the brilliant comedy he would soon contribute, his status was increasing at Keystone. He was no longer just another funny man on the lot. He was becoming the company's biggest star.

# CHAPTER 15

# *Twenty Minutes of Love*

**Alternate titles: *The Love Fiend; He Loved Her So; Cops and Watches***

Running Time: One Reel
Filmed March 19–24, 1914
Released April 20, 1914

**Credits**
Directed by Joseph Maddern (many sources credit Charlie Chaplin as director, but existing records indicate only Maddern)

**Cast**
Charlie Chaplin (Man), Minta Durfee (Girl), Edgar Kennedy (Boyfriend), Chester Conklin (Pickpocket Boyfriend), Eva Nelson (Pickpocket Date), Josef Swickard (Pickpocket Victim), Gordon Griffith (Boy). (Griffith's scenes were deleted from the 1918 rerelease and have not been restored.)

*Twenty Minutes of Love* is a standard Keystone park comedy, as well as perhaps the most important film Chaplin appeared in up to this time. Nearly every previous study of Chaplin's films would point out *Twenty Minutes of Love* as Chaplin's directorial debut, making this one-reeler a movie milestone. However, there is evidence that *Twenty Minutes of Love* was helmed by Joseph Maddern, with Chaplin receiving no credit in any existing records. Thus, when previous studies would examine this film with the perspective of its having been directed by Chaplin, they will attribute the subtlety of the situations, the cleverness of the gags, and the deftness of the pantomime to the comedian's vision.

Even with the understanding that Maddern directed *Twenty Minutes of Love*, this perspective could very well be true. Records were not as carefully kept on early cinema, and even the idea that Chaplin wrote any of his Keystone films is speculative. We have to base it on later accounts and comparisons to his approach in subsequent films where he is indeed credited. Chaplin's sudden, explosive popularity, coupled with his strong desire to contribute at a greater level to his films, caused Sennett to give him more control over production. Afraid to simply let a relative newcomer helm his own film, especially when theater owners were clamoring for more from Chaplin, Sennett was pragmatic. Not wanting the resulting film to be unreleasable due to the possibility of Chaplin's not fully understanding the filmmaking process, Sennett chose to assign a nominal director like Maddern, who would comfortably take orders and allow Chaplin as much creative input as he desired.

Unlike Lehrman, Nichols, Normand, or Sennett, Joseph Maddern had no real vision as a filmmaker. A Broadway actor, Maddern worked at Keystone for a brief period in 1914 and mostly helmed educational subjects rather than comedies. He later went into independent production, traveling around the country, shooting low-budget films in a community and showing them to that community. Little is known about his work, and there is no indication that he had any real merit as a director.

Thus, it is quite likely, especially evidenced by the resulting film, that Maddern was a veritable traffic cop while Chaplin created ideas for himself and suggested them for the other cast members. Since the supporting players were all Keystone regulars, such a structure was not difficult. Maddern was there chiefly to make sure things moved along, on budget and on time, and a releasable film was ready when expected. The creative aspect went to Chaplin, who fashioned a classic Keystone park comedy with the subtler bits of business that caused him to stand out from the others. In a letter Chaplin wrote to his brother Sydney, he refers to this film as "my own," indicating that he did indeed direct it. However, in his autobiography, Chaplin calls *Caught in the Rain* his directorial debut.

There is no real plot to *Twenty Minutes of Love*. Charlie wanders through a park and disrupts a series of romantic escapades among various couples on park benches. One lady expects a gift from her beau, who picks the pocket of a sleeping man. Charlie then picks the pocket of the pickpocket. The film concludes with a free-for-all. And while this is a very standard Keystone structure—a series of plotless escapades that conclude with a slapstick conclusion—that is precisely what Sennett would entrust to a director like Maddern, with the idea that the substance of this ordinary movie would be provided by Chaplin's input. Sennett, the pragmatist, was testing the comedian's skills before allowing him sole directorial chores on a subject.

*Twenty Minutes of Love* immediately establishes Charlie as the lovable rascal the moviegoing audience was suddenly finding so amusing. Entering the scene at the film's outset, Charlie spies two lovers on a park bench. He is childishly amused by their mushy romantics and starts mocking them by hugging and kissing a nearby tree. In later films, Charlie would be presented as the ultimate romantic, one who longs to find true love, but Keystone Charlie is a bit of a scamp, his reaction one of physical sarcasm. Charlie is filmed in a closer shot and

*Chaplin was allowed to contribute to the direction of* Twenty Minutes of Love.

the couple on the park bench from farther away. The emphasis is on Charlie. The couple on the bench is seen from his vantage point.

Within the structure of a standard Keystone park comedy, the subsequent dalliances with the various couples are executed quite brilliantly. When Charlie approaches the first couple, he cozies up and attempts to avert the girl's interest. There is a nice bit of business on the park bench as the girl's beau pushes toward Charlie, trying to knock him off the bench, but Charlie moves and causes the beau to fall off. Charlie takes his place and flirts with his girl. While the gag is standard, its execution is what separates it from the Keystone norm. The gestures are less florid, the action more natural. The Keystone comedy excess was significantly reduced, and it is unlikely this was director Joseph Maddern's idea.

Chaplin had been suggesting bits of business for his supporting players as early as his first film, *Making a Living*, in an effort to make the project more effective. These ideas were edited from the final release print by that film's director, Henry Lehrman. By the time Chaplin filmed *Twenty Minutes of Love*, only a few months later, his status at Keystone had improved, as did his understanding of the filmmaking process. Hence, any suggestions he might have of business for his supporting players would be encouraged by nominal director Maddern.

What is also interesting about this first couple is the amorous way they respond to each other. They embrace and kiss on the mouth, holding that kiss while Charlie, seated beside them, reacts with comic business. Their stillness offsets Charlie's movement. The Keystone method of framing the action in a medium shot is presented in a more subtle, more refined manner. It makes the scene that much more effective.

Another couple is shown in a much less amorous situation, as the woman wants her beau to prove his love with a gift. He is broke, so he picks the pocket of a napping man, stealing his watch. Charlie steals the same watch from the pickpocket. This slightly convoluted series of actions is followed by a particularly amusing sequence when Charlie is confronted by a policeman. While Charlie believes he is about to be arrested for the theft, the policeman, in fact, is merely admiring the watch. This is all done in pantomime (there are almost no title cards in this one-reel short). Charlie has the watch out, twirling it on its chain until it plops into his front pocket. The officer approaches and a frightened Charlie gives the watch to him and tries to hurry away. The policeman calls him back, returns the watch, and wanders off. Charlie displays an enormous sigh of relief.

What is most impressive about this sequence is how we, as an audience, react to Charlie's situation. Although he quite clearly has stolen the watch, we realize he stole it from another thief. We don't want him to be arrested for this petty crime. His appearance as a loner among sappy couples, reacting with sarcastic disdain to their various levels of romantic communication, is far more attractive to us than any basic sense of right and wrong. Charlie's sigh of relief upon realizing he is safe from arrest is our reaction as well.

The twirling of the watch chain so the watch lands in his pocket is one of several little bits of business Chaplin employs in *Twenty Minutes of Love*. He bumps into a tree and excuses himself by tipping his hat. Upon approaching a young lady, he creases his derby to make it look more distinguished. All of this business helps to further define his character, making it more attractive to the audience. This sort of thing would continue to be explored by Chaplin over the course of his Keystone work.

The standard free-for-all finish escalates when Charlie attempts to unwittingly sell the watch to the very person from whom the pickpocket had stolen it. One couple angry about being disrupted, another man wanting his watch back, and the original pickpocket reacting to Charlie having done him what he'd done to the first man all mesh into a frenzy of slapstick activity, where there are hits, kicks, near misses, and tumbles into a nearby lake. As the film concludes, Charlie walks away with one of the young women, emerging as triumphant amidst whatever situations he had stumbled through during the course of the reel.

Critics and moviegoers agreed that *Twenty Minutes of Love* was as triumphant as Charlie's character was in the film's conclusion. *Kinematograph Weekly* stated: "Plenty of the comic element is introduced and the person who does not laugh at the peculiar antics of Charles Chaplin—well—must be hard to please."

Chaplin's contribution to the film is obvious. *Twenty Minutes of Love* is consistently inventive, due not only to Chaplin's ideas for his own performances but to the general structure of each situation. What is worth notice, however, is the process of direction. Concentrating on comic bits of business and the series of situations with each set of characters, Chaplin does not appear to be approaching Maddern about camera angles. No series of shots adds up to any real composition as can be found in some of the work by previous directors like Lehrman, Nichols, or Normand. Maddern, a veritable traffic cop in the director's chair, simply points and shoots. Chaplin is sure that the action is worthy of the frame.

Chaplin is also concerned about the showcase for the comedy. The medium shots are effective in presenting the action as less frenetic, responding more completely to the stillness of the park surroundings. The movement of the couples is not broad. Chaplin's reactions are contained. The free-for-all conclusion is the only typical Keystone element in *Twenty Minutes of Love* that is presented in the manner of any of the studio's other comedy productions. And even that is much shorter, less the focal point than otherwise presented. The buildup to that conclusion is what appears to be most important in *Twenty Minutes of Love*. Chaplin was pleased at having more to do with the creative process of the comedy, and Maddern was quite likely following his directions in the same way as any of the cast members. While he receives no director credit, *Twenty Minutes of Love* is as much a Chaplin film as any of the subsequent Keystones that bear his name as director.

# CHAPTER 16

# *Caught in a Cabaret*

**Alternate titles: *The Jazz Waiter; Charlie the Waiter; Faking with Society; Prime Minister Charlie; Cafe Society***

Running Time: Two Reels

**Credits**
Directed by Mabel Normand (contrary to other sources, Charlie Chaplin did not co-direct)
Filmed March 27–April 2, 1914
Released April 27, 1914

**Cast**
Charlie Chaplin (Waiter), Mabel Normand (Society Girl), Edgar Kennedy (Charlie's Boss), Chester Conklin (Waiter), Alice Davenport (Mabel's Mother), Josef Swickard (Mabel's Father), Mack Swain (Boy's Father, Tough Customer), Gordon Griffith (Boy), Minta Durfee, Hank Mann, Billy Gilbert, Bert Hunn, Phyllis Allen, Eva Nelson (Cabaret Patrons), Grover Ligon (Bartender), Glen Cavender (Piano Player), Wallace MacDonald, Alice Howell, Dan Albert (Garden Party Guests), Bill Hauber (Thief in Park)

During the time that *Caught in a Cabaret* was being filmed, Chaplin's first eight Keystone comedies were already in release, with his ninth, *The Star Boarder*, ready to come out two days after production ended on this picture. Chaplin had become increasingly more fascinated with every aspect of making comedy movies. However unlike most Keystone comedians, Chaplin favored a subtler and more refined approach with his comedy. Sneaking in such bits of business in all of his previous films, Chaplin continued to feel that none of the directors understood his concept of comedy. They simply understood the established Keystone method, which Sennett often described as a plotless series of circumstances that led to a slapstick conclusion. It was a structure that worked, as the massive popularity of the comedies attested.

However, by the time Chaplin made *Caught in a Cabaret*, the ideas with which he was able to imbue his screen character were reaching the moviegoing audience. Theater owners inundated Sennett with requests for more Chaplin product. Wanting to oblige, and realizing Chaplin was becoming the most lucrative performer on the Keystone lot, Sennett ordered his directors to allow the comedian to offer creative suggestions. With all animosity between them resolved, Mabel Normand now had a rooting interest in Chaplin and gladly obliged. Thus it was perfectly appropriate that Chaplin's latest comedy be one Normand was directing.

*Caught in a Cabaret* contains so many solid examples of Chaplinesque ideas, it has often been cited as being co-directed by Chaplin and Normand. While it is Normand who is credited as sole director in existing Keystone records, it is quite obvious that she gives the same free rein to Chaplin that Joseph Maddern had with *Twenty Minutes of Love*. However, this two-reel production has a stronger narrative, greater character depth, better comic business, and a more effective composition of shots that use movement in both the foreground and background to greater effect than any of Chaplin's previous Keystone comedies. His ease in front of the camera is palpable. It is, thus far, the high point of his Keystone tenure, and it would remain among the best of his earlier films. It may be the very best Keystone Chaplin that the comedian did not direct himself.

*Charlie poses as a person of breeding for rich Mabel Normand.*

This time Charlie is employed as a sloppy waiter in a dive restaurant. While out walking his dog through the park during a break, he sees Mabel being accosted by a thief and runs to rescue her, while her foppish boyfriend stands by. Charlie gives Mabel, a society girl, a phony identification card that indicates he is a person of breeding. She invites him to her society party, much to her boyfriend's chagrin. The boyfriend follows Charlie afterward and discovers he's merely a common waiter. Charlie does attend the party, commanding most of Mabel's attention. After Charlie has left the party, the boyfriend suggests to the other partygoers that they go "slumming" and visit a seedy cafe. Charlie's ruse is exposed and the film concludes with a slapstick free-for-all.

Despite its convenient Keystone conclusion, *Caught in a Cabaret* is a very effective look at the American class system during the early part of the twentieth century. Having spent a difficult childhood on the streets of London, Chaplin had his own misgivings about the wealthy and their reaction to the have-nots. A film like *Caught in a Cabaret* would likely arouse his enthusiasm more so than many other comedies in which he had already appeared. Sennett himself was fully aware that the five- and ten-cent admission prices at the movies meant the lower classes were very well represented in his audiences, while many higher-ups dismissed movies in favor of live theater.

Charlie the waiter works comfortably within his surroundings. The diner is populated by all manner of boorish customers. Chaplin presents Charlie as one of those masses. Blowing his nose on his apron, keeping his dog in the kitchen area, Charlie remains the vulgar tramp despite gainful employment. He is immediately established as one who would not fit in high society.

Normand's eye for visual expression is borne out in the fact that a dachshund is chosen as the breed of dog for Charlie to take for a walk. With its long body, short legs, and a waddle to its walk, the dog has a shape and movement that correspond perfectly with its owner. Charlie's character is further defined when Mabel is accosted in the park and her boyfriend offers no protection. The rich boyfriend is presented as not masculine enough to dirty his hands against the thief who is attacking his girl. Charlie, however, has no such misgivings and comes to her rescue, but he must pretend to be a person of breeding in order for this friendship to continue.

At the garden party, Charlie's manner of dress—a shabby, loose-fitting suit and top hat—is inappropriate but accepted as eccentric by the wealthy. Charlie's lack of experience in societal circles would naturally have him choose an outfit that he would deem stereotypically of that nature. Chaplin presents Charlie as discernibly uncomfortable in these clothes, feeling conspicuous, for despite the clothing, his manner is the same. When he and Mabel sit on a garden bench and are served by a waiter, Charlie happily consumes both his drink and Mabel's. Noting that the waiter left the bottle behind, Charlie takes a few swigs. Mabel

*Charlie's manners belie his alleged breeding at a society party with Mabel.*

reacts with surprise at such undignified behavior, but Charlie's phony credentials save him from harsher judgment. Throughout this scene, there are cutaways to her boyfriend, who is fully aware that Charlie is merely a working-class lout. While he tentatively attempts to confront Charlie, he still does not fight. He must think of a way to expose Charlie without getting his hands dirty.

Perhaps the most effectively shot scenes are those that take place in the cabaret where Charlie works. Having the tables strewn about the area haphazardly, with no real semblance of order, is a most effective setting for the type of establishment that is being portrayed. Dancing occurs in any vacant spot, so dancers are scattered about the room in the same manner as the tables. Normand's mise-en-scène frames the entire setting, with the movement of the dancers offsetting the stillness of the seated patrons, so there is a sense of sloppy rhythm to the room. Later, when the society patrons are visiting, they are the still members seated at the tables while the dancers gyrate suggestively, even flirtatiously, around them. Now the setting also engages the underlying class system commentary. While most of the society people are fascinated, even entertained by this manner of "slumming," Mabel reacts as an appalled member of a much higher social class. Normand keeps herself in the foreground, but off to the side. Her framing of the scene makes room for Charlie's entrance. It is he on whom she focuses.

When waiter Charlie enters the dining area and sees Mabel and her society friends, he stops cold and drops the dishes he is carrying. It is not a typical Keystone reaction; there is no excessive double take or backward fall. The dishes fall to the floor simply because the shocked Charlie's arms drop to his sides. Charlie sits next to Mabel, very quickly rolling up his apron and hiding it in his arms. Initially she thinks he is also slumming, but his ruse is revealed only seconds later.

There are some especially effective scenes in *Caught in a Cabaret*. One that has little to do with the overall plot but reaffirms Chaplin's character in the film is a scene when a particularly large man bullies his way into the cabaret and demands service. None of the workers, including the rather large proprietor, wants to confront this behemoth and ask him to leave. Charlie rises to the occasion, slugging the guy with a mallet, which allows the others to carry him out into the street. This presents Charlie as a fighter in any context, so his saving of Mabel from the park thief was no fluke. It was a genuinely heroic gesture. At the cabaret, he is immediately surrounded by young women, as impressed with his prowess as Mabel had been. And they do not insist he be a person of breeding in order for any further acceptance.

*Charlie is actually a waiter in a seedy diner.*

Another of the highlights in *Caught in a Cabaret* features Charlie, back in the diner after having just met Mabel, listening to a cabaret singer warble a love song. The scene fades to show Mabel at the gate of her home, then fades back to Charlie, showing that he is thinking about the society girl he's just met. Charlie is placed, center frame, in the foreground. The singer is just off to the side and back slightly. The other patrons are strewn about at tables, reacting to the song. The only real movement is the singing. It is brief, but a particularly interesting use of a purely cinematic effect during motion picture's infancy.

While his comic business continued to exhibit subtlety and greater refinement, Chaplin still presented Charlie as crude and earthy. He is clearly uncomfortable in his society clothes, unable to adapt to societal behaviors, and suspicious when he is accepted as eccentric for his own natural boorishness. During the sequence when Charlie rescues Mabel from the park thief, he lets go of his dog's leash and the canine wanders into the arms of a small boy. Charlie later goes to retrieve his pet, but the youngster does not want to give it up. Charlie takes the dog and shoves the child to the ground. Of course this reads as being too mean to be funny, but it is quite an amusing presentation of the irascibility of Keystone Charlie. In fact, Charlie's reaction to both kids and dogs is significant here. Later films like *A Dog's Life* (1918) and *The Kid* (1920) would show Charlie reacting to, respectively, a dog and a small child in a most affectionate, supportive manner. But in the wholly unpretentious Keystones, the dog is merely a prop while the child is an intrusion.

Director Normand was now allowing Chaplin to mine the possibilities within his own character. She was receptive to his suggestions. His creative input was encouraged. *Caught in a Cabaret* is a perfect example of his efforts paying off. Normand was quite perceptive about comic talent and realized there was something beyond what Chaplin had been allowed to exhibit. She had previously gone to bat for Roscoe Arbuckle when the rotund comic was nearly fired for being slow to adapt from stage performing to screen acting. And while she had initially rebuffed Chaplin on the set of *Mabel at the Wheel*, Sennett's angry reaction to Chaplin's difficult behavior was calmed by Normand, who did not want Chaplin fired or removed from her film.

With so many superior moments throughout *Caught in a Cabaret*, its free-for-all conclusion is a decided letdown. Typical for Keystone, and frenetically funny in its own manner, it appears as a terribly convenient way to avoid resolving anything in the movie's plot. Perhaps Normand, and certainly Chaplin, could have come up with a better conclusion, but there were some hard and fast rules in a Keystone comedy. They would invariably end with a chase or some other slapstick style free-for-all, as that is what audiences expected. Chaplin, in his autobiography, would balk at this method of conclusion.

On the subject of Chaplin directing, Normand disagreed with Sennett. She believed Chaplin could indeed succeed as a director and privately told the comedian she would use her relationship with Sennett to help secure Charlie such a level of control. Throughout the filming of *Caught in a Cabaret*, Normand acted as mentor to Chaplin. She allowed him in the cutting room to view the rushes, listened to his suggestions as to which of the takes would be best to use, and indulged his editorial choices. By the time post-production was completed, Chaplin was especially eager to direct his own films. While he concentrated mostly on comedy, not the technical aspects of film direction that Buster Keaton would later employ, Chaplin wanted to most effectively stage his comedies for maximum impact. He was supremely conscientious about his work, and his interest in directing was to properly stage the scenes and hone the performances of his supporting cast.

Critics were very impressed with *Caught in a Cabaret*, as borne out in this review from *The New York Dramatic Mirror*: "Superlatives are dangerous epithets, especially when dealing with pictures. For that reason it is unwise to call this the funniest picture that has ever been produced, but it comes mighty close to it." With any animosity that might have existed between Chaplin and Normand having been dissipated, they could now work effectively together, as presented in this film. Even when they were at odds on the set of *Mabel at the Wheel*, Chaplin admitted he always liked Mabel. In his autobiography, Chaplin recalled:

> The "he-man" atmosphere of the studio would have been almost intolerable but for the pulchritudinous influence. Mabel Normand's presence, of course, graced the studio with glamour. She was extremely pretty, with large, heavy-lidded eyes and full lips that curled delicately at the corners of her mouth, expressing all sorts of indulgence. She was lighthearted and gay, a good fellow, kind and generous; and everyone adored her.

Mack Sennett, in his autobiography *King of Comedy*, stated:

> Mabel Normand and Charlie Chaplin had much in common. She was as deft at pantomime as he. She worked in slapstick, but her stage business and her gestures were subtle, not broad. Mabel Normand could do anything that Chaplin could do. To me she was the greatest comedienne that ever lived.

Chaplin recalled in later interviews that after the success of the films for which he enjoyed greater creative input, he practically pleaded with Sennett to be allowed to direct. Although Normand had spoken to the producer in support of Chaplin, Sennett was still not convinced that the comedian could helm a picture alone, and he could not afford to take a chance. Chaplin's films were becoming the studio's biggest moneymakers, and if Chaplin spent time on a project that was ultimately deemed unreleasable, it would bite into profits.

By this time, Chaplin had saved $1,500, quite a bit of money in 1914 (the standard budget for a Keystone comedy was $1,000). Desperate to be given the chance to direct, Chaplin gave the money to Sennett, stating that he could keep the entire sum if the picture Chaplin directed was not worthy of release. If it was, the money would be returned and Chaplin would have the opportunity to direct more of his own films. Chaplin did not want to simply become a company director for Keystone studios; he wanted to supervise his own films, make them from his own ideas, and film according to his own vision. Chaplin would later recall that Sennett asked him if he had any ideas for stories. Chaplin assured the producer that he had hundreds of ideas for comedy stories, for gags, even for filming particular scenes in their most effective manner. Wanting to keep his biggest star happy, and no longer concerned about finances since Chaplin put up the money himself, Sennett accepted the offer.

# CHAPTER 17

# *Caught in the Rain*

---

**Alternate titles:** *Who Got Stung; At It Again; In the Park* **(not to be confused with Chaplin's 1915 Essanay comedy** *In the Park***)**

---

Running Time: One Reel
Filmed April 4–13, 1914
Released May 4, 1914

**Credits**
Written and directed by Charles Chaplin

**Cast**
Charlie Chaplin (Flirt), Alice Davenport (Sleepwalking Wife), Mack Swain (Husband), Alice Howell (Girl at Hotel), Harry Russell (Desk Clerk), Slim Summerville, Grover Ligon (Cops), Ted Edwards (Cop outside Bar)

---

Any misgivings or casual dismissal of Chaplin's Keystone period will give at least marginal lip service to his having created the iconic Little Tramp character at the studio, and that it is where he began directing his own films. Unfortunately, most studies will claim that Keystone was a stepping-stone only, that Chaplin's direction was of little consequence because he did not have the time to work out and develop headier ideas. The fact that *Caught in the Rain* is Charlie Chaplin's directorial debut makes it a movie milestone. Mack Sennett's reluctance to allow him full directorial control, Mabel Normand's support for Chaplin to be allowed the chance, and Chaplin's continued clashes with previous directors like Henry Lehrman and George Nichols finally culminated with this opportunity. The result is the tightest and one of the funniest of Chaplin's Keystone efforts.

In one-reel comedies, plot narrative is usually replaced by situations and gags. Chaplin, however, in *Caught in the Rain*, does not keep it simple in an effort to investigate comic possibilities. The setups are many, the situations intricate, and the comic business is inspired.

In the opening, Charlie wanders into the park and attempts to get a drink from the water fountain. The power of the spray hits him in the face, causing a nearby woman on a park bench to laugh. Attracted, Charlie walks over, sits beside her, and flirts. Her irate husband returns, argues with the wife, and shoves Charlie. After a few drinks in a nearby saloon, Charlie checks into a hotel and discovers he is across the hall from the still arguing couple. The wife is a sleepwalker and ventures into Charlie's bed that night. When she awakens, Charlie tries to get her back into her own room, but they are caught by the husband.

By this time, Chaplin had already learned the basic rudiments of filmmaking, such as where to place the camera, how to work with actors, and the most effective methods of choreographing the physical comedy, by simply experiencing the handful of directors with whom he'd already worked. Mentored by Mabel Normand, Chaplin paid particular attention in the editing room, where he would view rushes and select the best possible scene. In later years, Chaplin would be notorious for doing an enormous number of takes just to get a short scene exactly the way he envisioned it. Certainly the budget-minded Sennett would not allow that luxury on a Keystone short, but Chaplin enjoyed full supervisory control despite having to adhere to a schedule.

Charlie's first appearance, at the water fountain and then on the park bench alongside the woman, is intrusive, but in a much gentler manner than he'd been in his previous Keystone comedies. He remains aggressive, kissing the woman's hand and placing both of his feet in her lap, but his manner is more playful than boisterous. When her husband returns, another dimension is added as he is played by burly Mack Swain, who towers over Charlie. Chaplin would frequently use Swain in his Keystone films, realizing his diminutive frame would effectively play off the much larger actor, and he would employ him most effectively in his 1925 feature *The Gold Rush*. Swain's appearance offsets the framing of the scene perfectly. The smaller wife on the right side of the frame is arguing with Swain in the center. The small Charlie stands behind them, bracketing big Swain with the wife. Swain's arguing is coupled with waving arms, one of which is holding a newspaper that keeps hitting Charlie in the chest. Before the couple exit, Swain pushes Charlie onto the park bench and the whole thing topples backward.

This opening scene is an immediate example of how Chaplin's direction of a typical Keystone slapstick scene in the park differs from the other directors at the studio. Chaplin's perspective relies on images. Swain anchors the scene as the larger person and is placed in the center, slightly to the left. Chaplin, further to the right, gives the husband and wife room to argue, allowing for Swain's arm gestures to reach back and hit Charlie, who falls and clutches his chest with each blow. It is all done with a sense of rhythm, and none of it appears overplayed, including Charlie's reaction to being hit. When the couple exit the scene, their argument continues.

In many Keystones, there appears to be a reliance on Chaplin's drunk act from the stage. In many of his previous films, excuses would be found for him to become intoxicated to the point where his actions and reactions could be culled from his finely honed stage performances. However in *Caught in the Rain*, Chaplin uses it to merely accent his character, not redefine it. Charlie leaves a tavern, obviously intoxicated, and immediately rests his elbow on a police officer. When the cop protests, Charlie lights a match on the man's badge and tosses the match in his face. The cop holds up his club, and Charlie hurries away. When one considers the broader gestures Chaplin used in, say, *Mabel's Strange Predicament*, where being drunk was the definition of the character, the approach in *Caught in the Rain* is far more subdued, and even more effective. Charlie was bold enough to flirt, but too small to fight the husband, and now that he is a bit tipsy, his resources are only slightly skewed. Rather than investigate opportunities for disruption, Charlie ventures to a hotel, planning to sleep it off.

As director, Chaplin decides to show the arguing couple enter the hotel before he reveals that Charlie has chosen to stay there also. The couple appear to be quite adversarial, arguing in every scene, extending far beyond what anyone would likely deem necessary for the failed dalliance in the park. When Charlie enters the hotel, he is more clearly showing the effects of his drunkenness and starts to ogle two attractive women in the lobby. He whispers something to the hotel clerk, who is shocked and appalled, leaving viewers to estimate if Charlie asked the women's price, or perhaps made an unsavory sexual comment. Chaplin then uses his slapstick prowess as Charlie climbs the steps, falls, and slides back down on his belly. He tries again, with the same result. Chaplin would again use intoxication as a detriment to his ability to conquer a staircase in the 1916 Mutual production *One A.M.*

Charlie staggers toward his room, tries to unlock the door with a cigarette, then realizes his key is in the other hand. He is surprised the room is not locked. When he walks in, he finds the arguing couple. The husband immediately recognizes Charlie and bodily throws him out. Charlie then goes to his room across the hall. Slight, amusing bits of business, such as attempting to unlock a door with a cigarette, are a good example of how Chaplin uses Charlie's intoxication for more delicate comic business. When he enters the couple's room, he does not immediately notice them. He instead pours liquor over his head, with his hat on, and starts brushing his derby with a hairbrush. That is when the husband physically removes him.

We now realize the adversaries are across the hall from each other. We realize the couple is still fighting over an incident involving Charlie. Chaplin lets that sink in as Charlie prepares for bed. The camera moves in more closely as Charlie removes each bit of clothing and sloppily discards it by tossing it over his shoulder. His cane, his hat, his removable collar, finally his coat, shirt, and pants are tossed about the small room. It is a simple, funny set piece that maintains the film's rhythm and pace, despite being a tangential sequence not directly related to the film's central theme. After Charlie climbs into bed, Chaplin cuts to the couple whose arguing appears to be at a stalemate. The husband leaves the building to get some air. The wife falls asleep and starts to sleepwalk. She enters Charlie's room and sits on his bed.

Chaplin's more refined approach is once again evident as Charlie slowly wakes from his slumber and finds the woman, seated at the foot of his bed, staring straight ahead, expressionless. He does not react in a flamboyant Keystone manner. Initially he is groggy and attempting to focus; then Charlie's face exhibits confusion, surprise, and, finally, fear as he realizes that this is quite a troublesome situation. Waking the woman, he attempts to get her back into the correct room, but the two are caught by her returning husband, who made his walk short because it's raining. A fight breaks out before anyone can explain, ending with gunfire and the police. Chaplin always balked at Keystone's penchant for relying on a plotless series of gags leading to a free-for-all or chase conclusion, so it is ironic that his first directorial effort concludes with a slapstick skirmish. It is quite short and simply tops off the situation.

The narrative for *Caught in the Rain* relies solely on situations but does not remain in one setting as did *Twenty Minutes of Love*. Settings include a park, outside a tavern, outside a hotel, the hotel lobby, and finally the rooms. That Chaplin had been mentored by Mabel Normand is significant in that his first directorial effort has some similarity to *Mabel's Strange Predicament* with its action in the hotel lobby, drunken Chaplin, confusion of rooms, and flirting couples. But while Normand's approach is carefully structured, Chaplin's is artfully so. *Caught in the Rain* never deviates from its brisk, steady pace. Gags and bits of business are timed and spaced out perfectly. Chaplin stages each scene as a separate vignette and blends them cohesively. The resulting film is a real triumph.

*Caught in the Rain* shows Chaplin using his body for comedy in a more effective manner, not just the funny walk, the right-foot skid, or the inebriated stagger. Chaplin is always aware of how his body should move. During the scene when Charlie is undressing for bed, he reminds us he is intoxicated by gently rocking from side to side. Again, there are no blatant gestures. His drunkenness is not at the forefront but is a subliminal part of his current state as he prepares for slumber in so haphazard a manner. Throughout the undressing, little bits of business, such as using a removable collar to wipe his brow, help sustain the sequence. Charlie is alone, center frame, commanding the scene with comic assuredness. It alone justifies his skyrocketing stardom.

Chaplin's direction of other actors was said to be very exacting. He would act out the part and expect them to imitate this presentation. This was especially offensive to an actor like Marlon Brando when Chaplin directed him over a half-

*Chaplin is finally given the chance to direct with* Caught in the Rain.

century later in *A Countess from Hong Kong* (1962), but at Keystone it does not appear to be a problem. Chaplin even stands back and lets Mack Swain improvise. One of the funniest brief gags is when the irate husband impulsively kicks an outdoor potted plant as he enters the hotel, still steaming over the continued argument he is having with his wife.

Mack Swain is a key ingredient as the husband. A very large man, his contrast with Charlie is an immediately impressive image. Charlie is very slight. Swain is a lummox. The diminutive Charlie is no match for the lumbering slab of dumb destructive strength, but he still shows no real fear. He stands up to the insurmountable obstacle of the larger man in the same way that the immigrant lower classes that Chaplin represented would persevere despite larger obstacles.

As Chaplin rarely discussed his filmmaking technique, it is difficult to determine specifically how he directed the actors in *Caught in the Rain*, especially Swain and Alice Davenport, who have the most footage other than Chaplin himself. Now established as the focal point of his comedy, Chaplin commands the spotlight almost completely in *Caught in the Rain*, but he would occasionally share it in his subsequent directorial efforts.

Mack Sennett, pleased with Chaplin's first film as director, returned the $1,500 life savings that Charlie had offered as insurance. After leaving the screening room, Sennett told Chaplin he would hereafter give him a $25 bonus for each movie he directed. But accounts which state that from this point Chaplin wrote and directed all of his subsequent Keystone films are false. What followed this interesting directorial debut was a lull in Chaplin's film career, where his next few films, directed by Sennett, returned to the fitfully funny status of his first few Keystone efforts. Chaplin wanted to explore more elaborate situations, comic business that required the close-up intimacy of the motion picture camera, large and small comparisons with objects and with people, and how he could somehow take the Keystone rough-and-tumble approach to another level. However, it would be a few more films before he was allowed the same supervisory control he had over *Caught in the Rain*.

# CHAPTER 18

# *A Busy Day*

**Alternate titles: *A Militant Suffragette; Busy As Can Be; Lady Charlie***

Running Time: Split Reel
Filmed April 11, 1914
Released May 7, 1914

**Credits**
Directed by Mack Sennett (contrary to some sources, this film was not directed by Charlie Chaplin)

**Cast**
Charlie Chaplin (Wife), Mack Swain (Husband), Mack Sennett (Film Director), Billy Gilbert, Ted Edwards (Cops)

After making a successful first venture as a director with *Caught in the Rain*, Chaplin was next shunted into this split-reel comedy, his first half-reel production since *Kid Auto Races at Venice, Cal.* several months earlier. Perhaps Sennett was waiting for *Caught in the Rain* to be released before allowing Chaplin to direct more films. Another factor may have been the feature-length film *Tillie's Punctured Romance*, which had started production shortly after Chaplin finished *Caught in the Rain* and remained active until June 9. Running a full six reels, *Tillie's Punctured Romance*, directed by Mack Sennett, has the distinction of being the first feature-length American screen comedy. Chaplin co-stars with stage actress Marie Dressler, making her film debut, as well as Mabel Normand, and the film features nearly the entire Keystone stock company. Chaplin did not return to directing his own films again until *Laughing Gas*, which went into production on June 11, only days after filming *Tillie's Punctured Romance* had been completed. In any event, the comedian's next several efforts were directed by Sennett while *Tillie's Punctured Romance* (which would not be released until the following December) was being filmed.

There is little opportunity in *A Busy Day* for Chaplin to stretch his creative muscle. This short effort is just an outrageous knockabout farce with a few great gags and the fact that Chaplin plays the female lead. Dame masquerade played for comedy is as old as Greek theater and turns up frequently at Keystone. Roscoe Arbuckle, with his cherubic face, was perfect for female roles and often played a woman for the course of an entire picture, as Chaplin does here.

Keystone was certainly not serious about this casting. In fact, during some of the slapstick skirmishes, Chaplin's wig noticeably loosens. But unlike other films in which Chaplin does a dame masquerade (the Keystone short *The Masquerader* and the 1915 Essanay production *A Woman*), Charlie is not playing a man pretending to be a woman in this short. Chaplin is not portraying Charlie at all; he is cast as the wife of burly Mack Swain. Chaplin continued to request Swain to play opposite him, believing the counterbalance with the much larger man was a good visual image, and it certainly works here. Of course this comedy is directed by Sennett, who also had an eye for visual contrast and might have been the one that decided to cast Swain opposite Chaplin. But since Chaplin continued this process in ensuing films for other studios (famously reusing Swain's services again for his feature *The Gold Rush* eleven years later), it can be assumed that Chaplin had some contribution in his supporting cast, even when he did not happen to be at the helm.

*Chaplin plays a woman and camps it up.*

The setting for *A Busy Day* is a military parade commemorating the opening of the harbor in San Pedro, California. It is another example of the Keystone crew attending an actual event and filming their comedy in and around it, with ready-made extras in the audience and activity in the background. There is no plot. Chaplin plays a jealous wife who reacts when her husband tries to sneak off with another woman from the parade they're attending. The film, then, is little more than a series of slapstick battles filled with wild pratfalls, intercut with the event taking place.

There is one particularly interesting bit where the wife notices a newsreel camera filming the event and is distracted enough to approach the director and attempt to get in the shot. It is something of an homage to Chaplin's breakthrough Keystone *Kid Auto Races at Venice, Cal.*, where the entire split-reel film features Charlie the tramp trying to do just that. In *A Busy Day*, this is just one of the sequences. The wife-husband skirmish is central to the film, and any action stems from it, with the parade and festivities in the background.

The diminutive wife smacking around her much larger husband is amusing in a purely visceral sense, but not enough to extend even a half-reel of footage. There is nothing special about Mack Sennett's direction other than his interconnection of the actual event and the Keystone slapstick. This had become such a

*Chaplin plays Mack Swain's jealous wife.*

natural manner of filmmaking at that studio, any prowess was, by now, learned. The basic method of medium-to-long shots containing all action in the frame is the directorial approach.

*A Busy Day* is a silly, sometimes amusing knockabout split-reeler that was produced to offer more Chaplin product to theaters (it was hastily filmed in one day while Chaplin was still working on *Caught in the Rain*). As with Chaplin's first few Keystone efforts, it was funny without any real cinematic flavor. The series of basic gags that permeated *A Busy Day* made it acceptable for moviegoers hungering for more product, but that is the extent of its interest.

However, Chaplin does not lazily phone in his performance as, say, Laurel and Hardy are sometimes accused of doing in their later films for MGM and 20th Century Fox (due to their having limited creative input at these bigger studios). Chaplin truly envelops his role as the battle-axe wife of Swain, displaying the same gusto and conviction he had when aping Ford Sterling in *Mabel at the Wheel*. While it had already been proven at this point that Chaplin's skills and creativity were above this sort of nonsense, he never shirks his role, no matter how offbeat, and he always tries his best to make each of his comedies as good as possible.

Unfortunately, Chaplin's next film, *The Fatal Mallet*, takes essentially the same approach with a slapstick battle as the film's only point, and it goes on for an entire reel. Chaplin once again exhibits a committed performance, but as with *A Busy Day*, the gag-strewn comedy becomes tiresome. This is especially disappointing, since the comedian's creative growth had been so discernible. This period remained a bit of a lull for Chaplin.

# CHAPTER 19

# *The Fatal Mallet*

**Alternate titles:** *The Pile Driver; Hit Him Again; The Rival Suitors*

Running Time: One Reel
Filmed May 10–12, 1914
June 1, 1914

**Credits**
Directed by Mack Sennett (contrary to some sources, this film was not directed by Charlie Chaplin)

**Cast**
Mabel Normand (Girl), Charlie Chaplin (Rival), Mack Sennett (Mabel's Beau), Mack Swain (Another Rival), Gordon Griffith (Boy)

While arguing against the casual dismissal of Keystone comedies as knockabout slapstick with little or no point to their comic violence, we are occasionally met by a film that follows this negative stereotype. *The Fatal Mallet* is such a film, made during what seems a creative lull for Chaplin's growth as a performer and director. The slapstick is superficial but has at least a marginal point of interest. This is Chaplin, Sennett, and Normand working within the parameters of a most basic Keystone situation. What they can do within the limited framework does not, however, result in anything that can truly be considered inspired.

Nevertheless, their personal lives had cohered along with their film collaborations. Chaplin recalled in his autobiography that his relationship with Mack Sennett and Mabel Normand had improved with his continued box office success:

> [Sennett] now practically adopted me, and took me to dinner every night. Because of Mack, I saw a lot of Mabel; the three of us would dine together and afterwards Mack would fall asleep in the hotel

lobby, and we would while away an hour at the movies or in a cafe, then come back and wake him up. Such propinquity, one might think, would result in romance, but it did not. We remained, unfortunately, only good friends.

In *The Fatal Mallet*, in a typical Keystone setup, Charlie is trying to distract Mabel from her boyfriend (played by Sennett) when a third suitor happens along. This causes Charlie and the boyfriend to team up against the third suitor in an effort to eliminate him so the two of them can continue their battle against each other. Whatever comedy exists in *The Fatal Mallet* is within this elementary framework. All of the onscreen talent is superior to this material.

While Chaplin, Sennett, and Swain figure prominently, this is Mabel Normand's film. She is central to the action. It revolves around her, not Charlie. The character Mabel is fickle, easily persuaded to accompany any of the men who give her attention. She initially seems happy with her boyfriend. Then Charlie spirits her away and she seems giggly and amused by his antics (such as rolling his hat down his arm and catching it with his hand). When her boyfriend sneaks over and kicks Charlie in the seat of the pants, he believes Mabel has done it and kicks her. This finds her back with her boyfriend. Charlie retaliates by throwing bricks at them. Mabel tosses a brick back at Charlie. While this is, indeed, standard Keystone violence, the tension doesn't build. There are no real situations to develop. It is just slapstick for its own sake, and while sometimes it is superficially funny, often it is simply dull. Perhaps such knockabout was acceptable for 1914 audiences, especially with performers as beloved as Mabel Normand and Charlie Chaplin. However, *The Fatal Mallet* is without any real significance.

Mack Swain is introduced as the third rival for Mabel's affections, probably in an attempt to add another dimension to the character structure. Sennett is larger than Chaplin. Swain is much larger than Sennett. The images contrast nicely. Swain is so large, however, that hitting him with bricks simply makes him mad. Charlie and the boyfriend discover a wooden mallet in a nearby barn and find this weapon effective on the bigger man. Now they are able to subdue him. After the two rivals drag Swain into a nearby barn, clever Charlie locks the door with the boyfriend still inside. The playing field is now clear for him to make a play for Mabel.

Another dimension is added when a boy with a crush on Mabel sits beside her and exhibits some level of innocent puppy love. The extreme opposite of burly Mack Swain, the boy (played by Keystone child actor Gordon Griffith) is a cute diversion to Mabel, but Charlie audaciously takes it seriously. Charlie comes over, shoves the child away with his foot, and tries to attract Mabel, who has clearly lost interest. Meanwhile, the boyfriend and the larger suitor escape the barn and go looking for Charlie. The ensuing battle among the three of them results in several tumbles into a pond as the film ends.

The staging of the actors here is perfunctory. Rivalries and alliances change, Mabel remains anchored in the middle of the action, and slapstick maintains the film's pace. Augmenting the images from large suitor to small boy is an interesting idea, but the comedy remains so utterly basic, it is difficult to appreciate that concept. Sennett directs in a point-and-shoot style without any creative vision.

Perhaps the only real distinction *The Fatal Mallet* has is its possible status as the weakest of Chaplin's Keystone efforts. One-dimensional violence can sometimes be funny, and the performers are all adept (this would be the only time Chaplin, Normand, Swain, and Sennett would appear in a film together). However the utter simplicity of *The Fatal Mallet* is compounded by its reliance on mindless slapstick without the necessary context to make it work on another level.

Some studies have indicated that the simple slapstick roughhousing in *The Fatal Mallet* might have been sufficient for 1914 movie audiences, but as we examine the critical success or historical significance of each Chaplin film for Keystone, it is disappointing to see so simple and unremarkable a comedy following the success of *Caught in a Cabaret* or *Caught in the Rain*. While it cannot be expected that Sennett would engage in presenting the sort of directorial vision one might expect from Chaplin, a film like *The Fatal Mallet* even appears desperate in its comic execution for any Keystone production. The fact that it features some of the best performers on the lot makes it even more curious that it is such a weak effort. It would still be a few films before Chaplin's creative vision was again allowed to be inspired.

# CHAPTER 20

# *Her Friend the Bandit*

**Alternate titles: *Mabel's Flirtation; The Thief Catcher***

Running Time: One Reel
Filmed May 11–18, 1914
Released June 4, 1914

**Credits**
Directed by Mack Sennett

**Cast**
Mabel Normand (Miss De Rock), Charlie Chaplin (The Bandit), Charlie Murray (Count De Beans)

*Her Friend the Bandit* is currently the only Charlie Chaplin film we know of that is lost. However, there may be other Chaplin appearances of which existing filmographies are unaware, while there is also some argument as to whether Chaplin did appear in this film at all. With silent cinema having such a poor survival rate, thus robbing us of a complete appreciation of the medium's development at an important part of our cultural history, we can be thankful that nearly all of Chaplin's work survives. Of course there is the possibility that this film will be found, but as of this writing, no print of *Her Friend the Bandit* is known to have survived. This makes it the holy grail of Chaplin films, but only if Chaplin is, indeed, in it.

Another factor to consider is the 2009 discovery of *A Thief Catcher*, a comedy in which Chaplin has a small part as a Keystone cop (see chapter 7). That production, although known to exist as per various published filmographies, was not known to feature Chaplin at all. The fact that *Her Friend the Bandit* was released under the title *The Thief Catcher* (the title's first word being different) caused further speculation as to this film's existence and origin.

Brent Walker, in his massive study of Mack Sennett productions called *Mack Sennett's Fun Factory*, offers a production number (KC-239) and a cast list (above) that differs from the one he gives for *A Thief Catcher*, and this is significant despite Walker's book having been written prior to the 2009 discovery of the film.

At this point, *Her Friend the Bandit* remains a curio.

# CHAPTER 21

# *The Knockout*

**Alternate titles: *The Pugilist; Counted Out***

Running Time: Two Reels
Filmed May 12–23, 1914
Released June 11, 1914

**Credits**
Directed by Mack Sennett (contrary to some sources, this film was not directed by Charles Avery)

**Cast**
Roscoe Arbuckle (Pug), Minta Durfee (Girl), Edgar Kennedy (Cyclone Flynn), Charlie Chaplin (Referee), Al St. John, Hank Mann, Grover Ligon (Multiple Roles), Mack Swain (Gambler), Frank Opperman (Promoter), Charles Lakin (Gang Member), Charles Avery (Cop), Glen Cavender, Harry McCoy (Society Singers), Mack Sennett, Rube Miller, Slim Summerville, Charles Parrott, Edwin Frazee (Spectators), Alice Howell, Eddie Nolan, Dan Albert (Society Guests)

Chaplin followed his directorial debut, *Caught in the Rain*, with a handful of curiously less interesting films helmed by Sennett. This odd lull in Chaplin's cinematic growth could be due to his also being active in the feature production *Tillie's Punctured Romance*, which was being shot concurrently during the time he also filmed the shorts produced between early April and early June.

One of Chaplin's more offbeat appearances was in *The Knockout*, a film that starred Keystone's other leading comedian, Roscoe Arbuckle. Some studies note that Chaplin would deviate from his Little Tramp character in films like *Tango Tangles* and *Cruel, Cruel Love*, citing these as obstacles rather than tangential expressions of other possibilities. In *The Knockout*, he is relegated to a mere cameo as a comic referee during a boxing match. What is most telling about this appearance is that Chaplin, in his one scene, manages to steal the production from the otherwise formidable Keystone cast.

The film stars Roscoe Arbuckle, the only Keystone star other than Mabel Normand, after the departure of Ford Sterling, whose popularity matched Chaplin's. However, Chaplin rocketed to stardom so quickly, it was probably only Sennett himself who realized the box office power of his films. By the time he was relegated to this small role, Chaplin's popularity was effectively soaring. Isolated from the commercial success and concentrating only on creative development, Chaplin remained immersed in the work and accepted even this small part as a welcome deviation, even a challenge of sorts. How could he effectively hold his own in a scene in someone else's movie when only allotted so much footage.

While this is Mack Sennett's film, Arbuckle's star status would allow him the ability to accept or reject a supporting player who may very well upstage him. However, Arbuckle was not egotistical to the point where he insisted all of the action be centered upon him. While he is the central figure of his comedies, including this one, he was benevolent enough to share the spotlight. After leaving Keystone, he cultivated the early career of Buster Keaton, who remained grateful to Arbuckle for the rest of his life.

Chaplin recalled, in his autobiography, a fondness for Arbuckle and believed it was reciprocated. Arbuckle, after having been already established, had appeared in small roles in some of Chaplin's earliest Keystones (*His Favorite Pastime*, *A Film Johnnie*), so Chaplin was interested in returning the favor. Chaplin likely agreed to appear in *The Knockout* realizing that Arbuckle as well as director Sennett would allow him to improvise. The results were an outstanding look at how much more effective a comedian Chaplin was against the other Keystone actors, including someone as layered and talented as Arbuckle. This is Arbuckle's starring film, and it is he who chiefly allows Chaplin to improvise freely. Arbuckle wisely understood that when another comedian upstaged him, it made the overall production funnier. This is what happens with *The Knockout*.

The boxing match in *The Knockout* is the culmination of a set of circumstances between Arbuckle and a character played by Edgar Kennedy. Burly Mack Swain has bet on Arbuckle to win and is standing at ringside making sure the fight goes on as planned. The director shoots the match so that all of these actors are in the frame, but the camera is close enough so any nuance from the comedians is detectable. Charlie enters as referee and spends the bout trying to officiate and also stay out of the flying fists from either pugilist.

Chaplin's diminutive body offsets the larger Kennedy and even larger Arbuckle, while Swain's presence just outside the ring (to the left) draws the scene away from the center. Because the action takes place in the ring, Swain's presence is not a distraction. He is evident and enhances the scene's dramatic effect as we realize this large tough guy is closely watching the results. It is Chaplin's

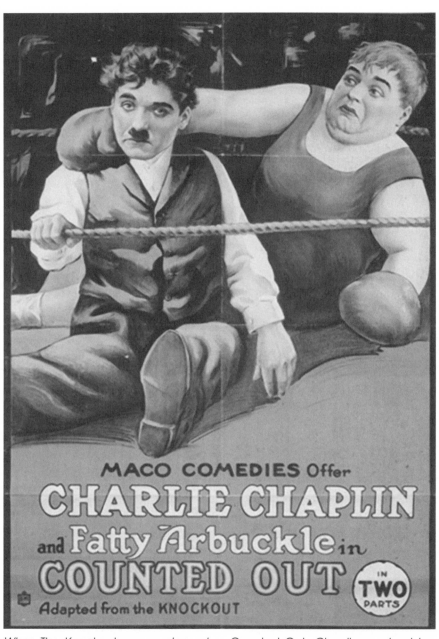

When The Knockout *was rereleased as* Counted Out, *Chaplin received top billing.*

movement—gracefully dodging the blows and reacting when he is frequently hit by an errant punch—that commands the pacing. Even more so than the actions of the fighters, Chaplin's balletic grace as referee is the focal point of the scene. There are some sequences that could be considered an early blueprint of what Chaplin would do with boxing scenes in later films like *The Champion* (Essanay, 1915) or *City Lights* (United Artists, 1931). Chaplin darts and weaves about the fighters, swings from a rope, knocks Arbuckle down, and even starts to fight Arbuckle, forcing Kennedy to step in as de facto referee.

*The Knockout* is pretty standard Keystone fare, and it ends with a wild chase, including a lot of spectacular spills by the Keystone Cops. But although it is pleasantly funny, it is one of Arbuckle's less interesting Keystones in that he does not direct it; Arbuckle was a much better director than Sennett. It is the boxing scene and Chaplin's participation that make this film most interesting today. In fact, as Chaplin's popularity soared, many of his Keystones were rereleased under different titles. When this comedy was rereleased under such titles as *The Pugilist* and *Counted Out*, it was Chaplin, not Arbuckle, who enjoyed top billing, despite being in the film for only one scene.

Chaplin manages to steal the film during the scene in which he appears. This goes back to Chaplin's first appearance in *Making a Living* only months earlier when his inimitable charisma managed to seep through despite his being an unknown in a role that was not characteristic of his special talents. In *The Knockout*, with greater creative freedom and a much loftier status as a recognizable movie star, Chaplin effortlessly overshadows such talents as Arbuckle, Kennedy, and Swain without resorting to mugging or attention-getting devices that his theater training probably taught him.

With his next film, Chaplin appears to have assumed more opportunity for creative input. Although Sennett was once again at the helm, the upcoming *Mabel's Busy Day* allowed for more opportunities for Chaplin, for co-star Mabel Normand, and for the director.

# CHAPTER 22

# *Mabel's Busy Day*

**Alternate titles: *Hot Dogs; Love and Lunch; Charlie and the Sausages; Hot Dog Charlie***

Running Time: One Reel
Filmed May 7–26, 1914
Released June 13, 1914

**Credits**
Directed by Mack Sennett (contrary to some sources, this film was not directed by Mabel Normand)

**Cast**
Mabel Normand (Mabel), Charlie Chaplin (Pest), Chester Conklin (Cop at Fence), Slim Summerville (Tall Cop), Harry McCoy (Taunting Freeloader), Edgar Kennedy (Tough Hot Dog Eater), Glen Cavender, Bill Hauber (Customers), Charles Avery (Small Cop at Entrance), Edwin Frazee (Freeloader), Mack Sennett, Billie Bennett, Charles Parrott, Frank Opperman, Alice Howell, Wallace MacDonald, Peggy Page (Spectators), Grover Ligon, Dan Albert (Vendors), Lou Sorrell (Driver)

*Mabel's Busy Day* is another effort produced during the period when Charlie Chaplin experienced a holding pattern while appearing in Sennett's ambitious feature-length production *Tillie's Punctured Romance*, which was being filmed at the same time. *Mabel's Busy Day* appears to have been made in haste to meet theater owners' demands for more Chaplin product. *The Fatal Mallet* was a barebones excursion into the most elementary slapstick. Chaplin's contribution to *The Knockout* was a mere cameo in a film starring the popular Roscoe Arbuckle. *Her Friend the Bandit* is a lost film and thus cannot be assessed. However, *Mabel's Busy Day*, a typical Keystone slapstick comedy directed by Mack Sennett, has enough appealing characters, moves so briskly, and contains so many interesting ideas, it can be considered a rebound.

The simple plot has Mabel trying to sell hot dogs at an auto race. Charlie is a troublemaker who has gained entry into the event through bullying. The comedy switches between Mabel's exploits and Charlie's, while also weaving in footage of the race. The rapid pace is consistent, the gags are funny, the performances are strong, and the supporting cast of Keystone regulars enhances the comedy. It is typically frenetic and has little depth, but as a Keystone production, *Mabel's Busy Day* is exciting and amusing.

Mabel opens the film by attempting to gain entry into the race through a fence that is being guarded by a cop. The cop allows entry after she gives him a free hot dog. Once inside, Mabel is annoyed by a man who picks up a hot dog from her vending tray and holds it up to her face, mockingly. She responds by punching him, and he falls to the ground, as does the sausage.

This beginning effectively sets the tone and pace for *Mabel's Busy Day*. At Keystone, a punch is delivered by hauling back and smacking someone in a straight-arm fashion. The reaction by the person hit is to kick both legs up and fall flat to the ground. It was such a mainstay in the Keystone slapstick battles, it had been perfected by all of the players. In *Mabel's Busy Day*, the slightest annoyance is combated in this manner. It adds to the comic outrageousness of this short, and is probably the most effective example of Sennett's method of direction.

Sennett's staging of Mabel's entrance into the race area is nicely composed. She is in the background, approaching the foreground where others are standing in a small group. When the man humiliates her, the reaction is explosively violent and presents Mabel as effective in protecting herself. Normand's small stature and cuteness often were used to belie her underlying ability to fight effectively with much larger opponents. An actor who never shied away from a violent gag or spectacular fall, Mabel Normand exhibits this ability most effectively here.

Charlie's initial appearance shows him at the entrance gate, in physical combat with the security cop and the ticket taker, as he tries to gain entry. Once in, he is followed by the cop, and their battle features so many twists and twirls, it appears as if they are dancing. As Charlie is confronted by a much taller cop, he slips through the officer's legs. It is all nicely timed and choreographed (probably by Chaplin) and maintains the film's pace as set by the scene with Mabel.

Mabel is then presented selling her wares. Plopping a wiener onto a bun, slathering it with mustard, and handing it to a customer, Mabel appears shy and friendly until one man walks away without paying. Her expression changes to one of angry defiance. She calls him back, and he gives her a coin. Normand's ability is displayed in this brief bit, showing that she is able to shift to a more commanding presence when necessary. When another customer comes along, a giggling Mabel explains she hasn't enough change to accept the larger bill with which he wants to pay. She is forlorn over losing the sale.

The layers to Normand's character are beyond the superficial comic role. While Chaplin would investigate similar possibilities before his tenure at Keystone expired, Normand, being the featured woman on the lot, already was allowed to present the weaker, more emotional aspects of her character. Audiences had already fallen in love with the plucky, determined, yet sometimes defeated Mabel by the time *Mabel's Busy Day* was produced, and her character offers a counterpart to Chaplin's as well as a harbinger to the sort of character depth that he would eventually explore.

When the picture cuts back to Charlie, he is out on the track where Mabel had earlier been accosted. Starting in the foreground, Charlie looks down and finds the sausage that had fallen to the ground earlier. He slyly reaches down, picks it up, and dusts it off. He eats it as he walks toward the background (moving in the opposite direction as Mabel had in the same setting), his gait changing to practically a skipping motion, exhibiting his merriment at finding the wiener.

While Mabel is endearing for her determined spirit, Charlie is loved for his audacity. He bullies cops to enter the race for free, and he picks up the discarded hot dog without worry about how much dirt it may have accumulated. Charlie remains the lovable scamp that attracted audiences from the first appearance of his tramp character. He wanders over to where three attractive women are watching the race. Sneaking a look in the purse of one, he pulls from it a hairpiece and starts playing with it. The woman snatches it back. However, rather than be annoyed, the woman is amused and responds to Charlie's flirtatiousness. This is the prime difference between Normand's and Chaplin's approaches to their respective characters. Charlie is found to be attractive by the women for his audacity, even though he is going through her purse and attempting to humiliate her by waving around her hairpiece. His puckish manner shows little respect for others, but his audacity is somehow charming. Mabel, on the other hand, is dismissed as a mere "girl" and taken advantage of by larger male customers.

Their characters are defined even more clearly in the next scene when a larger man approaches Mabel and demands service, bullying her considerably. Mabel's plucky determination is overpowered and she is frightened. Charlie comes to her rescue, leaving the women with whom he is flirting and knocking down the bully with a Keystone punch. Mabel is grateful but weeps over her plight. Charlie comforts her, crying with her, then diverts her attention, grabs several hot dogs, and runs away. Period moviegoers would not have reacted to Charlie for his meanness in the same way they would to Edgar Kennedy, who plays the bully. Charlie is a scamp, a rascal who puts one over on Mabel. Mabel would be perceived as the victim against the bully, but as simply outsmarted by Charlie. However, it is actions such as these that cause the latter-day response to Keystone Charlie as an unrefined portent to better things later. In fact, it is Charlie at his purest and most in touch with his first spate of fans. Even his bullying the police officers would generate a favorable response to the early twentieth-century immigrants in the movie audience, who would often feel bullied by authority.

Mabel chases after Charlie, feeling embarrassed and betrayed by his actions. As they run about in the foreground, the immediate background features the short cop sleeping peacefully. Once Mabel rouses him from his slumber, he joins their chase and engages in a free-for-all battle. However, unlike most free-for-all endings in Keystone pictures, it can be assumed that Chaplin and Normand combined their talents to choreograph this one more artfully. There is a precision to the thrown punches, the ducking, the weaving, and the falling. At one point, Mabel spits on her hands to start fighting Charlie, and when he raises a hand in protest, she reacts in horror that he dare consider striking a woman. Adding such subtleties to the usual slapstick conclusion places *Mabel's Busy Day* ahead of its similar predecessors.

Every ingredient of a Mack Sennett comedy is here. Mabel's plucky innocence, Charlie's audacity, a host of thugs and pretty young women, an actual event as a backdrop (a race and aerial show at Ascot Park race in Los Angeles), and a free-for-all slapstick conclusion. However, unlike some very typical Keystone comedies, every aspect of this comedy works. Normand turns in one of her strongest performances; Chaplin edgily investigates how far he can go with the character and still retain audience approval. The bigger men are accordingly

*Charlie is back at the racetrack in* Mabel's Busy Day.

menacing, the young women irresistibly cute. The pratfalls are spectacular, the slapstick is nicely timed and choreographed, and a sense of real fun permeates the entire short. A review in *Motion Picture World* summed it up nicely: "Any film with Charlie Chaplin and Mabel Normand as the leads is sure to be an immediate success. There is no plot at all, but the events that transpire in the one reel are side-splitting."

From this point until the end of his Keystone tenure, Chaplin would continue to make effective, interesting films that further solidified his mastery of the cinematic presentation of physical comedy and the method by which to most effectively film it. While he would continue to eschew any technological perspective, his staging of scenes, use of editing, and eventually even more relaxed approach would benefit his own work as well as Keystone's.

Sennett, however, still was not handing the directorial reins over to Chaplin. Perhaps he was waiting until the completion of *Tillie's Punctured Romance* before making that decision. Helming his first feature-length film at staggering costs, and with a Broadway star in the title role, Sennett no doubt was preoccupied with these matters while continuing to churn out his moneymaking short comedies. That a film as good as *Mabel's Busy Day* could be produced under these conditions is certainly impressive.

# CHAPTER 23

# *Mabel's Married Life*

**Alternate titles:** *The Squarehead; When You're Married; Charlie and the Mannequin*

Running Time: One Reel
Filmed May 30–June 2, 1914
Released June 20, 1914

**Credits**
Directed by Mack Sennett (contrary to other sources, neither Mabel Normand nor Charlie Chaplin directed this film, together or separately)

**Cast**
Mabel Normand (Mabel), Charlie Chaplin (Husband), Mack Swain (Man with Tennis Racket), Eva Nelson (His Wife), Charlie Murray (Bar Patron in Top Hat), Harry McCoy (Bar Patron in Straw Hat), Hank Mann (Bar Patron), Grover Ligon (Bartender), Frank Opperman (Worker at Sporting Goods Store), Alice Davenport, Dixie Chene, Alice Howell (People in Hallway)

One of the best of Charlie Chaplin's Keystone comedies that he himself did not direct, *Mabel's Married Life* is a quintessential exercise in refining standard Keystone clichés into a comedy that is perfectly paced and performed. Keystone frequently used a park as a setting for a series of gags and relationship mix-ups. *Mabel's Married Life* takes that premise and offers its usual gags, but with performances that enhance each situation. Chaplin and his formidable supporting cast of Keystone regulars are at their very best here.

The film opens with Mack and his wife kissing tenderly as Mack leaves for a quick errand. The wife looks at the camera, points to Mack, then to herself, gleefully acknowledging to the audience, "he's mine." Mack seems completely enamored of her. This contrasts with Charlie and Mabel on another bench in the same park. Mabel is noticing Charlie's unmended shoe with some disdain. Charlie reacts with embarrassment, looking around to see if anyone else is watching. Charlie then shares a banana with Mabel and complains that she has taken too big of a bite. He steps away to get a drink at a nearby tavern.

These first few minutes of *Mabel's Married Life* set up the characters perfectly with effective pantomimic expression. The woman's acknowledgment of Mack as hers is a nice piece of pantomime that reaches into the audience. Charlie's embarrassed reaction to Mabel investigating his shoe and his being bothered by the bite she takes from his banana (holding up his thumb and forefinger to indicate the size) are both funny and endearing. When Mack approaches Mabel while Charlie is in the bar, he sits beside her and flirts in a boisterous, obnoxious manner that befits a standard Keystone performance, and yet it still seems more refined than the norm. Mack's manner appears more natural, as if the character Swain is portraying is himself a bit forced and over the top. It is not florid Keystone acting as much as it is defining an obnoxious character. With his loose cap, pullover sweater, and tennis racket, Mack is the very definition of the sort of rube or schnook that Sennett himself enjoyed playing in cameos. Seated next to Mabel, he fidgets and chortles through his annoyingly animated conversation, while she projects a supreme lack of interest.

When a tipsy Charlie returns, Mabel is glad to see him. Big, burly Mack makes sport of the much smaller man and hovers over the equally small Mabel, attempting to convince her he is the superior of the two. Charlie's kicks to Mack's behind do not distract him. He treats Charlie as if he is a pest. In order to get rid of him, Mack removes Charlie's hat and tosses it away, continuing to flirt madly with Mabel. At one point, Mack pantomimes that he and Mabel should go dancing, by pointing to her, then himself, and bouncing around clumsily. It is a delightfully amusing bit of physical comedy, making it no wonder that Swain would be elevated from supporting roles to his own starring series by the end of the year.

Once the couples confront each other, Mack is forgiven by his wife, but Charlie angrily orders Mabel to go home. Despite her innocence, the jealous Charlie does not see beyond the act of flirtation taking place. Mabel responds by begging for Charlie's forgiveness, throwing up her hands in a defeated manner as she wanders out of frame toward home. When she happens by an athletic shop advertising a boxing dummy at a reduced price, she perceives it as a possibly effective outlet for her anger, purchases it immediately, and arranges for its delivery.

Charlie meanwhile is in the bar getting drunker and drunker. He gets in tussles with various toughs, and when Mack enters, a fight breaks out. Charlie's drunken adrenaline allows him to clear the bar handily and he returns home. There, the dummy is dressed similarly to Mack. Drunken Charlie thinks it is Mack and starts to hit it. Naturally, the dummy rocks back and knocks Charlie to the ground. Thinking he is in a fight with an intruder, he goes to the bed-

*Charlie angrily orders Mabel Normand to leave the premises.*

room and summons Mabel, who scoffingly reveals it is just a dummy. A giggling Charlie then makes up with Mabel as the picture fades.

In *Mabel's Married Life*, there are two interesting precursors to scenes Chaplin would later use in his 1916 masterpiece *Easy Street* for Mutual. As a rookie cop, Charlie attempts to accost big, burly Eric Campbell, but even his whacks with a billy club over the larger man's head are ineffective. Likewise, Charlie's equally ineffective kicks to Swain's posterior in *Mabel's Married Life* are presented to indicate Mack's physical superiority to the much smaller man. Also in *Mabel's Married Life*, Charlie fights off all other bar patrons. As they try to sneak back in, a mere look from Charlie sends them scurrying away. In *Easy Street*, upon eventually subduing Eric Campbell, Charlie gets the same reaction from the remaining street gangs. The smaller man is victorious. By comparison, Charlie is not drunk in the later film. By the time he was making films for Mutual, only two years later, Chaplin's onscreen character was honed to be far more sympathetic. However, the placement of these gags in *Mabel's Married Life* and their being reworked in a later production indicate how much supervisory control Chaplin was enjoying, even when he was not in the director's chair.

When Charlie confronts the dummy, it is evident that Chaplin is allowed to improvise freely. Except for a few brief cutaways to a giggling Mabel watching from the bedroom, this is Charlie's scene. He approaches the dummy warily. He is bemused at Mack's boldly standing in his apartment, but also cautious. When he orders him out of the house, naturally the dummy doesn't move. When he shoves it, the dummy rocks back and knocks him down. Charlie tries reasoning with the dummy, even attempting to cajole it into leaving. It appears Charlie does not believe himself to be quite as drunk as the dummy and expresses some level of empathy for his condition as he gently asks it to leave the premises. When this fails, Charlie is ready to fight, and the rocking motion again knocks him down. This isn't just a series of dull, predictable gags; Chaplin builds on the scene from a slow approach to a more violent reaction, until it becomes a veritable tour de force.

Each of the performances in *Mabel's Married Life* displays the effective nuance that Chaplin used to hone his own characterization. While Swain's performance is more inclined to Keystone exaggeration, even he comes off as more effectively boisterous than simply playing it as such. The slapstick battle in the tavern does not become a typical free-for-all and is not used as a conclusion; it is simply a sequence used within the context of this film to further the story and characters. The sequence with the dummy connects with and effectively culminates what occurs previously. Mabel explains to Charlie that he has been battling an inanimate object with the same matter-of-fact insistence that she'd tried to explain her innocence in the park. When Charlie giggles with the embarrassed realization that he has been foolish to fight with a dummy, he also appears to realize he has been wrong about everything. The tender kiss that concludes the film is a fitting wrap-up.

Mabel Normand again comes across as delightfully attractive as Charlie's cute, spunky mate. Mack's attraction to her is obvious and understandable, although his own mate is by no means unattractive. While she maintains her presence as more than just part of the ensemble, standing out as effectively as Chaplin does, Normand's strongest scene is while she is at home, before Charlie's arrival. She is awakened by the men delivering the dummy and throws a rug around her pajama-clad body as she answers the door. The cuteness of her modesty is further enhanced by her shocked reaction to the teasing of the delivery men when she drops the rug momentarily. Once the men leave, Mabel has a fun scene with the dummy, attempting to enjoy the catharsis of hitting it. It rocks back and knocks her down. Never one to shirk on a pratfall, Mabel flies back and flops to the ground. She gets back up and turns in for the night. It is this sort of balance between spunky strength and vulnerable innocence that continued to make her irresistible to audiences.

In their book *Charlie Chaplin at Keystone and Essanay*, Ted Okuda and David Maska observe:

> By this time, Charlie and Mabel had established an easy rapport as a screen couple. Mabel's subtle comic timing is used to good advantage. Her winsome facial expressions and body language convey a variety of moods; at one point she even does a precise imitation of

Chaplin's shuffling walk. *Mabel's Married Life* is one of her finest Keystone vehicles and a prime example of why she was referred to as 'The Female Chaplin.'"

For Mack Swain, appearing in most of Chaplin's films at this point, the enormity of his imposing presence is the perfect contrast to offset Charlie. Where Charlie nimbly flits about, Swain stomps and lumbers. When he confronts the equally diminutive Mabel in the park, his giggly flirting never seems to mask an ominous danger. His imposing presence notwithstanding, Swain comes off as a classic Keystone rube, whose schnooky attire and overbearing mannerisms are met with polite resistance from Mabel. While Bud Jamison and later Eric Campbell would provide this same counterbalance to Chaplin's character in his films for Essanay and Mutual, Swain would return years later to appear in a handful of films Chaplin would make for First National and for a star-making role in the comedian's brilliant United Artists feature *The Gold Rush* (1925).

The rest of the cast has little to do. Eva Nelson adds to the park scenes as Mack's wife, her pantomime bits showing the sort of nuanced refinement that Chaplin expected from his supporting actors. Bar patrons include Keystone stalwarts like Charlie Murray and Hank Mann, both of whom hold their own while Charlie remains in the foreground. Sennett's direction seems to be of little note here. This is really Chaplin's film, although Normand could have made some contributions. There is nothing about the composition of shots that is noticeably impressive. Sennett's direction appears to be little more than that of a veritable traffic cop, making sure things keep moving along and on budget while Chaplin himself investigates the film's comic possibilities.

Chaplin once stated, "I don't need interesting camera angles. I am interesting." Thus, he paid no attention to shot composition or mise-en-scène (the way a former director, George Nichols, had effectively). Chaplin was, like Sennett, preoccupied with what was happening on screen and only concerned that it remain in frame. On this film, it appears Chaplin is chiefly supervising the comedy, based on the style exhibited by the actors. Critics were quite pleased with this latest Keystone comedy. A 1914 issue of *Bioscope* stated: "The mix-up between Mabel, Charles and the dummy is extremely funny. . . . Mr. Chaplin gives a very excellent study in inebriation. This is certainly one of the best of the Keystone comedies."

With the understanding that Chaplin did not direct this film, but with so many Chaplinesque touches, *Mabel's Married Life* could likely have been another training film for Chaplin's abilities as *Twenty Minutes of Love* had been. From this point on, beginning with his very next film, Chaplin would write and direct all of his remaining Keystone productions other than the feature-length *Tillie's Punctured Romance*. Eager to express himself more completely, Chaplin also chose to use his background and rework stories he'd performed on stage in the Karno troop. Translating these ideas from stage to film could have resulted in limited productions (even more so than Keystone's usual fare), but Chaplin worked to open up the proceedings. The results are often quite impressive.

Along with being the last Keystone Chaplin that he did not direct himself, *Mabel's Married Life* is also the last short comedy produced while Chaplin and Sennett and Normand were also filming *Tillie's Punctured Romance*. Lifted from that distraction, Chaplin could now engage in sole responsibility for his own comedies, not only directing them but writing them as well (albeit this is speculative in that there are no surviving writing credits on these films and no documented evidence Chaplin did write them—except for interviews and writings he did years later when he claimed such credit).

But what is interesting about Chaplin's directing at Keystone is the fact that some of the films are typical Keystone comedies that might have been directed by Sennett himself. Chaplin does not always put his indelible stamp on a production. Eventually he would move away from the more typical Keystone method and attempt to incorporate different story ideas and character-driven scenes that rely on more than pure knockabout. But some of his subsequent self-directed Keystones are as frenetic and outrageous as, say, *Tango Tangles*.

Chaplin stated in his autobiography that while filming *Tillie's Punctured Romance*, he was "eager to get back to directing himself." And his next few films are interesting as how his vision worked within the parameters of the typical Keystone comedy.

# CHAPTER 24

# *Laughing Gas*

**Alternate titles:** *Tuning His Ivories; The Dentist; Down and Out; Laffing Gas; Busy Little Dentist*

Running Time: One Reel
Filmed June 15–22, 1914
Released July 9, 1914

**Credits**
Written and directed by Charlie Chaplin

**Cast**
Charlie Chaplin (Janitor), Mack Swain (Big Man by Drugstore), Slim Summerville (Man on the Street), Fritz Schade (Dentist), Alice Howell (Dentist's Wife), Josef Swickard (Patient), Fred Fishback (Patient with Beard), Peggy Page (Patient). (Contrary to some sources, neither Edward Sutherland, Joseph Sutherland, nor Gene Marsh appears in this film.)

Charlie Chaplin wrote and directed *Laughing Gas*, and he would write and direct all of his subsequent Keystone releases, save for the feature-length *Tillie's Punctured Romance*, which had completed filming just prior to *Laughing Gas* entering production but would not be released until the end of 1914. It is from this point that we are able to truly assess Chaplin's development as a filmmaker and not merely as an actor or gagman. What he learned from his previous directors, how his cinematic vision grew, and what he chose to investigate and eventually hone are all part of Chaplin's evolution from this point.

Some Keystone films that Chaplin did not direct actually seem more Chaplinesque than *Laughing Gas*, due to his uncredited input behind the camera. With *Laughing Gas*, the frenetic Keystone style is retained, there is little added nuance to the characters, and the slapstick is often violent. Further, this film concludes with a free-for-all, which indicates that Sennett's final say as producer was beyond Chaplin's decision. Chaplin did not like ending his films in such a manner, but at Keystone it was a staple and, according to Sennett, expected by his audience. Thus, there were things upon which Sennett insisted that Chaplin had to follow. Soon Chaplin would be lured away from Keystone with the promise that he could supervise his own productions more completely. Still the auteur, Chaplin now freely explored what he could do within the Keystone parameters.

Dentistry has long been a staple in comedy, used in such movies as Stan Laurel's *White Wings* (1923), Laurel and Hardy's *Leave 'Em Laughing* (1928), W. C. Fields's *The Dentist* (1932), the Three Stooges' *I Can Hardly Wait* (1943), and later features such as Roger Corman's *Little Shop of Horrors* (1960) and Steve Martin's *Novacaine* (2001). Chaplin chose to probe dentistry for comedy possibilities due to his own misgivings about going to the dentist. Family members have given accounts of how it was difficult to get him to see a dentist even for a checkup. Chaplin also had performed in a comedy dental bit on stage with Fred Karno's acting troupe. Opening it up for film, including outdoor scenes, Chaplin embellished on something with which he had complete familiarity.

Eschewing camera angles, and editing only to change sequences, Chaplin offers little in the way of interesting filmmaking in the manner of George Nichols or Mabel Normand. Chaplin's style here is closer to Mack Sennett's method of pointing and shooting, keeping the action within the frame. *Laughing Gas* is a plotless one-reeler of constant slapstick activity. It flies by quickly, contains some very funny gag ideas, and benefits from the performances of its players.

In the threadbare story, Charlie is a janitor in a dentist's office. He runs amok, getting into trouble with the dental assistant and the patients in the waiting room. When he is dispatched to a drugstore to pick something up, he gets into a brick-throwing fight that sends two townspeople to the dentist with their teeth knocked out. When they arrive and see Charlie, a free-for-all breaks out and the film concludes.

On this simple premise, Chaplin works hard to develop situations with a variety of different characters, placing Charlie in the middle. He also continues to enjoy presenting physical contrasts. The dental assistant, for instance, is much smaller, so he is bullied by Charlie. The two men Charlie battles in the street are much taller. One is big Mack Swain, who dwarfs Charlie and whom Chaplin nearly always cast in his films. The size contrasts extend to the waiting room, where the patients are all much larger. When Charlie clumsily runs a carpet sweeper in the waiting room, carelessly running into the toes of the waiting patients, he is confronted by a tall, imposing man with a thick beard. Unafraid, Charlie makes apelike gestures to mock the man's whiskered appearance.

Charlie continues to be the lone scamp, which initially endeared him to audiences. He is consistently defiant, maintains his tasks despite anything in his way, and is comically disruptive in a manner that causes moviegoers to feel a sense of triumph.

*Original movie ad, with no mention of the actors' names or that Chaplin directed.*

The title of the film figures prominently in that the dentist here uses nitrous oxide as an anesthetic. Of course "laughing gas" does not actually make one laugh, and by the time this film was made, nitrous oxide had been used for the purposes of dental anesthesia for about 70 years. But Chaplin takes the name seriously for comic purposes. A patient being prepared by the dentist for

*Patient Josef Swickard reacts to Charlie's anesthetic.*

an extraction has the gas administered and bursts into uncontrollable laughter. Charlie is dispatched to the drugstore to pick up an antidote, allowing for him to engage in a situation with the two men on the street.

The street confrontation is standard, again using enormous Mack Swain as Charlie's antagonist. Swain appears to be doing little more than loitering in front of the drugstore when Charlie accosts him. Mack the lummox is simply taking up too much room near the entrance. Mack responds in kind, and eventually things evolve into a brick-throwing battle. Mack gets hit in the mouth with a brick, as does a tall, gangly man, simply for being in the way. Each has his teeth knocked out by the blow, and they end up at the dentist where Charlie works. Meanwhile, trying to escape the battle in the street, Charlie has banged into a woman attempting to ascend a porch staircase, causing her dress to be ripped away in the process. When the woman rushes into her home, she discovers the minister and his wife have arrived for a visit. The sight of her bursting into the house with her dress ripped away causes the shocked holy couple to abruptly leave. The woman turns out to be the dentist's wife. The maid calls the dentist and asks that he come home because his wife has met with an accident. He leaves, and Charlie manages the office.

The conflicts presented up to this point allow Chaplin to use his various characters in the same series of conflicts as had been evident in *Twenty Minutes of Love*, for which he had creative input without actually directing the film. Here he appears to rest on the same creative inspiration for different comedy situations and conflicts. Charlie has no regard for other people. He bullies the smaller dental assistant, carelessly runs the carpet sweeper into suffering patients, hits patients in their sore jaws when they confront him, starts fights in the street, and offers no apology when he yanks off an innocent woman's dress. While his later character would be quite sympathetic, Keystone Charlie remains a scamp. By now Mack Sennett's most profitable star, Chaplin maintained the image for which he had achieved that popularity.

In the only scene in *Laughing Gas* that is not at all raucous, Charlie, in charge of the office in the dentist's absence, actually poses as the doctor upon discovering a pretty patient in the waiting room. While she is in the dentist's chair, Charlie makes every effort to flirt with her, from pretending to shine her shoes with the dental towel, to plopping his leg across her lap. Charming her with his disarming silliness, Charlie eventually is bold enough to use a dental tool to turn her head toward his so he can kiss her. She offers some weak, mock protests, but her smiles indicate she is enjoying this extra attention. While Charlie remains the boorish scamp, this scene comes off as a tender approach to his own special method of wooing.

The free-for-all climax seems like a pat way to end this funny one-reeler. Had it been directed by Sennett, perhaps one could better understand its reliance on slapstick gags. Since it was directed by Chaplin, we must focus on what might make it different from what Sennett could provide. *Laughing Gas* does show its Sennett influence, but Chaplin's own touches are discernible. Each character appears to have been carefully coached. Even Josef Swickard, as the hapless man laughing uncontrollably in the dentist's chair, lifts his legs and folds his arms in much the same manner as Charlie would. Everyone in the film, to some extent, acts like Charlie. It is said Chaplin directed his actors by performing the part himself and expecting them to mimic what he'd done. This is quite evident in *Laughing Gas*, which makes it more interesting but not necessarily funnier.

What makes this movie funny are its performances. Despite the careful, exacting approach of Chaplin as a director, an accomplished actor like Mack Swain, for instance, could still define the material based on his own ideas. He certainly must have responded correctly to Chaplin's direction, as he would be used as late as 1925 for *The Gold Rush*, which may be the finest performance of Mack Swain's career. The other performers are, at this time, limited to support and offer no real distinctions other than to enhance the performance of the film's star.

Charlie is the axis of the film. What he does dictates the pace and the action. He frantically tries to perform his custodial duties, hurriedly attempts to get the antidote the doctor needs, slapping and bullying his way in and out of situations. Even as he sweeps the waiting room carpet, he is completely focused on his task with no regard for the suffering patients seated about. When they confront him, and he pops them in the jaw, he is taking full advantage of their suffering. This sort of defiance was embraced by period audiences who loved slapstick.

Perhaps the most interesting aspect of *Laughing Gas* is how Chaplin takes a stage sketch from his days with the Karno troupe and re-creates it for the cinema. Without the original sketch's specifics, we cannot determine exactly how Chaplin revamped it. But it is likely the sequences that take place in the dentist's office are the bulk of the sketch, as they would play effectively on stage. The embellishment comes from Charlie's intrusive sweeping in the waiting room and the outdoor footage. The comedy is very broad, as would befit its stage origin, and for Keystone there is no reason to pare it down.

*Laughing Gas* is fitfully funny in the Keystone tradition and a good, earthy starting point for Chaplin's continued directorial career. Its primitive style and Chaplin's reliance on the Keystone formula are more interesting than funny. However, placing this film in its historical context, it is exactly the type of entertainment most moviegoers looked forward to seeing. *Bioscope* stated at the time of the movie's initial release, "This is an uproarious farce of a kind which is likely to create unrestrained mirth for its particular class of audience." With ensuing films, Chaplin would explore other possibilities as a director—not via technical achievement (Chaplin was never a director interested in cinema's technical capabilities), but instead with the proper structure in creating and executing comedy situations.

Occasionally Chaplin would experiment with shot composition, perhaps not at the level of previous director George Nichols, but certainly more so than his subsequent reputation as a director with limited technical scope would have one believe. Chaplin would never employ such a level of technical achievement as Buster Keaton or even Roscoe Arbuckle, but he did have a particular vision and was most interested in making the characters and situations seem interesting and involving for the audience.

Chaplin's popularity continued to grow, especially now that he was supervising his own productions. According to Brent Walker in his book *Mack Sennett's Fun Factory*, "By April, Sennett had given Chaplin the directorial reins to his own comedies. Like a snowball, the comedian's momentum of popularity continued to build."

The success of *Laughing Gas* allowed Chaplin to make a two-reel comedy, *The Property Man*, as his next project. That film continues to be singled out as his most violently abusive. It is also structurally sound and an excellent example of how Chaplin was able to refine slapstick vulgarity.

Around the time *Laughing Gas* was released, Charlie Chaplin's first seven Keystone films were made available in Great Britain. In an article titled "Are You Ready for the Chaplin Boom?" Keystone advertised their star comedian overseas with a press release that stated: "There has never been so instantaneous a hit as that of Charles Chaplin, the famous Karno comedian in Keystone Comedies. Most first-rank exhibitors have booked every film in which he appears, and after the first releases there is certain to be a big rush for copies." *Kinematograph Weekly* stated: "We have seen seven Chaplin releases, and every one has been a triumph for the one-time hero of *Mumming Birds* who has leapt into the front rank of film comedians at a bound."

Compared to the strides he was making at this point, Chaplin's first seven films might have looked comparatively crude. *Making a Living, Kid Auto Races at Venice, Cal., Mabel's Strange Predicament, Between Showers, A Film Johnnie, Tango Tangles,* and *His Favorite Pastime* all have their moments of interest, and some offer important lessons for Chaplin's eventual career as a director as well as a writer. But by the time he filmed *Laughing Gas,* Chaplin had learned much more, refined his screen character, and had a solid understanding of effective movie direction. More of Chaplin's Keystone films would be desired by overseas film distributors, making the Keystone company quite a formidable presence.

# CHAPTER 25

# *The Property Man*

**Alternate titles: *The Roustabout; Getting His Goat; Props; Charlie on the Boards; Vamping Venus; Hits of the Past***

Running Time: Two Reels
Filmed June 25–July 11, 1914
Released August 1, 1914

**Credits**
Written and directed by Charlie Chaplin

**Cast**
Charlie Chaplin (Property Man), Phyllis Allen (Ham Lena Fat), Jess Dandy (Garlico the Strongman), Fritz Schade (Singer), Josef Swickard (Elderly Assistant), Charles Bennett (Actor), Vivian Edwards, Cecile Arnold (Dancers), Mack Sennett, Harry McCoy, Frank Opperman, Dixie Chene, Dan Albert, Slim Summerville, Charles Lakin, Edwin Frazee, Peggy Page (Audience Members)

Something of a milestone in that it is the first two-reel comedy that Chaplin directed, *The Property Man* is one of his most impressive Keystone efforts, especially since it comes so early in his directorial career. Having twice as much footage to work in his various ideas, Chaplin chooses to parody something that he knows quite well—the inner workings of smalltime vaudeville productions. Chaplin takes his time during the full two-reel length to cover everything, from the unpreparedness of the backstage help, to the limited talents and huge egos of the performers, to finally the boorishness of the audience. Often relying on violent slapstick situations, *The Property Man* is a joy to watch.

There is no discernible plot to *The Property Man*. Charlie plays the title character in a seedy theater where several low-level acts are scheduled to perform. Since he is in charge of all props, the acts come to him more frequently than they do the stage manager. This puts Charlie in the forefront of the action, surrounded by a variety of different and interesting characters. A dramatic actress is chagrined about not receiving any billing on the outside poster. A temperamental singer is making demands. A strongman and his assistant are using strength to intimidate the other acts. An attractive female dancing duo is distracting Charlie from the job at hand. Meanwhile, Charlie is in charge of an elderly assistant, whom he physically abuses with punches, kicks, and shoving. Charlie's assistant is smaller, slimmer, and much older. His slow, stooped-over gait seems unlikely for a prop assistant who must carry large pieces of scenery. Charlie enforces his superiority by shoving the elderly man around, and the assistant's fragile appearance contrasts with his ability to take a spill (the actor playing this role, Josef Swickard, was only in his 40s at the time but was made up to look much older).

Chaplin calls upon his own veteran stage experience to exaggerate situations surrounding the production of a vaudeville show. The acts, although treading the boards in the seediest theaters, enter the premises quite haughtily. Charlie does not suffer these fools gladly. When a smalltime actor enters the backstage area while smoking, Charlie points out the "No Smoking" sign, even though he himself is smoking a pipe. When the dramatic actress comes in complaining about receiving no billing, Charlie puts cotton in his ears to ignore her.

Chaplin was always interested in presenting physical contrasts among his players, often pitting Charlie against a much larger antagonist. Along with Charlie's contrast with his elderly assistant, Chaplin continues to exhibit contrasts via his confrontation with Garlico the Strongman. Garlico bullies Charlie in the

*Charlie lazily takes a break in the first two-reeler he directed.*

same manner as Charlie bullies his assistant, pushing him around and treating him as a lackey, an underling whose status in life is as a subordinate.

Smoking a foul-smelling cigar, Garlico immediately starts barking orders as he enters the backstage area. Charlie, too intimidated by the man's presence, does not enforce the smoking ban; he instead turns the sign around. Garlico assigns Charlie the task of carrying his heavy trunk and boxes to his dressing room. After a few failed attempts, Charlie delegates the task to his elderly underling. Both men have the same problem maneuvering the heavy, bulky object, especially as they venture down the stairs. Charlie does a fall down the stairs, and later up the stairs as well. The elderly assistant carries the trunk on his stooped back while also using a cane—details in performance that Chaplin obviously felt would add to the humor. Making the man elderly is one thing, but adding such props as a cane to maintain his limited posture is the subtle emphasis that enhances the absurdity of his task.

Chaplin's directorial choreography is impressive. The steps that are necessary to get to the backstage area are not particularly steep, so in a medium shot he can contain the action and just enough negative space to make the pratfall effective. Charlie balances the heavy boxes and trunks on his back, creating a workhorse image that subdues his disruptive behavior and puts him at the mercy of the inanimate object. It is the portent to the opening scene in his 1915 Essanay production *Work*, where he pulls a wagon up a steep hill like a mule. The sequence in the later film is framed in a long shot, with more negative space. The comic situation is a good example of how Chaplin's earlier directorial efforts at Keystone were often the blueprint for work he would later hone at other studios.

In *The Property Man*, Chaplin seems particularly interested in hierarchy. The leading act, Garlico, bullies Charlie and the other acts. Charlie bullies his elderly assistant. The dramatic actress is an overbearing presence who dismisses her male co-star as an underling. With these situations, Chaplin appears to be investigating the general caste system that existed behind the scenes in the smaller show business venues. The performers limited to one-nighters in rundown theaters believe themselves to be worthy of star treatment, just as worker Charlie assumes superiority over his assistant.

Another interesting aspect of *The Property Man* is how Chaplin exhibits the comedy of humiliation. The elderly assistant is continually humiliated by Charlie's behavior toward him, from not sharing his beverage pitcher, to striking a match on the heavy trunk under which the assistant struggles helplessly. Charlie is humiliated in his attempt to attract the female dancers on the bill. Speaking to the young women in a flirtatious manner, while concealing his pitcher of drink in his baggy trousers, Charlie bends to pick something up and spills some of the beverage in his pants, resulting in a very embarrassing situation. The conceited singer is humiliated when his act is cut short by a prematurely falling curtain.

The strongman must perform sans his missing tights. The dramatic act is booed off the stage. Humiliation is a constant theme in *The Property Man*, where the fragile egos of the smalltime performers meet comic comeuppance.

Often *The Property Man* is discussed in terms of Charlie's sadistic behavior toward his elderly underling, so it is important to address the violence contained in this comedy. The slapping, kicking, and shoving are the same sort of violence found in many Keystone comedies (and would be elevated to a veritable art form by the Three Stooges years later). But an element of cruelty is discerned by some viewers when Charlie does not rush to his assistant's aid when the old man is trapped under a heavy trunk. He prefers to flirt with the pretty young woman who assists Garlico. While his assistant struggles, Charlie and the young woman whisper in each other's ear. Soon they engage in a balance challenge. First, Charlie grabs hold of his own ankle and raises one leg up as high as he can. When the woman shows she can do it as well, Charlie playfully pushes her down. Shortly thereafter, Garlico comes over and confronts the woman, putting his hands around her neck. Charlie braces to kick the strongman but backs off when Garlico turns around and sees him. Things settle quickly, and the strongman rescues Charlie's assistant from under the heavy trunk. Charlie's awestruck reaction to Garlico's effortless lifting and casting aside an object that seemed insurmountable makes it clear he is glad to not have come between the strongman and his assistant.

In his biography *Charlie Chaplin*, John McCabe responded to such violence in *The Property Man* thusly: "A cheerful cruelty characterized many of Sennett's films [and] Charlie became master of the process. . . . *The Property Man* is no exception. In his short films, Charlie's sadism is incessant. One does not laugh at a cartoon—which is what *The Property Man* is—because it is real, but precisely because it is unreal, a caricature of life's troubles."

All of this is merely the setup to the second reel of *The Property Man*, which presents the various acts in performance. Chaplin does a brilliant job crosscutting from the stage to backstage to members of the audience, this last ingredient being a key addition to the remainder of the film. The audience is indicative of the seediness of the theater and the limited skills of the performers. Audience members are sloppy, boorish, and disheveled. One lummox (played by Mack Sennett) is seated front and center. A sleepy drunk is at his left; a woman holding a small dog is on his right. Chaplin frames the audience and judiciously places particular people in the right spots, including Sennett to anchor the center frame.

Recalling the stage experience that extends back into his childhood, Chaplin presents a vaudeville show that is every bit as good and as bad as history would lead us to believe. The acts are particularly substandard. First, a conceited singer takes the stage, until a backstage error causes the heavy curtain to come down

on top of him, delighting the audience. Charlie comes out and sweeps the pros-
trate man off the stage; he rolls off as Charlie applies a broom. When the female
dance duo performs, Charlie continues his admiration for them by coming out
and standing at stage right, leaning against the curtain and smoking his pipe;
checking out their every move.

These are, of course, exaggerations of what did happen in some vaudeville
shows. Vaudeville lore has indicated that some acts were so bad, they were removed from the stage while performing. Vaudeville performers recall the hook,
which was a cane that would yank a performer off stage, and the hoop, a device
that would encircle a performer and yank him into the orchestra pit. Chaplin
parodies this by having Charlie literally sweep a performer off stage as if he were
relegated to so much dust, and Charlie then returns to the stage holding his nose,
indicating just why that performance was unceremoniously cancelled.

Charlie had earlier been entrusted to iron Garlico's tights, but they got lost
in the process. Thus, the strongman goes on without them. Yet another tussle
between Charlie and his elderly underling ends up with Garlico's female assistant
getting knocked out backstage. Charlie runs out to cover for her and makes a
shambles of the strongman's act. Charlie pushes weights onto Garlico's toe and
is unable to lift some of the props. Wanting to have some sly fun, Charlie tears
a handkerchief, imitating the sound of ripping pants, as Garlico bends to lift the
heaviest weight. He does this repeatedly, as Chaplin once again investigates the
comedy of humiliation. The audience is in on the joke, so the strongman mis-
takes their laughter for a derisive reaction to his plight. The humiliation endured
by Garlico during his act appears to be presented as his comeuppance for being
the most abusive character in the film.

The vaudeville show concludes with the dramatic act, featuring the woman
that so haughtily challenged not being billed on the advertising poster. The act
gets a poor reaction from the audience, who respond with gestures of displeasure,
while an argument backstage with Garlico, Charlie, and the assistant escalates
to the point where the strongman starts throwing weights at the others. In an
attempt to diffuse the situation, Charlie grabs a firehose and douses the acts and
the audience and destroys the stage. While *The Property Man* concludes with
essentially a Keystone free-for-all, Chaplin's choice to use a firehose as a prop offers something of a variation. The usual Keystone free-for-all conclusion was the
same sort of punching, kicking, and shoving that had permeated this film, but
Chaplin wisely did not go with the same sort of behavior for the ending. Pulling
out a firehouse to wash away all conflict is most effective.

There are many elements of Chaplin's creative vision evident in his first
two-reel effort. For example, he uses his penchant for contrasts in size and shape,
but instead of relying simply on larger actors as antagonists, he also incorporates objects, such as Garlico's large boxes and trunks with which Charlie must

grapple. Perhaps we can look back at his confrontation with the dummy in *Mabel's Married Life* as another example of battling an object, but in that case the object was mobile, Charlie was drunk, and his inebriated perspective anthropomorphized that which was otherwise inanimate. The heavy matter Charlie must carry as the title character is in contrast to the size of his own body.

Chaplin also taps into his own resources for gags and comic situations involving the staging of a show. Having experienced some of the seediest and most undesirable theatrical conditions, Chaplin was able to present comic variations on the smalltime performer with a far loftier opinion of his or her own status and skills, as well as the general tumult of what can happen backstage. The backstage setting is filled with conflicts over billing, dressing rooms, and other such externals. Chaplin perceived the man in charge of props as the focal point of these situations, thus casting himself in that role and presenting Charlie as central to nearly every one of these backstage conflicts.

The most effective and interesting portion of the film is the presentation of the acts themselves. The success or failure of each act, the activity backstage that has to be timed perfectly, and the reaction (and appearance) of the audience are all key ingredients to the effectiveness of this sequence. The timing of Chaplin's shots during this sequence assist in its presentation. He never holds his shots of the stage, the audience, or the backstage antics for too long, nor does he suddenly cut away too rapidly. Chaplin has the camera stay on the audience just long enough to present their reaction to the act and sometimes to each other. Sennett's appearance as a front-row lummox stationed comfortably at center frame, and surrounded by a fairly small crowd of similarly boorish types, is especially amusing. He reacts to the stage performances with varied enthusiasms, shrieking delightedly at such offbeat things as a curtain falling heavily on a performer while he is singing, or Charlie's remaining on stage to ogle the dancers during their act. With a drunken patron resting his sleeping head on his left shoulder, a woman with a small dog seated to his right, Sennett's rube character comes off as comparatively normal by comparison.

The longest shot is the strongman performing dull yet impressive feats of strength. When Charlie joins him as a substitute assistant and ruins his act with the practical joke of ripping a piece of cloth as Garlico bends to lift a weight, it amuses the audience more than the act itself. The camera shoots the stage with a far enough medium shot so that Charlie, Garlico, and some negative space at the left are in frame. The cut to the audience, crowded onto the frame with no negative space, not only presents their cramped quarters as they chortle with delight at Charlie's antics, but also contrasts with the amount of room on the stage for this sprawling act with its barbells and free weights.

With all of its brutal slapstick humor, *The Property Man* is consistently amusing and a remarkable piece of work for coming so early in Chaplin's directorial career. His intricate comic ideas, their abundance and structure, show Chaplin's status as a veteran of the stage since childhood. However, his impressive editing technique, especially when cutting between three different settings, is something he had learned only months earlier (mostly from Mabel Normand, who mentored Chaplin in the cutting room). While his filmmaking ability never reached the lofty level of Buster Keaton's—a far more technologically savvy filmmaker—Chaplin was quickly learning the basic method in spotlighting his comic ideas most effectively.

The sadistic violence in *The Property Man* is off-putting to some, as it had been at the time of this film's release. A 1914 issue of *Motion Picture World* stated:

> There are very few people who don't like these Keystones. They are thoroughly vulgar and touch the homely strings of our own vulgarity. There is some brutality in this picture and we can't help feeling that this is reprehensible. What human being can see an old man kicked in the face and count it fun?

Chaplin himself addressed the more vulgar and extreme aspects of slapstick comedy in an interview with Clarence J. Cane for *Motography*: "I believe I have been ridiculed for some of my actions, but whatever I have done to offend has been unintentional I am sure, for my one objective in life now is to amuse, and to do it in a clean way." Audiences, however, responded favorably, and *The Property Man* was yet another hit for Chaplin, and for Mack Sennett.

It is perhaps possible for one to approach a film like *The Property Man* as violence for the sake of violence, with the weaker being dominated by an uncaring stronger one. Since Charlie is the central character and the one for whom the audience should have something of a rooting interest, it might skew an audience's perspective if approached in such a manner. However, the best way to look at *The Property Man* is as another example of Charlie Chaplin exploring both comic and cinematic territory that he had not yet fully explored. Along with this being his first direction in the two-reel format, Chaplin also explores Keystone's penchant for violent slapstick purely from the class system aspect, with the higher up overpowering the lower. When searching beyond the surface gags, *The Property Man* has a fairly important place in Chaplin's filmography.

With his next film, *The Face on the Bar Room Floor*, Chaplin chose to go in a different direction entirely, tapping into literature as his inspiration and investigating headier areas of filmmaking. The result is one of the most intriguing films of his career.

# CHAPTER 26

# The Face on the Bar Room Floor

**Alternate titles: *The Ham Artist; The Ham Actor; Barroom; The Artist; Charlie Loses His Girl; Charlie Goes Mad***

Running Time: One Reel
Filmed July 13–20, 1914
Released August 10, 1914

**Credits**
Written and directed by Charlie Chaplin
Based on the poem by Hugh Antoine D'Arcy

**Cast**
Charlie Chaplin (Artist), Cecile Arnold (Model), Jess Dandy (Her Lover), Vivian Edwards (Model), Charles Bennett (Sailor in Bar), Josef Swickard, Chester Conklin, Fritz Schade, Frank Opperman, Edwin Frazee, Harry McCoy (Men in Bar), Eddie Nolan (Bartender)

With *The Face on the Bar Room Floor*, Charlie Chaplin offers the first example of ideas he has been harboring that might not fit the traditional Keystone style. Working from literary source material, using flashbacks, and for the most part, avoiding typical Keystone knockabout slapstick, *The Face on the Bar Room Floor* is one of Chaplin's most impressive Keystone one-reelers.

The source is an 1887 poem by Hugh Antoine D'Arcy, which begins:

> 'Twas a balmy summer evening, and a goodly crowd was there,
> That well nigh filled Joe's barroom at the corner of the square.
> As songs and witty stories came through the open door,
> A vagabond crept slowly in and posed upon the floor.

The patrons of the bar initially ridicule this stranger, who bears this "with stoical good grace." Then he tells them,

> "Give me a drink, that's what I want. I'm out of funds you know;
> When I had cash to treat the gang, this hand was never slow.
> What? You laugh as though you think this pocket never held a sou.
> I once was fixed as well, my boys, as any one of you."

After someone complies with his request for a drink, he tells them the sad story of his rise and fall. He was once a successful artist who fell in love with a beautiful woman named Madeline. But she left him for another man and he never recovered from the loss.

> "My friend had stolen my darling, and I was left alone.
> And ere a year of misery had passed above my head.
> That jewel I treasured so had tarnished and was dead."

The others in the bar are unexpectedly touched by his story, and the artist tells them that for another drink, he will draw Madeline's portrait for them.

> "Say boys, if you give me just another whiskey I'll be glad,
> I'll draw right here the picture of the face that drove me mad.
> Give me that piece of chalk with which you mark the baseball score;
> You shall see the lovely Madeline upon the barroom floor."

> Another drink, and with chalk in hand, the vagabond began
> To sketch a face that well might buy the soul of any man.
> Then, as he placed another lock upon that shapely head,
> With a fearful shriek, he leaped and fell across the picture—dead!

Chaplin uses portions of the poem as title cards to propel the narrative, and then, within the Keystone framework, acts out the story. His opening scene has him stumbling dejectedly into a bar, the title card offering enough of the D'Arcy poem to introduce him. As he is given a drink, Charlie begins telling his story, as does the vagabond in the poem.

This very first sequence is especially impressive for the way Chaplin composes the shot. Within Keystone's usual barroom set—the bar at the viewer's right, stretching into the background, with patrons in front of it—Chaplin places Charlie in the foreground, as the other drinkers surround him. The others are stationed carefully, with their contrasting sizes, shapes, and manner of dress helping to frame Charlie as he tells of his exploits.

His story is presented in flashback, showing Charlie the artist before a canvas, a pretty model posing for him. As he works on the painting, his attraction to the model is palpable. The composition of this shot is similar to the previous one at the bar, only this time Charlie is surrounded by inanimate objects of art, from hanging paintings to sculptures. The motionless live model is posing behind him to the left of the frame while he stands before his easel in the immediate foreground. The negative space between the artist and his model indicates the distance between them, contrasting with the drinkers in the barroom all standing close to Charlie, with any negative space relegated to outside their parameters.

These opening scenes point out Chaplin's ambition to explore comedy avenues outside of his experience at Karno or, thus far, Keystone. Any humor within the dramatic set pieces inspired by the D'Arcy poem is very subtle. While deep in thought, Charlie taps his wet paintbrush against his white shirt, marking it up. Continuing to ponder, he places the brush into his mouth, quickly spitting out its contents. Crude physical comedy, perhaps, but played with natural subtlety rather than in the more extreme manner as usually expected from a Keystone production.

The poem's stanza referring to the young man with whom the model becomes smitten, breaking the artist's heart, is used for an especially funny visual. As this portion of the poem is presented via title card, the next shot is of Charlie

*Charlie plays the offbeat role of a jilted artist.*

painting the portrait of a bald, pudgy, middle-aged fellow who is the antithesis of the "fair haired boy" referred to in the poem.

When the artist's young rival convinces the model that they should run away together, she leaves Charlie a note. Upon seeing it, he reacts in more melo-dramatic fashion than comic, which is part of Chaplin's subtle parody, save for the fact that he sits on a stool where he's placed his paints.

The dramatic sequencing is never dull, easily drawing in the viewer with the performances of the cast, while Chaplin further attracts the audience with his usual penchant for visual contrasts. Casting chubby Jess Dandy as the object of the model's affections is a neat bit of comic incongruity, especially since the poem describes a completely different type. Chaplin is also careful to present Charlie in different guises. During the artist's flashback, he is handsome, dis-playing creativity, surrounded by his accomplishments. During the barroom sequences, he is staggering, disheveled, and defeated. These contrasts, even if only noticed subconsciously by the viewer, assist with the success of the film's narrative message.

Chaplin offers yet another contrast by showing Charlie alone on a park bench, noticing the couple as they walk by. They do not present an idyllic im-age. The woman is yelling at the husband, as he pushes a baby buggy with five other children in tow. Once again Chaplin goes for a laugh with complete in-congruity with the poem, but he has Charlie react in a sorrowful manner as per the vagabond in the original verse. It is this incident that leads the heartbroken artist to the bar.

The only absolute connection to Keystone tradition in *The Face on the Bar Room Floor* is the tussle that Charlie gets into with the bar patrons once he prepares to draw her portrait on the floor with chalk. In the poem, the artist's rendering is accurate and beautiful, concluding with his dropping dead across the image. In the film, Charlie bends over to draw and falls over. He tries again, manages a circle with slashes for eyes, and falls into a somersault onto the floor. The other drinkers are unimpressed, and a short free-for-all erupts, as Charlie clears the bar with his fighting. He then does fall over as the last line of the poem indicates, but the title card augments the verse by stating "dead—drunk!"

With *The Face on the Bar Room Floor*, Chaplin reworks many of his standard traits for another style completely. His drunk act, dating back to his Karno days and relied upon often in his Keystone comedies, is shown less for comedy and more for drama. He is not simply a boisterous drinker who causes disruptions; he is someone whose drinking can be traced to a specific incident. The situations with different couples arguing, flirting, and betraying within a comic structure (often set in a park) are now relegated to just one situation that is played straight. Any comedy comes from subtle character traits, such as Charlie the artist using a long pole to move the male model's head.

It is interesting that Chaplin engaged in such a complete departure for this film, and surprising that Sennett agreed to produce a comedy that was quite different from what had been expected from the comedian. *The Face on the Bar Room Floor* certainly is not as superficially funny as something like *Laughing Gas*, the latter being more typically raucous and filled with wild slapstick gags. However, the more delicate presentation and its offbeat source material make *The Face on the Bar Room Floor* another departure for Chaplin that works effectively. The film's attempt to evoke sympathy from the audience as well as laughter portends how Chaplin would eventually define his film career.

Previous studies have not offered a great deal of accuracy in assessing *The Face on the Bar Room Floor*. For decades, the only readily available copy of this film was devoid of most subtitles and had some scenes placed in the wrong order. It was nearly impossible to comprehend the narrative, the only enjoyment being garnered by the subtlety of the performances. The British Film Institute restoration of Chaplin's Keystone films in 2009 have corrected the problems with *The Face on the Bar Room Floor*, allowing us to assess it properly as an ambitious breakthrough.

Period reviews and audiences fully accepted Chaplin's choice to make what was for him such a different film. Moviegoers were quite familiar with the various styles and methods of silent melodrama, so the accuracy of Chaplin's parody was quite a success.

*The Face on the Bar Room Floor* is to be commended on several levels. First, it allows us to see Chaplin's initial attempt to draw some level of sympathy from the viewer. Second, it is interesting for being so different from the other Chaplin Keystones up to this point. Finally, and most significantly, it draws from several ideas used previously but presents them in a different manner. Chaplin's versatility as a comedian and his eye as a director were, to this point, never more impressive.

# CHAPTER 27

# *Recreation*

**Alternate titles:** *Spring Fever; Fun Is Fun; His Recreation*

Running Time: Half Reel
Filmed July 21, 1914
Released August 13, 1914

**Credits**
Written and directed by Charlie Chaplin

**Cast**
Charlie Chaplin (Tramp), Charles Bennett (Sailor in Bar), Edwin Frazee (Small Cop),
Eddie Nolan (Tall Cop), Peggy Page (Girl)

Shot in one day immediately upon completion of *The Face on the Bar Room Floor*, and running less than a reel, *Recreation* was obviously thrown together to appease exhibitors clamoring for more Charlie Chaplin movies. Chaplin had rapidly increased his popularity with each new release. By the time he filmed *Recreation*, his movies up to and including *Laughing Gas* were all in regular distribution at theaters. Keystone never advertised its actors, so theater owners would simply put a photograph of Chaplin on display out front, which would attract customers, and audiences would stay for repeated showings of the Chaplin comedies, filling the nickelodeon with screams of laughter throughout. This continued success needed little marketing by theater owners, so they naturally wanted as much Chaplin product as possible. Sennett was naturally pleased with the financial success of the films and thus gave Chapin the creative control he so desired (and deserved). While Sennett preferred that Chaplin stay within the structure of the successfully established Keystone formula, he did allow the comedian to stretch, as indicated by *The Face on the Bar Room Floor*. In exchange for that creative control, Chaplin agreed to quickly produce another, more typical Keystone comedy immediately upon the other film's completion. The result is *Recreation*.

There is really nothing to this movie other than its situations. Charlie and a sailor fight over a young woman in a park, punches and bricks are thrown, a couple of cops get involved, and everyone ends up dunked in the lake at the end. Running under ten minutes, *Recreation* uses a simple framework and a series of typical Keystone gags. It is fast paced and funny, but of little note. Charlie is playing the typical Keystone scamp he usually portrayed—prone to disrupting other settings and exploding into violent brick-throwing fights. It is all rather predictable and unremarkable, even with the understanding that it is frequently funny.

*Recreation* is not completely devoid of interest beyond its superficial amusement. The necessity of its having to be produced is an indicator of Chaplin's immense popularity. Chaplin having to hastily assemble a comedy on short notice is a harbinger to another incident that occurred for the same reason once he left Keystone for the Essanay studios. At Essanay, Chaplin was allowed one thing Sennett would not give him—he could take as much time as he pleased with each production. Chaplin the perfectionist took a bit too much time with his film *The Tramp* and was instructed to put together a one-reeler in order to meet the demand by theaters, which had increased to enormous levels by this time. The resulting film, *By the Sea*, is one of his better Essanay one-reelers. *Recreation*, however, does not quite reach so lofty a level. It is not one of Chaplin's best Keystones but is instead one of his most typical and dismissible.

The timing of the performers, the execution of the gags, the cheerfully violent slapstick, and the rapid pace all combine to provide some basic amusement, but that is the extent of the film's aesthetic success. For all the time and care Chaplin took to compose his shots for *The Face on the Bar Room Floor*, it appears that with *Recreation* he does little more than instruct the cinematographer to keep the action within its frame. There is no composition, no investigating of contrasts, and any negative space is just what happens to exist, unplanned, within the sequence. Echo Park was a frequent setting for Keystone's park comedies, and that is the setting for *Recreation*.

Despite its having been hastily produced and little more than a series of superficially amusing gags, *Recreation* was nevertheless appreciated in its time. The 1914 issue of *The Cinema* stated, "Charlie has a peculiar manner entirely his own, and the way he tries to extricate himself from an awkward position is very whimsical."

With his next film, *The Masquerader*, Chaplin was able to get back into a production for which he could draw from loftier creative ideas. And the film would turn out to be another of his best self-directed Keystone efforts.

# CHAPTER 28

# *The Masquerader*

**Alternate titles: *The Female Impersonator; Putting One Over; The Picnic; Charlie at the Studio; Charlie the Actor; The Perfumed Lady***

Running Time: One Reel
Filmed July 25–August 1, 1914
Released August 27, 1914

**Credits**
Written and directed by Charlie Chaplin

**Cast**
Charlie Chaplin (Actor), Charlie Murray (Director), Roscoe Arbuckle (Actor), Mabel Normand (Actress), Chester Conklin (Actor Playing Hero), Jess Dandy (Actor Playing Villain), Minta Durfee (Actress), Frank Opperman, Harry McCoy (Actors in Makeup Room), Billy Gilbert, Dan Albert (Cameramen), Glen Cavendor (Director), Cecile Arnold, Vivian Edwards, Dixie Chene, Helen Carruthers (Actresses), Frankie Dolan (Boy)

One of Charlie Chaplin's best and most ambitious Keystone efforts, *The Masquerader* investigates the background of film production and uses it as a backdrop for comedy. Chaplin was clearly inspired by one of this own earlier films, *A Film Johnnie*, which had been helmed for Keystone by George Nichols. While Chaplin in later years completely dismissed Nichols as a veteran director with little vision, their films together belie this memory. Nichols composed his shots carefully, appeared to understand effective mise-en-scène, and spotlighted Charlie in the foreground. A veteran whose career dated back to the very first moving pictures, Nichols rebuffed newcomer Chaplin's ideas as too time consuming, but the director also had his own vision and believed the director should, as per his title, be in charge of the directorial process.

Perhaps *The Masquerader* is Chaplin's attempt to use the ideas he had been harboring since making *A Film Johnnie* some months earlier. While the previous film is one of his best from that early period before he started directing his own films, *The Masquerader* is one of the finest Keystone productions he himself directed. The immediate change is the role of Charlie in either film. Ted Okuda and David Maska, in their book *Chaplin at Keystone and Essanay*, point out that in *A Film Johnnie* he was a spectator, while in *The Masquerader* he is an active participant. This is true, but in both films he is disruptive and must formulate a way to enter the studio where he is not welcome.

In *The Masquerader*, Charlie is an actor in a movie being shot at the Keystone studios, but he causes a disruption with the production. When he is fired, he attempts to regain entry to the studio. After being unsuccessful, he dresses up as a woman and has greater success until eventually being found out.

As with most Keystones, there is little plot. But from this level, Chaplin does more with the premise of investigating the act of making movies as a basis for comedy than Nichols had. While Nichols did a good job in *A Film Johnnie* by showing noted Keystone actors like Roscoe Arbuckle and Ford Sterling out of character and sans makeup, reacting to fan Charlie's delightedly recognizing them, Chaplin offers another perspective in *The Masquerader*. He now presents Charlie as an insider, and the disruptions he causes are due to his inability to take direction, to respond to the studio's parameters, not because he is intrusively stalking a pretty actress.

*Charlie schemes to get back into the studio.*

It could stand to reason that Chaplin approached Nichols during the production of A *Film Johnnie* and offered some of what appears in *The Masquerader*, perhaps even its plot. Such changes would alter what had been already established for filming, so it would not be feasible to revamp an entire production. Nichols would be responding accurately that there was no time. Thus, a film like *The Masquerader* presents the level to which Chaplin's status had risen in his months at Keystone. Rather than offering unwelcome suggestions, Chaplin was now in full control of his production.

Expanding upon the previous film's presentation of what occurs behind the scenes at a movie studio, Chaplin was now able to probe more deeply from the perspective of Charlie being an active member as opposed to an outsider. While the Nichols film only shows what Charlie encounters outside and on the sidelines, Chaplin's own production takes the audience into the makeup room and presents the preparation necessary. Audiences were likely fascinated by seeing Charlie, sans mustache, preparing his character in the makeup room, with Roscoe "Fatty" Arbuckle doing the same nearby. The byplay between Charlie and Fatty, who are actually appearing as Charles and Roscoe in this opening sequence, is an amusing look at their noted characters. While applying his makeup, Arbuckle is casually sipping from a beverage. Charlie attempts to sneak it away, but Arbuckle catches him and replaces the bottle with one containing hair tonic. Charlie takes a swig and reacts.

Not a lot of time is spent on the evolution of Charles the actor and Charlie the tramp. It would be interesting to see the full metamorphosis of how the dapper, handsome, well-dressed performer becomes the devilish rascal he portrays on screen. When recalling the time he first applied the tramp makeup at Keystone, Chaplin remembered how the makeup itself assisted with creating the personality, allowing him to feel the part. The classy, stylish actor who enters the Keystone makeup room is far different from the comical tramp he portrays, so it is unfortunate that Chaplin does not choose to show the steps in creating the appearance. Instead, he does a comic bit with a powder puff, cuts away to another scene, and when he cuts back to Charles and Roscoe, his tramp makeup is in place. In fact, his comic byplay with Arbuckle has now evolved into a tussle with tossed makeup wares, their personalities both reverting to their respective Keystone characters now that they are in makeup.

Once we are on the set where filming is taking place, the similarities between Chaplin's film and Nichols's is more evident. Both attempt to present the crudity of motion picture production, the necessity to use the most accessible props and scenery, as well as the problems of the harried director in getting his ideas properly carried out, and the actors who cannot seem to completely grasp their roles. Chaplin adds backstage squabbles to the proceedings, presenting a conflict between Charles and fellow actor Chester Conklin. Unlike the physical contrast Chaplin usually presented in Charlie's encounters, frequently casting enormous Mack Swain as his adversary, Conklin is as diminutive as Chaplin, maybe even smaller. Their confrontational relationship would cross over into several Keystone films, Chaplin using him as an opponent of equal size and stature with whom he could engage in comic conflict.

Charlie's role in the film being shot is to rescue a woman and her child when a rotund villain prepares to stab them. The scene starts filming, and Charlie is accosted by two attractive female fans off screen. Distracted by their flirting, Charlie misses his cue and the director is livid. In later interviews, Chaplin would recall how Sennett was very budget minded, liked to keep things on schedule, and did not want to waste any production time. Naturally the director of each comedy would be responsible for staying within the allowed budget and schedule. Charlie's missed cue costs time and money. Thus, the nearby Chester is chosen as his replacement. When the scene plays again, Charlie holds Chester's coat and keeps him from meeting the cue, causing more havoc on the set. As a result, Charlie is fired.

Chaplin was often considered difficult (especially by George Nichols, who is said to have complained to Sennett about the newcomer's intrusive suggestions holding up the flow of production). While shooting *Mabel at the Wheel*, Chaplin was nearly fired after a conflict with director Mabel Normand. Perhaps casting Charlie as an on-set troublemaker indicated Chaplin was comfortable and secure enough to take comic issue with his past experiences. In any case, the comedy material that leads up to his dame masquerade is too often overlooked in film studies.

Chaplin's dame masquerade is usually the focal point in any assessment of *The Masquerader*. The initial comparison could be to *A Busy Day*, an earlier Keystone split-reel comedy directed by Mack Sennett in which Chaplin actually does play a woman (not merely a man dressing up as one to fool others). The earlier film is a standard pastiche of slapstick gags, a good example of Sennett's freewheeling directorial style that Chaplin would refine considerably. *A Busy Day* is little more than an example of how male Keystone actors would sometimes play boisterous female roles for comic effect (Arbuckle, for instance, would frequently appear in wildly humorous female guises). Chaplin's portrayal is a ruse by Charlie, and he effectively camps it up to the point where he engages in flirtatious dalliances with the director as part of his comic vengeance.

Charlie transforming himself into a female character in the makeup room is a metamorphosis we are not allowed to see in *The Masquerader*. In one scene, he is being kicked off the lot; in the next he has returned in full female garb. Unlike *A Busy Day*, this time Charlie presents himself as an attractive, classy, well-dressed woman, one who arouses the attention of the male cast and crew members. Chaplin was only 25 when he made this film, sported a small frame, and had delicate enough facial features so that his disguise as a female is effective (just as Arbuckle's frequent female roles were successful due to his round, cherubic face and roly-poly body).

Female impersonation in films is a continuing of comic theater tradition. Chaplin's performance is especially amusing in *The Masquerader* because his ruse has a genuine effect as well as a comic one. Often for the sake of outrageousness, a broad-faced comedian would do dame masquerade and receive an attracted reaction from males despite looking quite hideous as a woman. Charlie, however, could very nearly pass as pretty. When the director brings "her" into the office and makes a play for her, an office boy walks in and gets something thrown at him—the director responding in Keystone fashion to being interrupted. "She" is then given a contract. Upon signing it, Charlie leaves, runs into the makeup room, and transforms himself back into the tramp character. He removes the wig (with some trouble, as the spirit gum is sticking to his own hair) and some of the clothing, and hastily applies his comic mustache. When the director runs into the makeup room, he finds Charlie. Believing this fired actor has locked the pretty lady in the closet, he opens the door to find her clothes and wig. Realizing it was Charlie, and that a contract had now been signed as a result of the ruse, the director gives chase. It ends in typical Keystone fashion, with all of the duped males chasing Charlie, who plummets into a nearby well.

*The Masquerader* continues to show Chaplin's consistent development on several levels. He had become a popular and successful star on the Keystone lot after a matter of months, quite a lofty measure of success. And Chaplin also was continuing to learn more about effective cinematic structure. *The Masquerader* is another Keystone comedy that has no plot, and only a threadbare premise on which to hang comedy situations and gags. The film's rhythmic flow of Charlie's arrival, the makeup room, set disruptions, his disguise, and finally the chase remains steady and without the often haphazard presentation that marred some of the more hastily assembled Keystone comedies (a good example being the previous *Recreation*, which was fitfully funny despite its having been produced in haste).

While there are similarities to George Nichols's earlier Chaplin starrer *A Film Johnnie*, the one thing Chaplin rarely concentrated on, unlike Nichols, was the composition of shots. In *The Masquerader*, Chaplin does show an eye for composition, especially in the scenes where the film is being shot. The villain actor, the heroine, and the baby (a doll being used as a prop) are stationed at the full right of the screen, the director is shouting instructions from center frame, camera equipment is further right, and some negative space allows for Charlie's entrance. As Charlie enters the frame quickly, slapstick business takes place, and the framing of the sequence accurately maintains all of the activity within the shot. Thus, the placement of each actor and prop not only allows for the entrance but is equally effective once the frame fills up with action within the same shot.

In *A Film Johnnie*, director Nichols was offering an investigation of the effect movies already had on the public by 1914. In the film, Charlie was an avid fan of a particular actress with whom he was smitten. *The Masquerader* realizes this public interest and gives audiences an inside look at film production at a level that is much different from that in the previous film. While the Nichols effort shows busy Keystone workers quickly building a set in order to film a scene, Chaplin instead presents this preparation through characters, namely himself and Roscoe Arbuckle. Both were quite popular (Arbuckle's massive popularity rivaled Chaplin's), and their comic byplay while in the process of becoming their characters via externals like makeup and costume would likely have been found to be quite interesting by period audiences.

*The Masquerader* has so many levels, it is unfortunate that only one sequence is singled out. As with many film studies, period reviews centered on Chaplin's dame masquerade. A 1914 issue of *Bioscope* stated that Chaplin "gives a really remarkable female impersonation. The makeup is no less successful than the characterization, and is further proof of Mr. Chaplin's undoubted versatility." Chaplin would do the dame masquerade one more time for his 1915 Essanay short *A Woman*, this again being an attempt to fool another.

# CHAPTER 29

# *His New Profession*

**Alternate titles:** *The Good for Nothing; Helping Himself; Charlie the Nursemaid*

Running Time: One Reel
Filmed August 3–8, 1914
Released August 31, 1914

**Credits**
Written and directed by Charlie Chaplin

**Cast**
Charlie Chaplin (Charlie), Charles Parrott (Nephew), Jess Dandy (Invalid Uncle), Cecile Arnold (Girl with Eggs), Roscoe Arbuckle (Bartender), Bill Hauber (Cop), Glen Cavender (Man at Bar), Charlie Murray (Man at Bar), Vivian Edwards (Nurse), Dan Albert (Man at Bar), Peggy Page (Nephew's Date)

With *His New Profession*, Charlie Chaplin's skills as a director continued to improve while he maintained his already formidable talent as a comedian. Originally more concerned with theatrical skills such as blocking and choreography, by the time he made *His New Profession* he had begun to exhibit more in the way of shot composition. This was already evident with *The Face on the Bar Room Floor* and to a decidedly lesser extent in *The Masquerader*. With *His New Profession*, Chaplin's eye for composition is especially discernible.

The typically simple plot deals with Charlie being asked by a young man to watch his invalid uncle, who is confined to a wheelchair. The nephew has a date he does not want to break, and he offers to pay Charlie for his trouble, so Charlie agrees to the task. However, Charlie wants to get a drink at the bar, and his payment will not be forthcoming until the nephew returns. He puts a "Help a Cripple" sign over the sleeping uncle's wheelchair in order to obtain money for a drink and then goes off to a nearby saloon once the donations are forthcoming. The nephew, upon returning, is shocked and annoyed to find the sign.

The first thing to address is the character setup. To prevent the comedy from being perceived as too cruel, Chaplin presents the wheelchair-bound uncle as demanding and incorrigible. The nephew is caring, but weary. His hastily choosing stranger Charlie when he sees him at the park might give us, in the twenty-first century, a look at how people might have been easier to trust as far back as 1914. It still presents the nephew as selfish in spite of his uncle's unsettling personality. Charlie is simply an opportunist. He is broke, wants a drink, and needs money. He is also impatient and not content to wait for payment upon completion of his task. The ruse to gain funds is classically skeptical, but effective.

Chaplin's framing of the opening shots effectively introduces the principle characters. The very first shot is a close-up of Charlie on a park bench perusing the *Police Gazette*, a popular tabloid of the era that presented lurid details of murders, photos of scantily clad women, and the latest sports coverage. The close-up features only Charlie's head and shoulders as he first looks into the newspaper. Charlie glances and smirks toward the audience, then turns a few pages and starts to yawn. He pulls out the interesting portion and discards the rest of the paper. Presenting all of this in such a close shot allows us to see the subtlest facial expression.

*Charlie is instructed to care for invalid Jess Dandy by Charles Parrott.*

The film then cuts to the uncle, the nephew, and his girl. Nicely framed in a medium shot, the uncle is a heavyset man, sprawled out in his wheelchair, sleeping. The nephew is on a nearby park bench, dapperly dressed, and visibly whining over having to be saddled with the uncle's care. His girlfriend sits next to him, sporting a forlorn expression. Chaplin composes this shot with his penchant for differing contrasts. The uncle is large and imposing at the left of the frame, taking up space and blocking a portion of the idyllic park scenery. On a bench to his right sits the nephew, skinny and lanky, and the young woman, pretty and patient. The uncle seems to be shifting the weight of the frame in his direction, and the shot looks as though his presence is obtrusive.

Chaplin was certainly aware that he was acquiring a greater understanding of cinematic technique, and he addressed this awakening in *My Autobiography*:

> The mechanics of directing were simple in those days. I had only to know my left from my right for entrances and exits. If one exited right from a scene, one came in left in the next scene; if one exited towards the camera, one entered with one's back to the camera in the next scene. These, of course, were the primary rules. But with more experience I found that the placing of the camera was not only psychological but articulated a scene; in fact it was the basis of cinematic style. If the camera is a little too near, or too far, it can enhance or spoil an effect. Because economy of movement is important you don't want an actor to walk any unnecessary distance unless there is a special reason, for walking is not dramatic. Therefore placement of the camera should effect composition and a graceful entrance for the actor. Placement of the camera is cinematic inflection. There is no set rule that a close-up gives more emphasis than a long shot. A close-up is a question of feeling; in some instances a long shot can effect greater emphasis.

Once these establishing shots are presented, Chaplin goes right into comedy. The uncle is suffering from gout. His right foot is heavily bandaged and outstretched. Demanding that the nephew push his wheelchair, the uncle slaps the arm rests and yells for service. They approach the bench on which Charlie is sitting. Charlie tips his hat, but the wheelchair rests on his foot. Yet another contrast is presented here as the incapacitated uncle with the sore foot is now rolling with his full weight over the foot of otherwise healthy Charlie.

The comedy really gets going once Charlie is put in charge of the uncle's care. Responding to the object as an albatross, Charlie pushes, pulls, turns, and tugs at the wheelchair, the occupant's weight especially being a factor in its limited mobility. Pulling, unable to move the chair, falling over backward in his attempts, Charlie wrestles and struggles with the wheelchair in his first few moments with the uncle, obviously realizing this task is far more daunting than he'd anticipated. Chaplin concentrates on constant movement. The flailing protests of the incapacitated uncle, the apologetic fluttering of the nephew, the annoyance of the girlfriend, and the eagerness of Charlie soon flow into the movement of Charlie struggling with the wheelchair.

When he succeeds in the ruse to obtain money, Charlie parks the blissfully sleeping uncle near a pier and goes to the nearby tavern. The nephew and girlfriend return and react to the uncle being alone. The girl sulks off and the nephew goes after her as Charlie leaves the bar and returns to his responsibility with the uncle. However now, in his inebriated state, it is even more difficult to push the unwieldy wheelchair around. As the disgusted nephew goes into the bar, Charlie sits at the pier with the uncle, pulling out his *Police Gazette* photo and showing it to him. The uncle enjoys it, they nudge each other, and a relationship between them is established.

So as the film moves forward with comic business, greater dimension is added to each character. Charlie, in the center of the action, is the mainstay. The uncle warms up to the photo from the *Police Gazette* and strikes a surface-level friendship with Charlie. The nephew's girl turns out to be haughty and impatient. The nephew is irresponsible.

When the nephew's girlfriend returns, she sits next to Charlie and the uncle without really looking. Thinking Charlie is the nephew, she reaches back and tickles Charlie's thigh. He giggles, scratches the tickle, and pokes the young woman in the ribs. At first she is shocked, then laughs with embarrassment. Charlie has made another surface-level connection. The uncle has now become obtrusive, so Charlie kicks the wheelchair, which rolls down the pier and nearly tumbles into the lake. When the nephew returns from the bar and sees not only that his uncle is missing but that his girl is flirting with another man, it results in a slapstick free-for-all finale.

Under Chaplin's direction, this conclusion is far more artful in its execution. Escalating to the point of engaging Charlie, the nephew, the girlfriend, two cops, and two different people in wheelchairs, Chaplin again presents different contrasts within this slapstick finale. The uncle is shoved out of the way and wheels even closer to the edge of the pier. The girlfriend repeatedly slaps the nephew. Charlie gets in a tussle with another wheelchair-bound victim who has his own "Help a Cripple" ruse for money. The cops get somewhat involved in each of these situations. Cutting from one skirmish to the next—from one character doing a pratfall as he misses a kick, to another ducking from an oncoming punch—Chaplin uses more shots and quicker edits than the usual Keystone free-for-all conclusion. Charlie is taller than the wheelchair, the nephew is much taller than Charlie, and we see a variety of shapes and sizes moving at their own rhythm and pace, attempting to use comic violence to make a point.

Blocking the movements of the actors, Chaplin benefited from his stage background. As Chaplin stated in *My Autobiography*,

> There was a lot Keystone taught me and a lot I taught Keystone. In those days, they knew little about technique, stagecraft, or movement, which is what I brought to them from the theater. They also knew little about natural pantomime. In blocking a scene, a director would have three or four actors blatantly stand in a straight line facing the camera, and, with the broadest gestures one would pantomime "I-want-to-marry-your-daughter" by pointing to himself, then to his ring finger, then to the girl. Their miming dealt little with the subtlety or effectiveness, so I stood out in contrast. In those early movies I knew I had many advantages, and that, like a geologist, I was entering a rich, unexplored field. I suppose that was the most exciting period of my career, for I was on the threshold of something wonderful.

Chaplin often recalled how he would try to inject subtle bits of business in his earliest films in order to connect more completely with the audience. Now that he was supervising his own films, there are several bits of business constantly happening in *His New Profession*. As Charlie enters the tavern, he gets briefly caught up in the swinging doors. When he pushes the rotund uncle in the wheelchair, he pratfalls onto the sidewalk where another couple had just dropped a dozen eggs from their grocery bag. Chaplin also has Charlie use his cane more frequently here than in previous Keystone efforts. It is usually used to draw someone closer, either grabbing the uncle around the neck, or the nephew's girlfriend around the waist.

Although Charlie does have a few drinks in *His New Profession*, he does not rest on his drunk act as completely as he does in other films. He catches something of an alcoholic buzz and uses it to enhance the comic business of manipulating the bulky, unwieldy wheelchair-bound uncle, but it does not extend into a true "drunk act." The nephew, also having had a few drinks, makes no attempt to play drunkenness for comedy; he acts straight upon emerging from the tavern. Charlie's drinking does not affect his skills once the fight breaks out. He ducks, dodges, and fights back effectively. The last shot of the movie is as the first—a triumphant close-up of Charlie.

The uncle character has gout, with his foot bandaged and extended, but Chaplin does not overdo the gag where the uncle's sore foot gets hit or bumped. It happens a few times, and in such an accidental fashion, it is as much a surprise to the viewer as it is to the uncle (who always reacts big). The only time it appears to be done deliberately is after the nephew mistakenly rolls the wheelchair atop Charlie's foot and Charlie, to extricate himself, whacks the uncle's bandaged foot. Chaplin would revisit this situation with Eric Campbell, an even larger man, in his brilliant comedy for the Mutual studios, *The Cure*.

*His New Profession* received the same pleased response from the critics as had his other films. *Motion Picture News* stated: "Charlie Chaplin appears in this picture and, as usual, whenever he appears it is a laugh throughout." But it was Chaplin's own experience visiting a movie theater that helped him realize just how popular his films had become, as he notes in *My Autobiography*:

> The stir and excitement at the announcement of Keystone Comedy, those joyful little screams that my first appearance evoked, even before I had done anything, were most gratifying. I was a great favorite with the audience. If I could just continue this way of life, I could be satisfied. With my bonus for directing, I was making two hundred dollars a week.

# CHAPTER 30

# *The Rounders*

**Alternate titles: *Oh What a Night; Revelry; Two of a Kind; Going Down; The Love Thief; Greenwich Village***

Running Time: One Reel
Filmed August 12–15, 1914
Released September 7, 1914

**Credits**
Written and directed by Charlie Chaplin

**Cast**
Charlie Chaplin (Mr. Full), Roscoe Arbuckle (Mr. Fuller), Phyllis Allen (Mrs. Full), Minta Durfee (Mrs. Fuller), Al St. John (Bellhop), Dixie Chene, Jess Dandy (Diners at Front Left), Charles Parrott, Wallace MacDonald, Peggy Page (Diners), Eddie Cline (Man in Hotel Lobby), Billy Gilbert (Doorman), Bill Hauber, Harry Russell (Waiters), Cecile Arnold (Girl in Hotel Lobby). (Contrary to some studies, Fritz Schade does not appear in this film.)

With the release of *The Rounders*, it is evident that the comedian had truly hit his stride once he began directing all of his comedies. Each of his self-directed films is interesting, even a relative misfire like *Recreation* or those that rely on a more typical Keystone structure like *Laughing Gas* or *Caught in the Rain*. Chaplin had discovered ways to realize his ideas within the parameters of the established Keystone method of presentation, making his films superior to the others produced by the company. The massive financial success of his films caused Sennett to allow Chaplin the freedom of experimentation, as long as he remained within budget. A film like *The Face on the Bar Room Floor* is a good example of Chaplin creating a comedy that is decidedly different from the usual Keystone fare but that was wildly successful with moviegoers and supported positively by critics. Chaplin never felt the need to once again make a film based on a noted poem, but his one attempt to do so was quite successful despite its being very offbeat.

138

With *The Rounders*, Chaplin allows co-star Roscoe Arbuckle equal footage, as the two of them play a veritable comedy team. Chaplin did this very infrequently, but this particular pairing benefited both him and Arbuckle. They play off each other instinctively, and their pairing also allows for Chaplin's interest in presenting the physical contrast between himself, the smaller man, and a much larger one. While Arbuckle frequently appeared in Chaplin's films, and Chaplin returned the favor with a cameo in Arbuckle's *The Knockout*, the two never did any more than offer some marginal support to the other.

Again, the plot is simple. Chaplin is Mr. Full; Arbuckle is Mr. Fuller. Each comes home drunk one late night and is scolded by his wife. They meet up, realize they are lodge brothers, and go off together. After creating havoc in a cafe, they run off to the park and find solace in a rowboat. From this threadbare plot, Chaplin creates a series of comedy situations with ample assistance from Arbuckle, who appears to be allowed space to offer his own ideas. Arbuckle was also a director and created an endearing character that audiences applauded with a passion similar to their affection for Chaplin. As a result, Chaplin allowed Arbuckle more freedom than perhaps any other actor.

This benevolence toward Arbuckle is significant in that Chaplin's vision was very specific. His later, more prestigious feature-length films were made under conditions where Chaplin the director insisted on as many as 100 takes just to film an entrance exactly as he envisioned it. This sort of freedom would not be allowed by the budget-minded Sennett. But Chaplin did expect very precise mannerisms from his supporting cast and would frequently act out their part on the set and ask that they simply copy him. This does not appear to be the case with Arbuckle. His mannerisms are the same as can be found in his own films. Chaplin realized that a comedian receiving attention would not diminish his own starring performance but would enhance the comedy of the film overall. Arbuckle enhances this film a great deal.

Chaplin's drunk act from his Karno days was often fodder for his Keystone comedies, and in this case the film opens with an inebriated Charlie. Chaplin had discovered when watching his films at a theater that the audience would offer audible murmurs of delighted recognition the moment Charlie came on the screen. The framing of his entrance, then, is possibly with the understanding of such a reaction from moviegoers. Charlie enters at mid-frame, staggering toward the camera. His body movements obviously indicate his drunkenness; his body, his head, and his legs are all wobbling with a cohesive rhythm, flopping determinedly toward his destination. Charlie stops briefly, twists his ear, and spits out his cigarette, then proceeds to enter the rooming house where he lives. As he turns to climb the porch steps, he lifts his leg high to take the first step and falls face first. This opening is timed perfectly. Chaplin allows Charlie just enough screen time to allow for the initial audience recognition, and right about when

*Charlie and Roscoe Arbuckle drunkenly sink into the drink.*

that would be dying down, the pratfall on the porch steps would generate a solid laugh. This opening, only seconds long, is a clear indication of how effectively Chaplin was understanding how to successfully direct his Keystone comedies.

Body movement continues to be essential during the opening scenes of *The Rounders*. As Charlie makes his way through the lobby, he notices a pretty young woman and walks backward while keeping an eye on her. Once he is upstairs in the hallway, he walks carefully, as if on a tightrope, trying to maintain his balance. The film then cuts to Charlie's room, where his larger, shrewish wife awaits him. Chaplin's choice to cast tall, sturdy, broad-faced Phyllis Allen, over twice his age, as his wife is another good example of his presentation of contrasts. Charlie is small and easily bullied by this woman, but his drunken state helps him maintain an aloofness and occasional defiance.

The contrasts continue with the next shot of Arbuckle taking the same path to the same rooming house. Where Charlie's drunken staggering was rhythmic and nimble, Roscoe's is ponderous and bombastic. He stomps through the lobby with little regard to controlling his movements, at one point stumbling onto the lap of the same pretty woman Charlie had earlier noticed, as she angrily protests. His wife is long suffering, much smaller, not unattractive, and played by Arbuckle's real-life wife Minta Durfee. Roscoe barges into the room, his weeping wife unable to get much of an explanation. Chaplin's study in contrasts has now extended to the small wife and the much larger husband. The wife begins slapping him; he cowers defensively; she takes a full Keystone swing and knocks him to the ground.

Chaplin's method of getting the two established stars of the movie together is to have Charlie's wife alert him to the noise across the hall and insist he investigate. Roscoe's wife scurries out and confronts Charlie's wife. The contrasts continue still further as the two men recognize each other as lodge brothers, going through a silly secret handshake, while the two women argue animatedly in the hallway. Charlie cuts between these two sets of individuals, showing how the drunken men make a connection whereas their wives are in heated conflict. Roscoe uses his cane to sneak his wife's pocketbook, while Charlie goes to his room and pulls money out of his wife's purse. After the men sneak off, the women realize it and suddenly become comrades joined in an effort to find their errant husbands.

In Chaplin's presentation, the women are far less subtle than the men. Their arms flail, their bodies shift, and their argument becomes so animated that their pulled back hairdos start to unravel. When they discover the men have gone, they just as blatantly collapse weeping into each other's arms.

Now that Chaplin has teamed Roscoe with Charlie, he uses their contrasting figures to play off each other. Unlike in Charlie's confrontations with Mack Swain, which are always adversarial, Roscoe is presented as a buddy. As the two of them leave the rooming house, the much larger Roscoe has his arm wrapped around Charlie's torso and is dragging his sleeping friend down the street like so many library books. This puts Arbuckle's imposing presence at the forefront, while Charlie is being carried along. It is a striking, funny image that displays Chaplin's willingness to allow Arbuckle the majority of audience attention (something the benevolent Arbuckle was known to often do for his supporting players).

Chaplin's shot composition is especially noticeable during the scenes that take place in a cafe. The shot of the interior is very vast, with deep focus allowing us to see, well into the background, a stage where music is being performed. The deeper area of the shot is filled with extras playing patrons at tables. The background movement is discernible but not distracting. The action is contained in the forefront, where Roscoe and Charlie are stationed. Immediately to the left of the frame at the foreground, a chubby man and his date sit at a table. To the right, the larger Roscoe is seated at a table. This anchors both sides of the frame, allowing Charlie to perform at the center. Charlie leans on the chubby man's bald head, takes the napkin tucked under the man's chin to blow his nose, and simply acts as a nuisance. The man wants to avoid conflict and tries to ignore Charlie.

At the same time, Roscoe rests his feet on a wine holder, pulls the tablecloth over his body like a blanket, and falls asleep. Charlie, noticing Roscoe's comfort, decides to nap right on the floor. He uses the chubby man's tablecloth, pulling it forcefully from the table and covering up. Customers and waiters come to rouse the two slumbering drunks and are met with defensive hits and shoves. This erupts into a free-for-all as per the usual Keystone structure, but a far briefer and more concentrated one. The battle lasts only seconds, remains in the foreground (with startled onlookers in the background), and is quickly broken up by the wives, who have entered the cafe. Charlie and Roscoe run away and scurry to a nearby park, pursued by the wives and most of the customers from the cafe. They retreat to a rowboat, and the last shot is of the two of them sleeping soundly as the boat sinks beneath the water.

The shot of Roscoe and Charlie in the boat contrasts perfectly with the action at the edge of the ground near the water where the others stand. Yelling, shaking fists, and weeping wives are contrasted by a serene-looking Roscoe and Charlie, floating in calm waters. Asleep, they simply allow the waters to consume them.

The difference between the drunk portrayals as essayed by Chaplin and Arbuckle is yet another interesting contrast, but not one that was specifically staged by the director. Charlie's drunk maintains a boldness and an awareness. Roscoe's drunk is lumbering and destructive. The look on Roscoe's face presents him as completely unaware of whatever damage he might be causing. For Charlie, drinking allows him a greater edge. Roscoe's senses are dulled.

For such a large, imposing man, Arbuckle had a great deal of control over his body. His pratfalls were hard and stunning. His manner of walk had an agility that belied his size. His expressions and reactions were never too blatant. Arbuckle would arguably do his best work once he left Keystone for his own starring series at Paramount via Joseph Schenck's productions, where he enjoyed full supervisory control even beyond what Sennett allowed. The fact that his performance in *The Rounders* is more subtle than in most of his other Keystone appearances would indicate that Roscoe was responding well to working with Chaplin. In later years, Arbuckle would recall in a *New York Post* interview: "I have always regretted not having been Chaplin's partner in a longer film than these one-reelers we made so rapidly. He is a complete comic genius, undoubtedly the only one of our time, and he will be the only one who will still be talked about a century from now."

With *The Rounders*, Chaplin also presented his ability to work with larger groups in settings that were busy and vast. Chaplin's previous directors, including Henry Lehrman, George Nichols, Mabel Normand, and Sennett himself, usually kept their shots tighter. Even Nichols, who had a reasonably good eye for shot composition, never exhibited the sort of ambition displayed by Chaplin in *The Rounders*. The cafe scene, though only a small portion of the film, opens things up in a most impressive way. There really is no negative space in this shot. Customers, waiters, and a band performing on the stage take up all manner of the background, so the comic business both Charlie and Roscoe are engaging in at the foreground is effectively backed up by something other than dull space. Nichols often dwelled on close-ups of Charlie, for instance, but never prepared the background of the shot so impressively.

The comedy in *The Rounders* is less reliant on excessive slapstick gags and is essentially character driven. The main characters and immediate supporting ones are funny and are placed in amusing situations. Arbuckle and Chaplin play off of each other nicely. There is not the absolute cohesion one can find in, say, Stan Laurel and Oliver Hardy (perhaps the first duo one thinks of in regard to a fat-to-skinny contrast). Laurel and Hardy developed their cohesion through working together over a period of time. Chaplin and Arbuckle, though, present a certain chemistry that was discernible during their brief slapstick encounter during *The Masquerader*. Arbuckle's assertion that he and Chaplin might have made a formidable team had they the opportunity to work together more frequently, or in a longer subject, is a pointed one.

Chaplin would very rarely work in a team situation. He did, however, re-work this very film while at Essanay, with Ben Turpin as his drinking buddy. Running two reels in length, it modified and perfected some instances in *The Rounders* but may not be the better film.

Of course the one-reel length of *The Rounders* does not allow for a deeper character development than the stereotypes presented here (irresponsible men, shrewish wives, etc.). And while period reviews would point out the cheerful rowdiness of *The Rounders*, the film was much less rowdy than the usual Keystone fare. It further presented Charlie Chaplin's continued development as cinema's finest comedian and one of its best filmmakers.

# CHAPTER 31

# *The New Janitor*

**Alternate titles: *The New Porter; The Blundering Boob; The Custodian; The Window Washer; Capturing the Robber; Charlie the Janitor***

Running Time: One Reel
Filmed August 18–26, 1914
Released September 24, 1914

**Credits**
Written and directed by Charlie Chaplin

**Cast**
Charlie Chaplin (Janitor), Jack Dillon (Clerk), Al St. John (Elevator Boy), Glen Cavender (Luke Connor), Jess Dandy (Bank President), Frank Hayes (Accountant), Peggy Page (Secretary)

*The New Janitor* is among Charlie Chaplin's best and most important Keystone films, and among the most significant of his career. Perfectly structured with a balance of slapstick humor and dramatic sequencing, *The New Janitor* is another milestone in Chaplin's filmography. While he had experimented with dramatic structure with *The Face on the Bar Room Floor*, presenting Charlie as a hapless victim rather than a wily perpetrator, in *The New Janitor* Chaplin redefines his approach to comedy and offers a portent to the method that would transform him from popular funnyman to worldwide superstar.

Usually when Chaplin portrays a working-class individual, the character is sneaky, energetic, and dealing with a variety of conflicts with co-workers while trying to complete his tasks (*The Property Man* is a good example). This time, Charlie is dismissed as the lowest-level employee at a bank—a mere janitor whom even the elevator operator finds so insignificant, he refuses to hold the elevator door for Charlie, forcing him to climb to the top floor via the stairs. The usual spring in Charlie's step is not evident. He plods along, unhappily but

*Charlie evokes sympathy as the hardworking janitor.*

productively. He is easily overlooked, but a distraction when he attempts to do his work too near where others are active.

Chaplin separates Charlie from the other characters quite brilliantly. The underlying plot of *The New Janitor*, where a banker steals from the safe to pay off an overdue gambling debt after being threatened by gangsters, does not directly involve Charlie. While he is the center of the film, Charlie is on the periphery of the plot. Thus, his being overlooked by those directly involved with the film's story is a fascinating way to make Charlie the star of the film, as well as being completely separate from its narrative course of action.

That we are seeing a new Charlie is evident by the first few seconds. Gathering his cleaning supplies, Charlie hurries to the elevator. The operator sees him but quickly shuts the door. In any other Keystone, Charlie would have somehow retaliated. In *The New Janitor*, we see the forlorn Charlie plodding up the steps until he reaches the top floor. For much of the film, at least until the end, Charlie maintains this slower pace. He is tired from climbing the steps, and the physical labor necessary to perform his custodial tasks requires more effort than his energy allows. He becomes sloppy. As he picks up discarded paper from next to a desk in an office, a large bank statement book falls to the ground. Charlie picks that up and throws it away, until told by the banker to retrieve it. It is all timed quite beautifully. The book falls right where Charlie is picking up paper, and he places the book in his wastebasket just as it hits the ground.

Chaplin always tried to offer subtle bits of comic business through Charlie, exhibiting greater refinement than the more florid Keystone style. In *The New Janitor*, his comedy is even more natural. As he empties wastebaskets, he casually holds them upside down so that their contents spill on the ground. When he is assigned to wash windows, he has trouble multitasking in his position on the top floor. In an effort to keep his balance, Charlie ends up dumping his water bucket on the bank manager, who is standing on the sidewalk below. This too is done naturally, Charlie being as much a victim of his own clumsiness as he is of the general mistreatment by his co-workers.

The only person to give Charlie any attention, and this is marginal at best, is the pretty secretary. Before going to his window-washing task, Charlie sits and ogles her flirtatiously, but his actions seem more like an innocent crush than the more salacious meaning these same actions might translate to in any earlier Keystone. Often Charlie is aggressive in other films, and yet the women are amused and responsive. Here, Charlie is coy, and the secretary's faint smile shows little more than tolerance.

Charlie is discharged by the manager for dumping the bucket of water on him. Rather than start a fight, as he might have in other films, this time Charlie pleads his case with dramatic conviction. He is refused and sadly backs out of the office.

Chaplin recalled in his autobiography that this specific scene was very important to his career:

> I was playing in a picture called *The New Janitor*, in a scene in which the manager of the office fires me. In pleading with him to take pity on me and let me retain my job, I started to pantomime appealingly that I had a large family of little children. While I was enacting the mock sentiment, Dorothy Davenport, an old actress, was on the sidelines watching the scene, and during rehearsal I looked up and, to my surprise, found her in tears. "I know it's supposed to be funny," she said, "but you just make me weep." She confirmed something I already felt: I had the ability to evoke tears as well as laughter.

Chaplin's memory was faulty in his recalling Dorothy Davenport as the "old actress." At the time *The New Janitor* was being filmed, Dorothy was 19 years old and not employed at Keystone. Her mother, however, was a Keystone actor and was around 50 (over twice Chaplin's age at the time). Hence, it is more likely that Alice Davenport was the "old actress" who confirmed Chaplin's belief that he could be effective with tragedy and comedy, and that the two would blend cohesively.

The dramatic plot appears in earnest once Charlie has been fired. A bank employee attempts to rob the safe, but the secretary walks in, thwarting his plan. He leaves until he believes she is gone, and then returns. She, however, is suspicious, so she hides and catches him in the act. Responding to her angrily, the employee pulls out a handgun. A struggle ensues during which their bodies bump the janitor call button, which alerts Charlie. The woman faints, and the thief goes back to emptying out the safe.

This particular scene from *The New Janitor* plays like a typical silent screen melodrama. Chaplin offers no comedy here, just a purely dramatic scene about a desperate bank worker stealing from the company safe, an innocent secretary who witnesses his crime, and the violent struggle that follows.

There is also nothing funny about Charlie's response to the call button. Down in the janitor's quarters, Charlie is preparing to leave, having been fired. He does not know if he should answer the call or not. He ponders. The scene cuts back to the violent situation between the criminal and the secretary. Rather than build this scene for comedy, Chaplin builds it for suspense. Reports from the era indicate moviegoers would yell frantically at the screen for Charlie to hurry and get upstairs. During cinema's infancy, when moviegoers responded so completely to what was on the screen, suspense of this nature was extremely effective.

Once Charlie finally makes it upstairs and sees the safe being robbed and the secretary lying on the floor, he confronts the criminal, who pulls out his gun. Using his cane, Charlie easily knocks the gun from the man's hand and takes it himself. When he bends to see how the secretary is, he sticks the gun through his own legs to keep the criminal at bay. However, attempting to call the police while still holding the gun proves difficult (telephones in 1914 needed two hands for operation). In order to alert a cop on the street, Charlie simply fires the gun a few times. Soon the bank manager and the police are on the scene. But they believe the shabbily dressed Charlie is the criminal and the better dressed, white-collar worker a victim. The secretary explains, and the correct man is taken into custody. Charlie is given his job back and a reward.

Presenting the powerful as crooked and the worker as the hero, *The New Janitor* shows how aware Chaplin was of his moviegoing audience. Their initial attraction to Chaplin's audacity now runs deeper. They see him here as a victim due to his lower working-class status, the judgment further manifesting itself when he is wrongly accused of a crime that he just thwarted. Chaplin understood his impact, and he added depth to the character. Chaplin has allowed us to understand Charlie much better, and also see how society perceives him. In his haste to rescue the secretary, Charlie has no time to ponder or plan—overpowering the criminal and keeping him at bay stems from pure instinct. It further increased his popularity and was the harbinger to his later work. While his remaining Keystones would certainly not abandon the typical slapstick approach for which the brand was best known, Chaplin had now established another layer to his screen character. It would serve him well in future productions, especially after leaving Keystone.

The closest thing we have to a free-for-all in *The New Janitor* is the brief slapstick battle that ensues once the police arrive and mistake Charlie for the burglar. He defends himself in the same manner as in his earlier films, by ducking punches with perfect timing and delivering kicks that cause his combatants to fly backward. This skirmish is quickly interrupted by the secretary's identification of the real culprit and the real hero. It is a triumphant use of a standard Keystone practice in that it serves to enhance the action rather than be something on which the film could lazily rely for an easy conclusion. Chaplin's filmmaking savvy was becoming even more impressive, especially as he assumed greater and greater creative control over his productions.

There are fewer solid laughs in *The New Janitor* than can be found in more raucous Keystone productions like *Laughing Gas* or *The Property Man*. The strength of those earlier films was their reliance on nicely executed gags and the way they were edited and framed. *The New Janitor* concerns itself with narrative structure and Charlie's character development. The other characters, in fact,

*Charlie subdues the burglar.*

register as mere stereotypes. The secretary is the pretty, innocent heroine; the banker who robs the safe is the typical crook; the managing banker is rotund and pretentious, gloating merrily over his success with every step. Chaplin wisely maintains this balance with these characters so that Charlie can be central to the film without being central to the story.

This is the first time Chaplin used an element of suspense for one of his comedies, mostly because this is the first of his films to have enough of a dramatic basis to do so. Suspense was an early method in filmmaking. Edwin S. Porter used crosscutting between the action of a crime and the oncoming cavalry in *The Great Train Robbery* (1903), while D. W. Griffith employed similar methods to excite the moviegoer with his earlier short films like *Musketeers of Pig Alley* (1911) and *The Lonedale Operator* (1911). Rather than use quick edits to zip up the pace of the film, Chaplin uses suspense in a far more concentrated and methodical manner. Charlie spends several seconds pondering whether or not to answer the janitor call buzzer. This offers a contrast to the action happening on the top floor where a crime has taken place and a witness is being held at gunpoint. He finally decides to investigate, but not until after several long, suspenseful seconds.

While Chaplin had already exhibited a good eye for cinema's mise-en-scène, the shot composition in *The New Janitor* is serviceable and effective but not particularly remarkable. When showing Charlie going up and down the steps, Chaplin frames the scene so that it is evident the elevator door is nearby. Charlie is shown in the foreground while performing his custodial duties in the banker's office, but it is the secretary in the foreground at the left with Charlie in the background to the right as he casually flirts. Chaplin films the window-washing sequence in a closer shot, so that Charlie's leaning backward while trying to wash the outer area seems more dangerous. (Ten years later, Harold Lloyd would make this sort of comedy an art unto itself.) These shots are perfectly effective, but Chaplin appears to be concentrating more on character and narrative, again causing us to reference his later comments of not needing interesting camera angles if the character was interesting.

There is no record of Mack Sennett having any misgivings with Chaplin making occasionally offbeat films that strayed far from the definitive Keystone structure. This is probably because Chaplin's films were so enormously successful. Even the intelligentsia started to recognize something more than boorish, knockabout humor in his subjects, as in Chaplin's literary inspiration for *The Face on the Bar Room Floor*.

*The New Janitor* was applauded in the press for being "a rippingly good comedy," while critics noticed there was "more plot than usual." Audiences were ecstatic, and as Chaplin presented a version of Charlie that was deeper and more layered, moviegoers responded with a greater appreciation for his work. *The New Janitor* was not only a comedy film, but an example of Chaplin's interest in turning motion pictures into a comprehensive presentation of different ideas and genres within the same one-reel subject.

Chaplin revisited this premise a year later at the Essanay studios with his film *The Bank* (several Essanay productions were reworkings and redefinitions of films Chaplin had made at Keystone). *The Bank* is a two-reeler that expands on Charlie's janitorial status, but it goes further in that his affection for a pretty teller is merely a fantasy, and the unscrupulous man she does love, whom he fantasizes about heroically beating up to avenge her, is a part of the same daydream. In *The New Janitor*, Charlie's world is quite real. It is a working-class existence, where the upper classes think nothing of the lower ones.

In his biography *Chaplin: His Life and Art*, David Robinson states:

> Only seventeen days separated *The Rounders* and *The New Janitor*, yet in that short space of time, Chaplin's art seemed to take a massive leap forward both in approach to film narrative and in appreciation of the character that was developing within the tramp makeup and costume. The film conforms to the basic Keystone rules, using only eight static camera set-ups, yet out of his material, Chaplin fashions a brilliant little narrative; clear, precise, with drama, suspense, and an element of sentiment that goes deeper than the flirtations of Westlake Park. The editing creates a real dynamic in the Griffith manner rather than simply providing a step-by-step progression of narrative incidents. Gags and character touches are developed without the Keystone rush and integrated into the story.

Tight, succinct, filled with depth of character, funny comic business, and a dramatic narrative that supports the action but never becomes dull or intrusive, *The New Janitor* is a consistently brilliant look at Charlie's perseverance and his ability to triumph over the most adverse conditions. It would remain one of Chaplin's finest short films.

# CHAPTER 32

# *Those Love Pangs*

**Alternate titles:** *Love Pangs; The Rival Mashers; Busted Hearts; Oh You Girls; Love Pains; Charlie and His Rival*

Running Time: One Reel
Filmed September 14–17, 1914
Released October 10, 1914

**Credits**
Written and directed by Charlie Chaplin

**Cast**
Charlie Chaplin (Flirt), Chester Conklin (His Rival), Cecile Arnold, Vivian Edwards (Girls in Park), Fred Fishback (Boyfriend), Billy Gilbert, Grover Ligon, Fritz Schade, Slim Summerville, Charles Parrott, Wallace MacDonald, Norma Nichols (Movie Patrons), Edwin Frazee (Cop), Peggy Page (Landlady)

Charlie Chaplin followed up his milestone *The New Janitor* with a much more typical one-reel comedy that includes rivals for the attention of women, escapades in a park, tumbles into a pond, and a slapstick finale in a movie theater. Compared with *The New Janitor*, *Those Love Pangs* seems emptier and less satisfying because it contains few of the layers its predecessor offered. Many dismiss the film as a mere distraction that comes between the superior *The New Janitor* and *Dough and Dynamite*. However, *Those Love Pangs* is a clever Keystone comedy, and Chaplin's refinement of the studio's noted methods is clearly evident.

The plot is, as usual, quite simple. Charlie and Chester are initially rivals for the attention of their pretty landlady. They soon find themselves at the park, where Chester gets the attention of a blonde, and Charlie pursues a brunette. Chester scores. Charlie does not. The brunette has a tall, lanky boyfriend, so Charlie retreats. After some slapstick in the park, Charlie manages to sneak away and meet up with both women in a movie theater. He is eventually discovered by

151

Chester and the boyfriend, who pick him up and throw him through the movie screen as the film ends.

While its reliance on pure comedy may make it seem unremarkable, it is, in fact, superior to most of the Chaplin Keystones that rely on knockabout humor. Perhaps the most interesting thing about *Those Love Pangs* is how Chaplin presents his screen character following *The New Janitor*. Having given Charlie a deeper and more sympathetic personality in the previous film, Chaplin no longer sees Charlie as the victorious scamp who successfully makes his way through life due to his audacious disruptions. He does not exhibit the aggressive behavior that causes women to giggle with interest. He is now the one who is, at first, left without a girl. And when he does manage to end up with both women, this dalliance is quickly thwarted with Charlie on the receiving end.

That *Those Love Pangs* is so basic in its premise has a valid explanation. Chaplin had originally conceived that the plot would feature Charlie and Chester extending their rivalry from the boardinghouse to the bakery where they are both employed. However, the scenes at the bakery started to offer more possibilities for creative comedy and went on too long. Both Chaplin and Conklin were coming up with interesting gags and ideas, and any thought of paring them down to fit a one-reel format along with footage already shot seemed infeasible.

*Officer Edwin Frazee catches Charlie by the seat of his pants.*

Chaplin decided to continue production with the bakery idea and build an entirely new film around it. The result is *Dough and Dynamite*, a two-reeler released just after *Those Love Pangs*. Chaplin concluded the one-reel *Those Love Pangs* rather hastily upon completion of *Dough and Dynamite*.

Chaplin moves Charlie and Chester into a park, which is a very typical Keystone setting, but here Charlie is the least successful aggressor. Chaplin's interest in visual contrasts comes into play when the boyfriend enters the scene. He is tall, lanky, and very much unlike Charlie's diminutive stature. As he leans over a park bench talking to his girlfriend, Charlie is able to crawl under the man's resting arm and scurry away. When he is confronted by the man near the lake, Charlie, with his back to the water, uses his cane to yank the man in. The gesture is quick, and the fall into the lake is forceful. Charlie may not be successful in love during this film, but he holds his own.

Perhaps the most amusing scene takes place in the movie theater. Charlie is sitting between the two women, with an arm around each. He is talking to both and making gestures with his feet, his arms being preoccupied. It is a brief, but delightful, presentation of Charlie using his body for comedy. The entrance of Chester and the boyfriend interrupts this sequence with a free-for-all and the final slapstick conclusion.

Some film studies have ventured the guess that the two women may very well be prostitutes. Glenn Mitchell in his book *The Chaplin Encyclopedia* addresses it directly:

> When Charlie decides to follow the brunette instead of buying a drink, he examines his money as if to decide which commodity to purchase. Similarly, one might query Chester's status with blonde Cecile Arnold (herself sporting a stereotypical "streetwalker" kiss-curl) when she gives him a sum of money retrieved from her shoe. Such references appear in several non-Chaplin Keystones of the period, and must have been quite shocking to contemporary audiences.

While the gags in *Those Love Pangs* are familiar, they are undeniably funny, and reviews were favorable. One review, from the *New York Dramatic Mirror*, stated: "In a comparatively short time, Charlie Chaplin has earned a reputation as a slapstick comedian second to none. His odd little tricks of manner and his refusal to do the most simple things in an ordinary way are essential features of his method, which thus far has defied successful imitation."

Even in this simple slapstick comedy, there was discernibly more to Charlie now. No longer just an attractively disruptive comic presence, Charlie was now a more fully developed character with a personality that extended beyond the superficial. Sennett was careful not to alter the established and successful Keystone formula. That he allowed Chaplin to experiment to the level of reinventing comedy presentation under the Keystone banner shows his respect for the comedian's ideas and happiness with the success of his films. Now able to extend beyond his previous limitations, Chaplin was eager to continue experimenting. His subsequent films for Sennett would further investigate his expanding comic vision.

# CHAPTER 33

# *Dough and Dynamite*

**Alternate titles:** *The Doughnut Designers; The New Cook; Bakers Dozen; Charlie Caught Out; Charlie's Hot Spot*

Running Time: Two Reels
Filmed August 29–September 11, 1914
Released October 26, 1914

**Credits**
Written and directed by Charlie Chaplin

**Cast**
Charlie Chaplin, Chester Conklin (Waiters and Bakers), Fritz Schade (Boss), Norma Nichols (Boss's Wife), Cecile Arnold (Waitress), Jess Dandy (Female Cook), Vivian Edwards (First Customer), Glen Cavender, Slim Summerville, Ted Edwards, Edwin Frazee, Frankie Dolan (Striking Bakers), Charles Parrott, Phyllis Allen, Wallace Mac-Donald, Charles Bennett (Customers)

Another of Charlie Chaplin's best Keystone comedies, *Dough and Dynamite* further presents how much the comedian had learned about the cinematic process in a few short months. Since hitting his stride when he began directing each of his starring films, Chaplin had built upon the established Keystone method, exploring different ways he could move past its limitations and incorporate greater depth to the comedy. Offbeat efforts like *The Face on the Bar Room Floor* and *The New Janitor* exhibited a more expanded cinematic vision than that of Sennett or other talented filmmakers on his lot.

*Dough and Dynamite* could very well be a culmination of these ideas. Not only does Chaplin create some of his most inspired comedy, but his method of cinematic presentation enhances each sequence. There is an increased number of shots, and with greater composition, more edits, and an underlying serious message inspired by then-current headlines. As far as the comedy goes, Chaplin and Chester Conklin drew on their inherent skill for riffing comic sequences, and the improvisational gifts of each inspired the other.

The idea for *Dough and Dynamite* emerged while Chaplin was filming *Those Love Pangs*. In that film, a rivalry between rooming house acquaintances Charlie and Chester was to extend to their place of employment, a bakery. During filming, the bakery scenes began taking on a life of their own, Chaplin and Conklin coming up with ideas that required more time. Wisely, Chaplin chose to expand these scenes into a separate film. The conclusion of *Those Love Pangs* was rewritten, less effectively, and that film was completed after filming wrapped up on *Dough and Dynamite*.

With *Dough and Dynamite*, the simple premise dovetails into a more detailed plot. Charlie and Chester are waiters in a bakery that has a small restaurant area. When the bakers go on strike to protest their working conditions, Charlie and Chester are asked by the boss to take their place. The striking bakers place a stick of dynamite in a loaf of bread, then dupe a little girl into returning it as stale. Charlie unwittingly places the bread in the oven, blowing up the bakery.

At the time *Dough and Dynamite* was filmed, striking workers and unionization were topics in the news. When Chaplin realized he would be expanding the bakery footage, he used the current interest in striking workers to add an underlying plot to the comedy. While there are loose ends that are not tied up once the two reels have elapsed, the plotline does allow for the concluding explosion. It also uses a newsworthy event as the catalyst to move Charlie and Chester from their waiter duties into the bakery.

There is no initial character development once *Dough and Dynamite* begins. Chaplin's establishing shot is a busy dining area with Charlie in the background and a man and woman being given their dessert by a waitress in the foreground. Charlie is clearing tables, dumping discarded meals onto a larger plate. He enters the foreground and dumps the plate of garbage onto the man's dessert, picking it up as being among the discarded meals. The man protests. Charlie apologizes and returns the dessert to the man, picking away the assorted debris. The man continues to protest, so Charlie dips his finger into the dessert and tastes it, assuring the man it is still okay.

This very first gag establishes Charlie's character. As with his previous Keystone appearances, Charlie is a bit of a rascal. But unlike, say, *The Property Man* or *Laughing Gas*, where Charlie does not appear to be too concerned with keeping his job, in *Dough and Dynamite* he is attempting to be conscientious. Cleaning up a meal before the man has finished is perhaps an example of Charlie doing his job a bit too well.

This is not to say that the conscientious Charlie is suddenly well mannered. Upon ruining the customer's dessert, Charlie responds as if dumping garbage onto the man's plate was a marginal error that is easily fixed. He laughs through his apology as he returns the dessert and picks away debris. When the man protests, Charlie does not appear to understand just why he is upset, pointing out that the garbage has been removed. Charlie starts to get angry with the man, believing the customer is overreacting, and when he jabs his finger into the dessert and proves it still tastes fine, he casually brushes the finger off on the man's jacket. However, unlike earlier Keystone films, Charlie is not doing this in the manner of a troublemaker merely causing a disruption. It is his awkward way of being helpful, of correcting what he believes is a minor error. It sets the tone to what we might expect from the character throughout the two-reel comedy. Charlie is uncouth, perhaps prone to poor judgment, but retains a conscientiousness about wanting to do his job well.

In a following scene, Charlie is behind the counter, waiting on a female customer whose flirtatious manner and walk is obviously flaunting all that she has. A sign against the counter, clearly visible in the immediate foreground, reads "Assorted French Tarts." Charlie, looking toward the camera (the viewing audience), nods his head toward the sign and then to the woman. In his effort to respond to her as a customer, he finds himself absentmindedly placing his hand into the gooey frosting on the confections in front of him.

This scene maintains Charlie's character but also shows Chaplin using the background and foreground. First is the placement of the sign and the acknowledgment of the woman whose appearance creates the irony. Charlie remains in the foreground, behind the counter (facing from the left) while the woman shops in the background. As she bends to look in the display case, Charlie leans to get a better look and chortles to himself.

Charlie's adversarial relationship with his co-workers comes into focus when he goes down to the preparation area and engages in a slapstick brawl with Chester and a heavyset woman doing dishes (played by rotund male actor Jess Dandy, whom Chaplin used frequently in his quest to present a physical contrast to himself). While it is all broad Keystone gestures, it establishes Charlie's character by showing him as the usual scrapper. However, these are not the same disruptions as can be found in, say, *Laughing Gas*, where his scrapping extends to the patients in the dentist's waiting room. Charlie's disagreements are limited to staff.

Working with the disgruntled bakers, Charlie comes up with some amusing bits of business that enhance his character and the comedy. When he places his hands in some sticky dough, he must brace himself with his foot against the table to pull his hands out. As he is given instructions by a very tall baker, Charlie stands on his tiptoes to hear him more clearly, calling attention to yet another physical contrast.

In these first moments of *Dough and Dynamite*, establishing shots and character-driven gags are used to set the tone and the pace. It all moves very quickly, flowing from one scene into the next, the comedy drawing the viewer in immediately. Along with the gags at the forefront, Chaplin continues to enhance each one by the subtle bits of business that further define Charlie's character. In a 1915 issue of *Photoplay*, writer Harry C. Carr stated:

> As a director, Chaplin introduced a new note into moving pictures. Theretofore, most of the comedy effects had been riotous boisterousness. Chaplin got his effects in a more subtle way and with less action. By making the most of the little subtle effects, Chaplin enlarged the field of all motion picture comedies. It goes without saying that the simpler effects a man needs for his fun-making, the more effects he has to draw on.

Chaplin's sense of composition is seen in the first shot of *Dough and Dynamite* and continues into the proceedings when Charlie, Chester, and Jess are battling. Charlie and Chester are the immediate opponents, fighting in the foreground with Jess anchoring the background. Charlie remains in the foreground with Chester, hastily washing dishes and throwing them to his partner to dry, but deliberately doing so in haste so that Chester is unable to catch them. Jess, in the background, reacts to every dropped dish.

The striking bakers leaving the bakery provide an easy narrative method to get Charlie and Chester into an area that offers greater comic potential than their duties as waiters. With gooey dough, hot ovens, heavy sacks of flour, and trays of bread, there are many opportunities for the comedians to continue riffing on the original premise and maintain their adversarial relationship. Chaplin also uses the current events to allow for transition in his narrative. And rather than simply have the bakers announce a strike, perform a walkout, and be gone, Chaplin offers closure to their situation when they plant the explosive in a loaf of bread and dupe a little girl into making the delivery.

Once Charlie and Chester are sporting their baker's aprons and hats, the film shifts gears and concentrates on their efforts to improvise in their new positions. Chester, upon being given his instructions, looks to the camera and throws up his hands, obviously unqualified for this activity. Charlie has been down in the bakers' area and has picked up at least some basic knowledge.

Throughout *Dough and Dynamite*, Chaplin gives a great deal of attention to what Charlie can do with various objects: placing his roaming hands in frosting, getting stuck on a mound of dough, dropping dishes on the floor upon washing them, and in a longer sequence, carrying a heavy, unwieldy sack of flour on his back, through the dining room, and down the ladder into the bakery area. Charlie staggers, bumps into an angry woman seated at a table, then stumbles down the ladder, dropping the heavy flour sack on Chester, who waits below. It is an interesting comparison to *The Property Man*, where Charlie forced his elderly underling to carry a large trunk that was also heavy and bulky. This time, Charlie is the workhorse. He has no authority to delegate the task to another, including

Chester, whose status is the same. While the heavy flour sack is used for a gag, the situation further defines Charlie's interest in doing a good job at the bakery.

The adversarial relationship between Charlie and Chester is interesting for the amount of footage Chester is allowed. The *Photoplay* article mentions Chaplin's being benevolent enough to allow supporting players some time in the spotlight in an effort to make the production better:

> As a director-actor at Keystone, Chaplin had the reputation of being the most generous star in the movie business. Every comedian was allowed to grab all the laughs he could get. Chaplin always insisted on having them do the comedy stuff his way, but he always built up their parts for them without regard for the fact that his own work might suffer.

This is especially evident when Chester gets ample footage alone to gather up Charlie's discarded hat and jacket and take them out to the trash. Chester indulges in evil giggling as he accomplishes his task. Chaplin uses a tracking shot to follow Chester up the ladder, through the kitchen area, and out to the trash, putting the supporting player at the immediate forefront. The gag is a loose end, as Charlie never does discover what Chester has done, despite having a scene of his own out by the trash only moments later.

Another brief bit that Chester does alone shows him with his hands stuck in a mound of gooey dough. He tries to extricate himself by pushing with his shin, then tries to set the mess on a table, only to have it continue to stick to his hands as he walks away. Chaplin was noted for a very exacting style of directing his players, insisting they perform according to his specific vision. This bit is brief, but it gives Chester Conklin a chance to respond more completely to Chaplin's direction. Conklin was usually the nominal star in his own Keystone films but understood his supporting status in a Chaplin picture. Always pleased with his friend's work, Chaplin would continue to use Conklin's services over 20 years after this film's release. (For more on Chester Conklin or any of the Keystone supporting players in Chaplin's films, see appendix A.)

A confrontation between the proprietor and his wife also sets the stage for a supporting player to have the spotlight. The wife has some dough on the back of her dress, and the proprietor jumps to the wrong conclusion, suspecting it is the mark of Charlie's dough-covered hands. They argue in the dining area, with a customer (Charles Parrott) in the foreground. While the argument is central to the frame, it is Parrott's reaction that draws the viewer's attention. His amused smirking in reaction to the arguing couple steals this particular scene, and Chaplin lets him improvise freely. Parrott, who had already appeared in a few films with Chaplin (most notably as the nephew in *His New Profession*), would later achieve his own fame as a comedian and director under the name Charley

Chase. The proprietor is animated in classic Keystone manner, flailing his arms and jumping up and down. Parrott, by comparison, is subtly reacting and, with little effort, drawing viewer attention.

Chaplin gives Charlie a number of solo set pieces in *Dough and Dynamite*. One in particular is discussed by Gerald Mast in his book *The Comic Mind*:

> Holding aloft a tray of bread loaves, he runs, dances, twirls, pirou-
> ettes, and somersaults without spilling a single loaf. Then, when he
> stoops down casually to pick one loaf off the floor, the whole tray of
> loaves slips and falls. Charlie does the supremely difficult balancing
> act with great ease; it is the simple, ordinary task that boggles him.

Charlie also balances the full tray on his head, walking forward and turning about-face without it falling. His technique has become fully refined; his approach to the comedy has matured. While the premise of *Dough and Dynamite* relates directly to Keystone's established slapstick style, Chaplin fills it with narrative depth, creative gags, character-enhancing bits of subtle comedy business, studied shot composition, and a consistently brisk pace, making it among the finest comedies ever to be produced by the company.

*Charlie balances a tray of loaves while Fritz Schade looks on.*

The limited contrast between Charlie and Chester is interesting in that Chaplin always preferred to pit Charlie against much bigger men, including Mack Swain, Fritz Schade, and Jess Dandy. Charlie is actually slightly taller than Chester. Chester is the same kind of scrapper. They had already been at odds in *Those Love Pangs* (the film from which this one stemmed), but it is *Dough and Dynamite* where this relationship is more thoroughly explored.

The title of the film refers directly to the substance that is central to much of the comedy business. While the dynamite gives the movie its conclusion, the dough is the chief object most frequently in use. In two skirmishes between Charlie and Chester, the sticky substance does not lend itself well to being tossed, as it sticks to the person's hand. So the two of them engage in a slap fight with dough on their hands, but this appears to soften the blow and make it less painful. A bit of absurd movie magic is used at one point when Chester rolls the dough into a ball and throws it at Charlie, who ducks and causes it to enter an open oven. Charlie reaches in and pulls out a fully cooked loaf of bread. While Chaplin did not engage in such cinematic surrealism often (it is more tantamount to the style of Buster Keaton and, to a lesser extent, Stan Laurel), in this case it is especially amusing because there is no real reaction. When the cooked loaf of bread is pulled out of the oven and allowed to fall to the floor, the fight continues. This lack of a reaction adds greater humor to the absurd event.

Charlie creates rolls by kneading dough, tossing it backward over his shoulder, and catching it in a container. He makes donuts by wrapping the dough around his wrist and rolling it off. At other times, the dough is used as a boxing glove, a bracelet, a mallet, a slingshot, and a discus. Chaplin's comic creativity explores these options as either central comic set pieces or subtle bits of business. But the dough is tantamount to artistic modeling clay as Chaplin transforms it as a comedy prop.

When the loaf of bread containing the dynamite is returned to the bakery, the bread feels exceptionally heavy, so the proprietor concludes that it is undercooked. Charlie and Chester are ordered to place it back in the oven. This causes the explosion that concludes the film, following the slapstick battle between the proprietor and Charlie, which extends throughout the dining area, the kitchen, and the bakery ovens. The impact of the explosion is concentrated in the bakery area. Chester, covered in debris, is shown in close-up, calling for help. Charlie, covered in the sticky dough that had plagued him throughout the film, forcefully pushes his head through the substance, which has now consumed him.

Because *Dough and Dynamite* developed out of Chaplin's and Conklin's improvisations in the bakery scene that had been intended for *Those Love Pang*, it is likely that a written scenario for *Dough and Dynamite* would not have existed. When the decision was made to expand the footage for a bakery comedy, much of the ideas were improvised. Since the comedy and filmmaking are exceptional here, the idea that it may have been accomplished with little preparation is even more impressive.

*Dough and Dynamite* was the first of Chaplin's Keystone films to go over the studio's set budget of $1,000. As Chaplin noted in his autobiography:

> *Dough and Dynamite*, a most successful film, took nine days, at a cost of eighteen hundred dollars. And because I went over the budget of one thousand dollars, which was the limit for a Keystone comedy, I lost my bonus of twenty-five dollars. The only way they could retrieve themselves, said Sennett, would be to put it out as a two-reeler, which they did, and it grossed more than one hundred and thirty thousand dollars the first year.

Chaplin, going by memory 50 years after the fact, was slightly off on the nine days of production, as records indicate it took 14 days to shoot, was finished with post-production a week after shooting completed, and received for distribution another six days later. Chaplin scholar Doug Sulpy also takes some issue with the comedian's memory as to *Dough and Dynamite* initially being presented as a one-reel comedy:

> Chaplin had already made *The Property Man*, so a two reeler wasn't anything new, and I'm sure Keystone planned things out far enough in advance so they knew whether they were making a one or two reeler at the point the cameras started rolling. *Dough and Dynamite* doesn't show any signs of a one reeler being padded out to two reels. At its full two reel status, nearly every account written during this era cites *Dough and Dynamite* as Chaplin's most successful Keystone film.

The brisk pace of *Dough and Dynamite* is maintained with Chaplin's editing process, using far more cuts per scene than he had used in his other Keystone efforts. The film's stepping over budget is most likely due to retakes, which were infrequent on Keystone productions, as Sennett considered them a waste of time, film, and money. Chaplin would eventually become notorious for making hundreds of takes just to get a short scene according to his exact vision. Such luxuries were not allowed at Keystone, and Chaplin never exceeded budget limitations again, despite the fact that *Dough and Dynamite* was enormously successful. But even in a *Photoplay* article written as early as 1915, Chaplin's penchant for costly retakes was noted: "Chaplin is a great waster of film. He never leaves a situation until he is thoroughly satisfied with it, and he is hard to satisfy. He is very much given to retakes, which is the most expensive habit in the movies."

That *Dough and Dynamite* did go over budget may be the first example of Chaplin's being so into his creative process that he completely overlooks the business aspect of the picture and continues to shoot without any heed to production costs. All ended well, but as Chaplin graduated to larger budgets and fewer restrictions, he would notoriously take tremendous advantage of such freedoms.

Along with greater concentration on performance, pacing, and structure, Chaplin explored different ways to further enhance certain scenes from a technological perspective. Chaplin was always about performance. He would occasionally use some level of composition for his scenes, liked to present visual contrasts among his players, and made good use of the background and foreground in his shots. But with *Dough and Dynamite*, he used an effect to enhance the concluding explosion, shaking the camera and causing the picture to vibrate as the explosive goes off. It perhaps seems like a very minor touch in this more sophisticated era, but during cinema's infancy, such an idea was able to influence the imaginations of many whose ideas gave more attention to technology than Chaplin's usually would.

Ted Okuda and David Maska in their book *Chaplin at Keystone and Essanay* cite *Dough and Dynamite* as "an artistic and financial victory" for Chaplin:

> With *Dough and Dynamite*, Chaplin reveals his most sophisticated filmmaking techniques thus far. The editing is particularly ambitious; there is a lot more intercutting within scenes, as he uses close-ups for comic effect and to complement the narrative. Chaplin is no longer just filming the action—here he's using cinematic technique to enhance the visuals. . . . The antics are effectively integrated into the film's storyline; the plot points may be thin, but it's a vast improvement over the Keystone crew showing up at a public event and trying to ad-lib a story to fit the surroundings.

While Chaplin would eventually become the darling of the intelligentsia when his work enjoyed even greater depth and refinement than could be accomplished under Sennett's tutelage, his best work at Keystone enjoyed popularity only with the mainstream moviegoing audience. They responded to *Dough and Dynamite* as just another funny Charlie Chaplin comedy from the Keystone studios, with *Motion Picture World* proclaiming: "Two reels of pure nonsense, some of which is very laughable indeed. This is well-pictured and very successful for this form of humor."

However, another issue of that periodical noted Chaplin's emergence as a motion picture figure that surpassed the dramatic performers of the same era:

> Mr. Chaplin has made a thorough, painstaking study of comedy in pantomime and this was a sort of preparatory course for his moving picture work. He is the exponent of realism and spontaneity in moving pictures, and his work has made him the best known actor on

the screen today. This does not bode well for the serious stars of the silent drama. Whenever there is a Chaplin booking, it is there the public flocks.

Much of the comic and filmmaking genius for which Chaplin would eventually be praised got its roots at Keystone, and *Dough and Dynamite* is among the very best examples. Stemming from his initial experiments as a director in films like *The Face on the Bar Room Floor* and *The New Janitor*, *Dough and Dynamite* maintains his continuous artistic progress. All of the elements Chaplin had learned about filmmaking, ideas we can see evolving as we watch each of these early films, culminated nicely in this two-reeler. His use of action within the frame, his depth of character, his presentation of conflict through visual contrast, even his interest in using topical events as part of the base narrative are all included here. To fit that much activity in a two-reel comedy was nothing short of genius. *Dough and Dynamite* remains one of the funniest and most significant films of Charlie Chaplin's entire career.

# CHAPTER 34

# *Gentlemen of Nerve*

**Alternate titles:** *Some Nerve; Charlie at the Races; A Gentleman with Nerve; Gentlemen with Nerves; Charlie Sneaks In; Charlot et Mabel aux Courses*

Running Time: One Reel
Filmed September 20–27, 1914
Released October 29, 1914

**Credits**
Written and directed by Charlie Chaplin

**Cast**
Charlie Chaplin (Mr. Wow Wow), Chester Conklin (Walrus), Mabel Normand (His Girl), Mack Swain (Ambrose), Phyllis Allen (Flirt), Glen Cavender, Charles Parrott, Tammany Young, Harry McCoy (Men Standing by Entrance), Dixie Chene (Girl with Pop Bottle), Cecile Arnold (Blonde Spectator), Alice Davenport (Woman by Beverage Counter), Ted Edwards (Man by Beverage Stand), Vivian Edwards, Morgan Wallace, Dan Allen, Slim Summerville, Fred Fishback, Eddie Nolan, Frank Opperman, Fritz Schade, Norma Nichols, Billy Gilbert, Bill Hauber, Peggy Page (Spectators), Ralph Hamlin, William Reuss, John Wiese (Drivers)

Even in comparison to the enormously successful *Dough and Dynamite, Gentlemen of Nerve* is another of Charlie Chaplin's strongest Keystone productions. Building on ideas he had been honing since first allowed to supervise his own films, Chaplin once again shows how effectively he could make a rewarding comedy even when working within the parameters of the established Keystone structure.

It would seem that following up something as ambitious and significant as the two-reel *Dough and Dynamite*, which was not only Chaplin's best Keystone production to date but also the company's most profitable film, would be daunting for any filmmaker. *Gentlemen of Nerve* is a one-reeler, relies almost completely on slapstick, and uses the old Keystone tradition of shooting a story around an actual event that is taking place, in this case, an auto race. But *Gentlemen of Nerve* continues Chaplin's progress as a comedian and filmmaker.

When we compare *Gentlemen of Nerve* to any previous Keystone one-reeler that relies specifically on slapstick comedy, it is remarkably superior in its cinematic structure, its staging of sequences, its presentation of characters, and especially its conclusion, not relying on a chase or a free-for-all. While shooting a film at an actual event is a typical Keystone practice, Chaplin does more than simply film a series of gags with the race as a backdrop. He chooses to juggle different characters, each performing different set pieces and connecting tangentially. Charlie does not appear for the first several minutes.

The beginning of *Gentlemen of Nerve* allows the characters of Walrus (Chester Conklin), Mabel (Mabel Normand), and Ambrose (Mack Swain) to develop rather fully prior to Charlie making the initial entrance. Conklin was even smaller than Chaplin, so the contrast between him and the very large Swain is immediately noticeable and amusing as Walrus and Mabel enter the auto race grounds, and the flirtatious Ambrose tries to attract the girl's attention. They skirt past Ambrose, who remains at the gate, unable to enter without the admission money. Once inside, Walrus takes his seat on the bleachers in the foreground with Mabel, and an imposing woman starts flirtatiously eyeing him.

During this setup, Chaplin uses conflicts among his initial characters and begins to define their characters. Although Walrus is with cute Mabel, he responds to the advances of the rather homely woman flirting with him. At first Mabel giggles at the very idea, but soon she finds it offensive that her date is giving attention to another when Walrus gives the woman his phone number.

The flirting woman is played by Phyllis Allen, a frequent Keystone player given to portraying shrewish, domineering wives. At 5 foot 8 inches tall and 180 pounds, she was typecast by her stature. She had a good comic sensibility within her casting parameters, so playing a kittenish flirt is certainly playing against type. Chaplin, with his eye for contrasts, uses her in this manner and she rises to the occasion with a real commitment to the very offbeat role. Allen flutters her eyes, winks, and smirks at Walrus, moving closer to him and shifting her position when he and Mabel stand up, so that when they sit back down, she is next to him. That Chaplin has Mabel initially react with giggling further points out the outrageousness of Walrus being at all interested in this attention. At the same time, why cute Mabel would be with the aptly nicknamed Walrus is another bit of absurdity.

When Charlie finally does appear, a title card introduces him as Mr. Wow Wow, an homage to Chaplin's stage years with the Fred Karno troupe, his having appeared in a play called *The Wow Wows*. Charlie, along with Ambrose, does not have the necessary admission to get into the race. Seeing an opening in the fence, the two decide to sneak through. Ambrose insists on going first but gets stuck due to his large frame. For the next several minutes, Charlie tries all possible methods of pushing Ambrose into the park area. There never appears to be any attempt to pull him back, but only to get him into the park. Ambrose is stuck and helpless as Charlie kicks, pushes, and head butts him to no avail. He even tries pushing him through with a baseball bat as one would stuff a turkey. Nothing appears to work. Meanwhile, Ambrose grimaces in pain on the other side of the fence, and a small group of onlookers at a concession stand giggle merrily at his predicament. A few try to help, but it is just as difficult to move the big man from one end as the other.

A gag featuring a large man stuck in a fence and a smaller man attempting to help him through seems awfully basic, but Chaplin augments it with a series of interesting ideas, approaching the situation with several creative methods. As a result, the scene extends, but it never seems to go on too long.

Charlie finally gives up on Ambrose and crawls under the bigger man to get into the races himself. Still willing to help his heavyset acquaintance, Charlie attempts to pull Ambrose through. Meanwhile, a cop comes along from the other end, sees the large man trying to sneak into the races without paying, and pulls on him. Charlie and the cop engage in a tug of war with poor Ambrose, who continues to howl in pain. Ambrose is finally through the fence. Charlie staves off the officer by squirting him with a seltzer bottle from the nearby concession stand.

Charlie eventually makes his way to the bleachers. Sitting next to a pretty lady, Charlie plops his feet in her lap. When she shoves him away and looks up at the race, Charlie leans toward the pop bottle in her hand and slurps through her straw. As with much of Charlie's boorish behavior in his Keystone films, the woman reacts by giggling rather than taking offense.

In this film, Chaplin is examining the flirtatious dalliances of the principal characters. There is really no reaction to the race itself, save for some minor footage that likely has significant historical interest. But with each subject, there seem to be different levels of romantic interest. Ambrose notices Mabel but is fought off by Walrus. Walrus responds to the attentions of a homely woman despite being with pretty Mabel. Charlie succeeds by his boldness, his aggressive behavior. Each sequence is in the foreground and not isolated. Walrus, Mabel, and Phyllis are seated on the lower level of the bleachers, surrounded by others. So are Charlie and the woman with the pop bottle. Ambrose, who has ventured from the gate area, finds himself near the bleachers. His large frame becomes intrusive as he walks through and tries to meet women. However, Ambrose does not present himself in as aggressive a manner as does Charlie. Ambrose removes his hat, holds out his hand, tries to be friendly. His big, freakish appearance is what works against him, while Charlie's behavior is forgiven because there is a cuteness about him that allows for an initial attraction. While Ambrose seems to be on the periphery of the action in *Gentlemen of Nerve*, the contrast between his behavior and that of the others (he is more mannerly with women than either Charlie or Walrus) offers as discernible a contrast as his physical appearance.

When Charlie and Mabel finally notice each other, it seems the match is perfect. Charlie has a playful boorishness that appears more amusing than disruptive. Mabel is cute and unappreciated by her less-than-attractive date. Chaplin uses crosscutting to show us that Walrus is continuing to be flirty with Phyllis, not realizing Mabel has wandered off in disgust. Charlie loses his attraction to the woman with the pop bottle when he notices Mabel. Mabel exhibits, with a coy smile, an attraction to Charlie and sits next to him, right on his hat. Charlie's reaction to this is an especially impressive bit of pantomime. It is not an over-the-top Keystone reaction, and it is more than just typically refined Chaplin. Charlie does a bit of an eye roll, moving his head only slightly. It registers cohesively with Mabel's accidental crushing of his hat and is a perfect reaction. Mabel acts apologetic, with innocently raised eyebrows and fluttering eyelashes, attempting to dust off the hat that is obviously ruined. Charlie shows her that the top of his derby is now detached by moving it up and down like a puppet's mouth. Rather than causing an argument, both end up giggling at the predicament.

Chaplin nicely sketches the relationship between Charlie and Mabel as one of initial attraction that quickly builds to a comfortable and forgiving one. Charlie is not merely attracted on a superficial level. He likes this young woman. The other he confronted more aggressively, with feet in her lap or slurping on her soda. Mabel does not receive such treatment. When her clumsiness ruins his hat (Charlie is not dressed in a manner that indicates he can easily afford another), his reaction is more comical than angry. Chaplin crosscuts back to Walrus and Phyllis. Chester has decided to be bold enough for what we might determine is a sexual advance. He whispers something in her ear. She responds in shock and disgust, starts beating him with her purse, and storms away. Left alone, he notices Mabel is no longer with him and sets out to find her.

Chaplin then allows the film to shift gears briefly and offers an amusing cutaway where Ambrose is shown happily enjoying the races on the sidelines. Suddenly, he is approached by the cop who had found him stuck in the fence earlier. The cop uses his club to smack Ambrose on his backside. Ambrose's mannerisms descend from celebration to stillness; the big man does an "uh-oh" double take, realizing the jig is up. With limited screen time, and not being directly involved in the central action of the film, Mack Swain shows with his exceptional performance that his imposing presence need not be limited to villainous heavies. By the end of 1914, he would be starring in his own series.

When Walrus attempts to reclaim Mabel, she appears uninterested and keeps her attentions toward Charlie. Walrus lifts her from her seat and starts arguing and alternately shaking her. Mabel looks back to Charlie, still seated, for assistance. Rather than jump up and slug or kick Walrus, Charlie stands and goes through an entire litany of preparatory gestures. Turning away from the

*Mack Swain tries to take Mabel Normand from Charlie.*

frenetically arguing Mabel and Walrus, Charlie carefully removes his coat, flexes his muscles, does a bit of stretching, and is ready to brawl. This bit of business is another example of Chaplin engaging in contrasts. Walrus and Mabel's arguing is all flagrant gestures and boisterous actions, while Charlie's preparation is studied and methodical. Each offsets the other. When Charlie does begin to fight, he places his outstretched hand, palm first, onto Walrus's face to hold him still, rears back with his arm, and smacks him into the audience. Walrus's attempts to retaliate are thwarted when Charlie boots him over into the area of Ambrose and the cop. The cop decides that Ambrose's sneaking in and Walrus's disruptions are both worthy of ejection by police. Chaplin cuts back to a close-up of Mabel and Charlie laughing. Their laughter slowly descends to flirtatious giggling as the film ends with Charlie attempting to steal a kiss and Mabel playfully squeezing his nose.

When Chaplin returned to the one-reel format, filming a breezy slapstick comedy on location at an actual event, it is evident he had no plans to simply follow the established Keystone pattern and explode with a series of isolated gags and conclude with a comically violent free-for-all. Instead, he concentrates on characters, giving as much attention to his supporting players as he does his own starring performance. In fact, Walrus and Mabel have about as much footage as

Charlie. It is they who open the film and establish the setting. Their relationship is pretty well defined before Charlie makes his first appearance.

One of the significant factors of the project is being able to create different situations with a myriad of characters and tying them into each other effectively. This was attempted in other Keystone films, but not with the cohesion Chaplin offers here. Charlie and Mabel's attraction is natural. Perhaps showing Walrus responding to the flirtation of an unattractive woman is Chaplin's method of conveying that Mabel's demure acceptance has resulted in her less worthy beau taking advantage of her easy acceptance of his behavior.

Ambrose is a study in contrasts. He is big, imposing, boorish, and potentially violent. He is broke, and he is crooked in that he wants to sneak into the races without paying. Charlie is all of those things, except small instead of big. However, when Charlie approaches someone he finds attractive, he is quite aggressive. To offset his imposing size, Ambrose is more delicate. Even in the opening scene, when Ambrose approaches Mabel and is fought off by Walrus, he does so because Mabel briefly wanders from her beau and appears to be alone. She ventures toward the gate entrance as Walrus is preoccupied with searching his pockets for admission money. He does not notice when Ambrose approaches Mabel. When he does, he reacts violently to the much bigger man and fights him off. For his part, Ambrose approaches Mabel in a mannerly way, not aggressively, and even registers shock and embarrassment when discovering she is indeed at the races with a date.

There are a few isolated elements in *Gentlemen of Nerve* that show up in later Chaplin films. The most noted would be when Charlie sneaks sips from a woman's soda. In a classic scene from Chaplin's brilliant 1928 feature *The Circus*, the Little Tramp, broke and hungry, sneaks bites from a child's hot dog in much the same manner. Chaplin would frequently revisit, rework, and refine sequences from his Keystone days throughout his career, and he would often use actors he had worked with at this studio (Swain would offer a career-defining performance in Chaplin's *The Gold Rush* in 1925, while Conklin would be appearing with Chaplin as late as 1940).

Chaplin also has an awareness of each actor's stature in films. Chester Conklin would often be the star of his own vehicles, and Mabel Normand was quite popular and established. Thus, Chaplin's idea to offer them at the outset of his picture, establishing their characters and their relationship before Charlie makes his entrance, further displays how Chaplin was more interested in the success of the overall production rather than simply advancing his own prestige. Chaplin realized that audiences identifying the initial characters and knowing something about their situation would add backstory depth to the subsequent scenes after Charlie makes his entrance. There is a reason that the overlooked Mabel allows herself to be attracted to Charlie, for instance.

*Mabel and Charlie together at the races.*

Along with the contrasts in Mack Swain's character, Chaplin's use of larger, homelier Phyllis Allen as the flirt is another inspired choice of offbeat casting. Allen's comic prowess is also a matter of record in other Keystones (she registered effectively as Charlie's wife in *The Rounders*). Her imposing presence offsets the smaller Walrus, while Mabel, sitting one over from Walrus, offers a variety of reactions. The initial flirting seems incredulous. Walrus's responding to it favorably is absurd. His being obviously more attracted to her than Mabel is outrageous.

Allen's general performance was to present herself as the classic ugly duckling. Older, bigger, and usually angry and uncompromising, even her mannerisms present her as little more than obtrusive. Chaplin could have easily cast any one of many attractive Keystone actresses in the role and maintained the same narrative effectively, but the offbeat casting of Allen makes it more visually amusing. Allen's winking, mincing mannerisms provide as much amusement as the situation itself, and the narrative progression is maintained.

While Chaplin's methods are more refined than in standard Keystones, this does not mean he completely eschews the more violent slapstick. There is plenty of punching, kicking, and slapping going on. At one point, Charlie burns Ambrose's nose with a lit cigarette; in another instance, he bites Walrus on the nose. Certainly the sequence where Walrus is physically shaking Mabel as they argue is of a more blatantly violent nature, especially since Walrus has already been identified as a scrapper. Chaplin having Charlie perform a series of preparatory gestures before physically rescuing Mabel is a nice contrast, especially the audience's anticipation of Walrus being effectively punished for his continued bad treatment of Mabel.

What should also be noted about this film is Mabel's attraction to Walrus, which seems incongruous. Walrus is a small, boisterous, rather ugly man with a large mustache covering most of his face. His bulging eyes and wild gestures are hardly indicative of his carrying himself in an attractive manner. The title card that introduces the couple states that Mabel is skittish about her situation with him. Her apprehension is justified. Further, there is the attraction of Phyllis to Walrus. While we can determine that the homely woman is willing to settle for the homelier little man, Walrus actually does have an attractive date accompanying him when he responds to this woman's advances. Chaplin's presentation of these various potential relationships and their situations follows a general pattern, but the details are restructured to offer something other than that which is standard.

Charlie is again a loner, but the fact that he ends up with cute Mabel appears to be a happy ending for both of them. The title card identifies Charlie as disruptive. He did sneak into the races without paying, as did Ambrose (with Charlie's help). He aggressively bothers a female spectator. He engages in slapstick battles with others. But still Chaplin chooses to allow Charlie to make it through the movie unscathed, and ultimately victorious. Despite his actions earlier in the film, his championing the unfairly neglected Mabel makes him a hero.

Period critics took note of the several Keystone favorites being allowed to shine in *Gentlemen of Nerve*. *Motion Picture News* stated: "Charlie, Chester and Mabel attend an auto race. Results? As laughable as ever were pictured." Any subtleties, offbeat casting, and varied ideas Chaplin had were lost on early movie audiences, who would only respond to the superficial humor of the subject. But the fact that Chaplin made these choices as a filmmaker is the reason for the success of a film like *Gentlemen of Nerve*, even if period moviegoers did not consciously appreciate it past simply finding Chaplin's movies funnier than those of other comedians.

Chaplin's box office popularity continued to increase as rapidly as his inspired ideas. His films were among the most popular being made, and certainly the most successful being produced at Keystone. Other studios were taking notice, and some discussions were already taking place as to the possibility of such an important star perhaps being won over to making films elsewhere. Chaplin was not preoccupied with such matters. Content with the $200 weekly paycheck he was receiving, the allowance of greater creative freedom, and the acceptance he now enjoyed on the Keystone lot (extending beyond longtime friends like Normand, Conklin, and Roscoe Arbuckle), Chaplin simply wanted to do a good job. In an interview with *Motography*, he stated: "Audiences will look at our pictures and sometimes say we should have done this or that. They do not realize that we do not do things at the spur of the moment. We spend many days and nights concentrating on what would work best and be most effective."

Chaplin's choices were sound ones. His only limitation now was budgetary, as Sennett's limitation of only $1,000 per short could be difficult for a filmmaker like Chaplin, whose exacting vision often required retakes. It was a limitation he did his best to work within.

One of many key factors in the success of *Gentlemen of Nerve* was Chaplin's ability to make such an effective comedy by offering his own version of a standard Keystone comedy. The structure of performing gags and conflicting situations at a racing event could not be more typical Keystone. How Chaplin uses these ingredients more effectively than the usual Sennett-produced knockabout farce is why the film stands out as one of the comedian's best from this period. This film continues to show how Chaplin was doing the proverbial thinking outside the box by extending past the usual raucous gag fests that Keystone was noted for producing. Each of the characters in *Gentlemen of Nerve* has an identifiable depth and purpose. These are not so much the superficial characters going through a litany of overplayed gestures and facial expressions. Each of the central characters in *Gentlemen of Nerve* is an individual. Their situations are believable. The comedy comes naturally from the characters and their situations.

While eschewing the more frenetic pacing that Keystone was noted for using, Chaplin maintains a briskness that is quick enough to keep interest, and relaxed enough to allow for character development and to play out important situations. *Gentlemen of Nerve* remains one of the comedian's strongest Keystone films.

# CHAPTER 35

# *His Musical Career*

**Alternate titles:** *The Musical Tramp; The Piano Movers; Charlie the Piano Mover*

Running Time: One Reel
Filmed October 1–10, 1914
Released November 7, 1914

**Credits**
Written and directed by Charlie Chaplin

**Cast**
Charlie Chaplin (Charlie), Mack Swain (Ambrose), Fritz Schade (Mr. Rich), Cecile Arnold (Mrs. Rich), Charles Parrott (Piano Store Manager), Frank Hayes (Mr. Poor), Bill Hauber (Servant), Billy Gilbert (Store Worker), Peggy Page (Mrs. Poor)

Charlie Chaplin's stardom happened quickly, rose rapidly, and increased when he began directing his own Keystone films. Moviegoers found his films funnier than other comedies of the time, and they felt his character offered a stronger connection with themselves. They may not have been able to assess his work at a critical level, but the stylistic technique Chaplin utilized had at least a subliminal effect on his audience by making his movies funnier and better structured. Moviegoers would not notice how many edits Chaplin used or the number of different camera setups. But Chaplin's creative choices did matter to his work, and audiences could appreciate, even if only superficially, that the Charlie Chaplin Keystone comedies were constantly getting better.

*His Musical Career*, however, can be called a marginal disappointment. There are some wonderful ideas, and some amusing moments, but the film's chief interest is in how differently Chaplin chose to structure the one-reeler, using fewer shots and concentrating on a more leisurely pace. Chaplin also continued to investigate cinema's possibilities for visual contrasts with *His Musical Career*. Not only is Mack Swain, as Ambrose, once again offering his enormous physical contrast to the diminutive Charlie, but so is the film's central prop. Pianos are large, heavy, and bulky. The initial premise of Charlie working for a company that delivers and collects these instruments conjures up comic possibilities. That he, and Ambrose, must deliver one to a residence that rests atop a steep flight of stairs is a quintessential comic obstacle.

The premise of *His Musical Career* has Ambrose and Charlie assigned to pick up a piano from Mr. Poor and deliver a piano to Mr. Rich. The piano to be picked up, due to lack of payments, is at 999 Prospect Street. The piano to be delivered is scheduled for receiving at 666 Prospect Street. Naturally, Charlie and Ambrose mix the addresses up, delivering a piano to Mr. Poor and taking a piano from Mr. Rich.

What can first be observed with *His Musical Career* is the relationship between Ambrose and Charlie. Chaplin promotes Mack Swain to full co-star status here, and the two comedians operate as a cohesive team. Swain usually portrayed an adversarial presence in Charlie's world, but here he reaches the level of partner. Their physical contrast of big man and little man therefore works at another level.

When Ambrose and Charlie attempt to deliver the piano, Chaplin presents the heavy, bulky object as much for its fragile nature as its heft. Initially, Charlie and Ambrose are compared as to each one's individual strength. Ambrose pulls the piano while Charlie, at the other end, merely hangs on as the soles of his shoes skid along the pavement, showing how the bigger man can handle the instrument alone if necessary. However, when Ambrose must tie the rope underneath the piano and Charlie tilts it upward so that he can do so, the smaller man tires easily and drops the heavy instrument on his partner's head. Before extricating Ambrose, Charlie must catch his breath.

To make the delivery, the piano is balanced precariously on the back of a small mule-driven cart, with Charlie and Mack sitting in front. The mule pulls diligently, but eventually the weight of the object causes the cart to tip backward and take the mule off its feet, hanging above the street. Chaplin shoots these street scenes from different angles, from a deep focus long shot to a close-up tracking shot with Ambrose and Charlie framed tightly. As they ride, Charlie uses his pipe to sneak spoonfuls of Ambrose's beer.

Once they have reached their destination, there is a nice shot of Ambrose and Charlie untying and preparing the instrument for transport. Their economy of movement is offset by a background with a great deal of movement in and around the street.

Next comes the noted gag of Ambrose and Charlie transporting the piano up the steep flight of steps. Comedy film enthusiasts will immediately think of Stan Laurel and Oliver Hardy's classic three-reel comedy *The Music Box* (1932), an Oscar-winning short that features the comic duo trapped like Sisyphus in their repeated attempts to maneuver a piano up a long flight of stairs. There is even a connection through Charles Parrott, who appeared in *His Musical Career*. By the time the Laurel and Hardy film was being shot, Parrott was, as Charley Chase, one of the top comedians at the very same studio, Hal Roach Productions, and his brother, James Parrott, is credited with directing *The Music Box*. Of course Laurel himself directed the Laurel and Hardy films by this time, with the credited director acting as a veritable assistant, but still it was James Parrott on the set, Charles Parrott at the same studio, and Laurel was not above listening to ideas from others.

Ted Okuda and David Maska, in their book *Charlie Chaplin at Keystone and Essanay*, argue against the idea that *The Music Box* was inspired by this film:

> While *His Musical Career* has a passing resemblance to Laurel and Hardy's piano-moving classic *The Music Box*, it's debatable as to whether it can be considered a true forerunner. There are similarities, particularly in a scene when Charlie and Mack attempt to deliver a piano up a staircase. But whereas Chaplin uses it for a brief gag, Laurel and Hardy based their whole picture around moving a piano up a ridiculously long flight of stairs. Actually, it has always been understood that *The Music Box* was a later, longer, more detailed version of an earlier silent two-reeler Laurel and Hardy made in 1927 entitled *Hats Off*. At the time of this writing, no known print of *Hats Off* survives, but judging by existing stills, written material, et al., this silent comedy with Laurel and Hardy attempting to deliver a bulky washing machine up a long flight of stairs appears to be the true portent to *The Music Box*. It is noteworthy that comedian Edgar Kennedy, another Keystone regular at this time, also remade *Hats Off* as *It's Your Move* (1945) with the silent film's director, Hal Yates, once again at the helm. Finally, the Three Stooges offered another variation in *An Ache in Every Stake* (1941), when they attempt to carry a large block of ice up a long flight of stairs, only to discover the ice has melted in that much time.

In *His Musical Career*, the piano up the stairs is indeed an isolated gag on which this film does not focus completely. An inspired setup, Charlie is at the bottom, while Ambrose is at the top. Charlie pushes and Ambrose pulls. Naturally a lost grip causes the bulky instrument to come rolling back down the steps relentlessly, bullying Charlie down with it. Chaplin does a nice job of having two very large contrasts to Charlie, the piano and Ambrose, slanted upward as they go up the staircase. When Ambrose loses his grip, the heavy piano rolls down and shoves Charlie back to square one. This happens more than once, Charlie being creative by attempting to push the obstacle with his cane and other maneuvers.

The next shot presents big Ambrose entering the delivery area, followed by small Charlie with the entire piano balanced sideways across his shoulders and back. Standing there as Mr. Poor slowly decides exactly where to place the instrument, Charlie watches Ambrose enjoy a refreshment. Charlie's knees tremble and finally buckle in a nice, dragged out scene. First, Charlie's legs slowly spread under the weight of the piano. Ambrose and Mr. Poor come to his rescue and hold the piano steady. Finally, Charlie emerges from beneath the instrument, hunched over and unable to straighten up without his partner's assistance.

Here the contrasts are clearly evident. Mack, so much larger, is allowed to enter the room carrying nothing. Charlie, the smaller man, must perform the bulk of their task alone. Contrasting little Charlie with the large object and the larger man forces Charlie into the center of attention, surrounded by bigger objects, standing in the forefront throughout. Chaplin also allows Charlie to attain sympathy from the audience as the ambitious working man whose struggle is greater than that of those in charge or wealthy enough to afford such a large item.

When Ambrose and Charlie then retrieve a piano from Mr. Rich, their initial obstacle is that the wealthier man's home is well furnished, unlike Mr. Poor's rather barren studio. Maneuvering the large piano through a living room filled with furniture causes broken crockery, and a servant who gets in the way is shoved to the floor. Mr. Rich's home has only a small set of porch steps in front of the house. However, they are as daunted by this obstacle as they had been by the longer, steeper staircase that led to Mr. Poor's studio. Ambrose, going backward, stumbles down the steps until he falls. Once he gets up, he drags the piano, pulling Charlie down the steps and to the pavement.

The conclusion of *His Musical Career* is too convenient and too pat. The film ends with the piano getting away from Ambrose and Charlie as they attempt to take it down a steep walkway. It rolls mightily down the walk, where it ends up destroyed in a lake. It almost appears as though Chaplin had run out of time, and allotted film, for a one-reel production and was careful to not go over budget. While his spending on the elaborate *Dough and Dynamite* would be rectified by its massive box office success, that film had not yet been in general release by the time Chaplin was filming *His Musical Career*.

Here Chaplin relies perhaps a bit too much on formula, ending *His Musical Career* with an unnecessarily convenient wrap-up. The events leading up to this perfunctory ending, however, are quite inspired and filled with interesting ideas. As with *The Music Box*, the piano in *His Musical Career* can perhaps be called another supporting character. Unlike the later film, which concentrates the delivery of just one piano over the course of three reels, *His Musical Career* has different assignments for two pianos in the course of one reel. While the

*Charlie responds to a statue.*

major reliance is on size and heft, the mix-up is also a good, solid basis on which
to hang comedy situations.

While it lacks the substance of *Dough and Dynamite*, or even *Gentlemen of
Nerve*, *His Musical Career* is still a much more ambitious one-reel comedy than
the shorts on which Chaplin had cut his teeth earlier in his Keystone tenure. Its
ending is disappointing, but the body of the film is a series of creative ideas based
on an interesting situation rather than a simple premise on which to hang violent
comedy and a free-for-all conclusion.

The characters in *His Musical Career* are all quite obviously coached by their
director. Charles Parrott, who as Charley Chase would eventually enjoy solid
stardom with his own series at the Hal Roach studios by the early 1920s, is a
perfect example. Parrott plays the manager of the piano company where Charlie
and Ambrose work, and his mannerisms, whether confronting his underlings,
his well-paying customer Mr. Rich, or the slacking Mr. Poor, are all reminiscent
of Chaplin's style. Upon making the sale to Mr. Rich, Parrott smiles and rubs
his hands together in a mannerism that Charlie himself uses shortly afterward
in another scene. Parrott would soon leave Keystone, eventually end up at the
Roach studios, and be able to develop his own distinct style. Some of Parrott's
own films as Charley Chase are among the classic short comedies of screen his-

tory. His later direction of such Three Stooges comedies as *Mutts to You* and *Violent Is the World for Curly* (both Columbia, 1938) would solidify his legacy for generations. However, at Keystone, Parrott was given far too little opportunity. (For more on Parrott, see appendix A.)

Aside from the comedy and the way the characters are presented, what may very well be most interesting about *His Musical Career* is that Chaplin uses much fewer shots. David Robinson, in his book *Chaplin: His Life and Art*, observed of *His Musical Career*:

> The single reel consists of a mere twenty-seven shots; usually Chaplin and the other Keystone directors used up to ninety shots in a film of the same length. Here, as Buster Keaton was later to do, he bypassed the current fashion in editing, recognizing that each shot needed to be a stage for his own extended comedy routines. He declared this early that cutting was not an obligation but a convenience.

Most of Chaplin's shots would be of the journey to the first house. The scene of the mule pulling the cart on which the piano is precariously balanced employs a tracking close-up of Charlie and Ambrose, and both long and medium shots to show the counterbalance between the mule and the piano, with the instrument eventually outweighing the mule and lifting the animal from the street.

Chaplin relaxes the pace, just as Laurel and Hardy would do with *The Music Box*. The difference here is that Laurel and Hardy had a naturally relaxed pace, while Chaplin was employed at the Keystone studios, where frenetic activity was the norm. With under 30 shots, *His Musical Career* allows Chaplin to rest on each sequence and frame his shots in longer takes. For instance, when Charlie comes into the home of Mr. Poor with an upright piano balancing across his shoulders, the contrast between his small frame and the large inanimate object draws attention, but it does not anchor the shot. There are three other people, including the imposing Mack Swain as Ambrose, who are also part of this scene. The contrast is merely a visual effect. The laugh comes when Charlie's knees buckle under the weight of the piano, due to his having to wait in this position while Mr. Poor takes his time deciding just the right spot for it.

But it is not the relaxed pace or fewer shots that cause *His Musical Career* to be less amusing than *Dough and Dynamite* or with more limited scope than *The New Janitor*. *His Musical Career* shows Chaplin venturing past the standard Keystone trappings with a structure that was unlike the studio's standard method but does not challenge this style as did *Gentlemen of Nerve*. The former film took a Keystone premise and concentrated on character development, adding layers of personality to each individual. *His Musical Career* concentrates more on gags and gag situations. The characters are basic (successful Mr. Rich contrasting with

Mr. Poor, who cannot keep up payments on his piano), while anything Charlie and Ambrose do is in reaction to their prop more so than to each other.

This is not to state that *His Musical Career* is a complete failure. Chaplin was still using his relatively new freedom at Keystone to explore the myriad different comedy and filmmaking ideas that were circulating in his mind, and he was relying less often on his Karno troupe background. Within the scope of his investigation, Chaplin would sometimes attempt methods that would not have the same success as others. With *His Musical Career*, Chaplin perhaps learned more about limiting his pace and structure in a way that assisted him once he began directing feature-length films several years later.

Period critics certainly welcomed *His Musical Career*. *Variety* stated: "One of the best short comedies in a month. Funny piano moving skit." Chaplin had clearly hit his stride, continuing to do more than simply rest within the Keystone parameters and add funny bits of business to separate his character from those that were more conventional. His superior comic vision was becoming more and more evident with each production he supervised, even a film like *His Musical Career*, which was not quite at the lofty level he had now established. Along with fewer shots and a more leisurely pace, *His Musical Career* extends Chaplin's interest in presentation contrasts by the film itself contrasting greatly with something like *Dough and Dynamite*, a film that uses many shots and is paced more briskly.

Still not committing himself completely to a specific cinematic style, Chaplin continued investigating different cinematic ideas, especially after he left Keystone. A film like *His Musical Career* is a good example of Chaplin honing his craft and probing different approaches to cinematic structure.

# CHAPTER 36

# His Trysting Places

**Alternate titles:** *His Trysting Place; The Family House; Family Home; Very Much Married; The Henpecked Spouse; The Ladies Man; Papa Charlie*

Running Time: Two Reels
Filmed September 19–26, 1914
Released November 9, 1914

**Credits**
Written and directed by Charlie Chaplin

**Cast**
Charlie Chaplin (Charlie), Mabel Normand (Mabel), Mack Swain (Ambrose), Phyllis Allen (Ambrose's Wife), Glen Cavender (Cop), Nick Cogley (Bearded Customer at Diner), Peggy Page (Clarice), Frank Hayes, Ted Edwards, Billy Gilbert (Diners), Edwin Frazee and Vivian Edwards (Couple outside Diner). (Contrary to some studies, Gene Marsh did not play the role of Clarice.)

In *His Trysting Places*, a film that could battle with *Dough and Dynamite* for the title "Best Chaplin Keystone," Charlie Chaplin examines married life and jealousy by once again reimagining the standard Keystone structure. There are mistaken encounters, jealousies, mix-ups, and petty fights, but the method to Chaplin's presentation of these typical Keystone plot elements is what separates *His Trysting Places* from the norm. This is not the first time Charlie was married in a Keystone comedy (shrewish Phyllis Allen had played his wife in *The Rounders*), but this is the first time that the character is placed in a structured domestic situation. Chaplin explores what can be done with Charlie as a married man with a child, but he soon shifts focus to the mix-ups and mistaken identities that are the basis of this film.

It is worth noting that while *His Trysting Places* was released after *His Musical Career*, it was filmed before *Gentlemen of Nerve*, just after Chaplin completed

*Those Love Pangs*, a production he had started but delayed finishing until he completed *Dough and Dynamite*. It appears that upon completing *Those Love Pangs* rather hastily, Chaplin then exploded with a burst of creativity that resulted in some of his best work.

In *His Trysting Places*, Chaplin takes issue with the seedy underbelly of domestic life by tightening his shot around Mabel, Charlie, and their infant child. While Mabel attempts to do the ironing with a crying baby in her arms, Charlie sits nearby reading a magazine. The area is so cramped, Charlie keeps bumping into the flaming stovetop that sits imposingly at the right of the frame. Mabel, with the child, is at the ironing board at the left of the frame, while Charlie anchors the center. The shot is tight, with no negative space, showing the cramped quarters as uncomfortable and inconvenient. Charlie feels closed in, perhaps metaphorically by his domestic situation, while the long-suffering Mabel does her best to persevere.

With our concentration on Charlie, it is easy to neglect the talents of Mabel Normand, whose versatility allowed her to play all manner of heroines, feisty scrappers, innocents, and savvy opportunists throughout her tragically brief screen career. Her close friendship with Chaplin and their mutual respect allowed them to work together well. Here, Chaplin presents Mabel as tired, overwhelmed, but determined. She does not take much from husband Charlie, willing to lash out if his laziness or grumpiness becomes intrusive.

Mabel insists Charlie take the baby so she can get some housework done. There is a neat bit of business in which Charlie, carrying the baby by the back of its shirt, like a suitcase, goes into the living room, fluffs up the pillow on the child's cradle, then sits in it himself, plopping the infant on the hardwood floor. These actions are very different from his sentimental approach to child rearing in *The Kid* (1920) but fall neatly in line with the established Keystone character.

Charlie later goes to get a baby bottle for the child, which allows Chaplin to introduce the next set of characters. Cutting away to Ambrose and his wife, two large, homely people unlike the attractive Charlie and Mabel, Chaplin shows this other couple cooing, pinching, and tickling as Ambrose prepares to leave. Their marriage remains on its honeymoon. The two of them appear to be very much in love, while Charlie and Mabel seem overpowered by the very structure of domestic living. Here Chaplin's interest in presenting physical contrasts is given something of a new twist. Rather than compose shots with large and small people, the contrast is between the unhappy marriage of the attractive couple and the happiness of the unattractive couple.

Ambrose is asked by his secretary to deliver a love letter she has written to her beau. He cheerfully agrees and sticks it in his pocket. Chaplin, in an effort to bring the characters together, sets up a scene in a diner where Charlie goes to have lunch. Ambrose is already there, waiting to be served his soup. Upon his entrance into the diner, Charlie casually wipes his hands on a customer's long

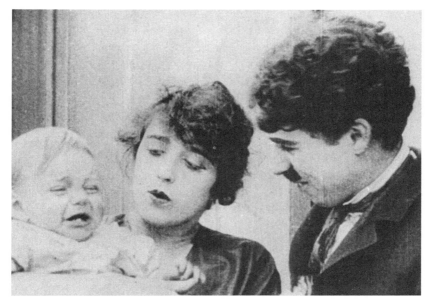

*Charlie, Mabel Normand, and baby.*

beard, causing the offended man to leave in a huff. This is puckish, rascally Keystone Charlie, being troublesome for the very sake of disruption and channeling it through clever visual comedy.

Charlie and Ambrose's encounter in the diner is a throwback to disruptive Charlie and his slapstick boldness. First there is the initial contrast between enormous Ambrose and diminutive Charlie, made even more evident as the shot Chaplin uses has them facing toward the camera, seated behind a lunch counter. Ambrose towers over Charlie, seated at his right. As Ambrose concentrates on the bowl of soup in front of him, Charlie responds to the slurping noises and the splattering. Of course this being a silent film, we cannot hear any of the noises Ambrose might be making, so Chaplin has Charlie plug his ears in response, conveying to the audience that the visual sloppiness is accompanied by audible sloppiness. In order to convey the splattering, Charlie lifts his jacket as a veritable shield.

Ambrose reaches across Charlie's dinner to obtain salt. Charlie bites Ambrose's arm. The comic mayhem includes flinging soup with the spoon, slaps, and ultimately a classic Keystone slapstick free-for-all, where Charlie's punches, pivots, and kicks to subdue all the customers. A thrown pie flies out the door and into a man preparing to enter.

Even this far into his Keystone tenure, and doing his best work thus far, Chaplin did not stray completely from the trappings of the studio's basic comic elements. While he eschewed chase scenes, he would engage in free-for-all slapstick battles, maybe only to pacify Sennett, whose name still remained as producer. But Chaplin's sequences of this sort were comparatively brief, able to accent the overall structure of the film and add energy to a scene rather than distract from it. Once it ends, Chaplin returns to plot exposition.

The free-for-all here has a distinct point. Amidst the hubbub, Ambrose and Charlie carelessly grab each other's jackets. Neither tries to wear it; they simply grab and go. Once Charlie gets home and Mabel searches for the baby bottle he went out to buy, she finds the love note that Ambrose was delivering, and she believes it was sent to Charlie. Having staged the free-for-all in the diner, Chaplin's next presentation of a slapstick conflict builds upon that scene's rhythm by allowing the film to relax before Mabel lashes out. She violently slaps and shoves Charlie, busting the ironing board over his head. He leaves the apartment, wandering to the park in utter confusion as to what he has done wrong.

Meanwhile, Ambrose and his wife are billing and cooing on a park bench. Ambrose leaves the area, and his wife finds a baby bottle in his pocket. Convinced that this means Ambrose has fathered another woman's child, Mrs. Ambrose bursts into tears. Charlie, wandering into the park with no understanding as to his wife's tirade, takes a seat on the bench beside Mrs. Ambrose. Each tells the other their respective tales of woe. When Mabel comes to the park, leaves the baby with a cop, and finds Charlie being consoled by Mrs. Ambrose, she jumps to the conclusion that this is the other woman.

In the realm of Keystone comedies, this weaving of different character mix-ups, each dovetailing neatly into the next, is actually quite intricate. When Charlie flees the scene, Mabel confronts Mrs. Ambrose. The contrasting dynamic is even greater here, as Mabel is so much smaller than Mrs. Ambrose. In fact, Ambrose's wife seated is nearly as tall as a standing Mabel. That does not stop the diminutive Mabel as she lunges for Mrs. Ambrose's throat. As Mabel and Charlie start to fight, the cop with their baby comes along, hands the baby to Ambrose, and tries to break up the fight. Ambrose, holding the baby, wanders over to his wife to show her. Naturally his wife believes this to be his child and lashes out at him. Ambrose is just as confused as Charlie had been.

This tangled web of character confusion is straightened out at the end, with a delightful close-up of Mabel and Charlie concluding the production (not unlike the final shot of *Gentlemen of Nerve*, which had not yet been filmed). The film's intricacies are impressive, while the performances feature this ensemble at somewhere near their collective best. Not spending a lot of time on shot composition other than the physical contrasts that exist between different actors, Chaplin choreographs the confusion, especially in the park scenes where the characters remain within yards of each other even as they leave a specific area, with a pace and rhythm that probably stem from his stage training.

*His Trysting Places* became one of the more noted examples of Chaplin's Keystone period when scenes were used in the 1960 Robert Youngson production *When Comedy Was King*, an anthology of silent screen comedians. While briefer shots from *Gentlemen of Nerve* and *The Masquerader* were also used, the footage from *His Trysting Places* was lengthier and established Chaplin with new audiences. The film remains a good introduction to Chaplin's slapstick comic style, leading the viewer to the comedian's later career, where his style and character would become more refined.

In *Charlie Chaplin at Keystone and Essanay*, Ted Okuda and David Maska point out that Chaplin investigated domestic life in this manner only once more, in the 1919 First National release *A Day's Pleasure*. They also notice some tangential similarities to French comedian Max Linder, whom Chaplin often cited as a major influence. According to Okuda and Maska, "The films of the debonair, top-hatted Linder deftly combined subtle farce with imaginative visual gags. Though Chaplin's later comedies would be closer to Linder's style, *His Trysting Places* clearly reveals the Linder influence taking hold." Critics of the era embraced this comedy in the same manner as they had all of Chaplin's films. *Moving Picture World* stated: "Chaplin does some particularly amusing stunts in this and the fun runs high through the entire two reels."

However, in *His Trysting Places*, we see further development in Chaplin's comic presentation. The diner sequence is particularly impressive in how Chaplin approaches a typical situation with potential for Keystone-style slapstick and re-creates it according to his own vision. The disruptive Charlie who boisterously enters and wipes his hands on a customer's long beard soon becomes more sensitive when responding to the sloppiness of Ambrose slurping his soup and sneezing toward his bowl. The fight that eventually erupts between them is not sudden. It builds gradually from minor confrontation to all-out battle. Rather than explode into a free-for-all, it builds to that point. Then, once it reaches that level, the scene concludes and the narrative continues.

The tightness of this ensemble is notable in that the performers are all actors Chaplin enjoyed using. Swain's contribution was, at first, a physical contrast to Charlie. But Swain's abilities extended beyond simply stereotyping, and he would use his larger presence to work against type. In more than one Keystone comedy, including *His Trysting Places*, Swain will bop and cavort in a most silly, playful manner. This sort of cavorting is made more amusing by his large size. His female complement would be Phyllis Allen, whom Chaplin would enjoy casting against type, never presenting her as merely a homely woman even in instances where she is made up to be just that. Her larger frame also contrasts with Charlie and with Mabel. When Mabel attacks her and Phyllis cowers, the image is surrealistically funny.

*Charlie responds to Mack Swain's noisy eating habits.*

Mabel Normand is the most impressive performer in this film after Chaplin. As usual, she commands her role completely, exhibiting the worn-out manner of a long-suffering wife at one point, and gritting her teeth with feisty determination in another. Her diminutive size never negates her charisma. The opening scene where Chaplin presents the cramped kitchen quarters gives Mabel at the left of the frame more to do than Charlie in the center. While Charlie responds to the flaming stove by inadvertently putting his foot on it, backing into it, and so on, it is Mabel who responds more effectively to Chaplin's attempt to present the frame as uncomfortably cramped without negative space. Mabel is balancing between holding an active, crying baby and trying to do the ironing. The iron is hot, the ironing board is bulky, the baby takes up space or the use of her one arm, and her being so small would cause one to imagine the child also being rather heavy.

Regarding Mabel Normand, Chaplin wrote in his autobiography:

> Once when Mabel, Roscoe Arbuckle and I appeared for some charity at one of the theaters in San Francisco, Mabel and I came very near to being emotionally involved. It was a glamorous evening and the three of us had appeared with great success at the theater. Mabel had left her coat in the dressing room and asked me to take her there to

get it. Arbuckle and the others were waiting below outside in a car. For a moment we were alone. She looked radiantly beautiful and as I placed her wrap over her shoulders I kissed her and she kissed me back. We might have gone further, but people were waiting. Later I tried to follow up the episode, but nothing ever came of it. "No Charlie," she said good-humoredly, "I'm not your type and neither are you mine."

Chaplin would garner a more sordid reputation with women a few years later, but in these times, the friendship and professional relationship he enjoyed with Normand would survive the flirtation he described. This would not be the last film in which Chaplin and Normand would appear together. She would work in his final film produced at Keystone, *Getting Acquainted*.

*His Trysting Places* was another portent to what Chaplin would accomplish upon leaving Keystone, a situation that was slated to happen not long after the release of this film. It has a tighter plot and more carefully developed gag sequences. Some of the situations recall the plot of *The Rink* (1916), one of the comedian's Mutual productions, and arguably the most aesthetically creative period of Chaplin's career. *The Rink* also features flirtations and dalliances among various characters who eventually meet up in the end, with the enormous Eric Campbell now filling in for Mack Swain, while rotund Henry Bergman played his wife in a dame masquerade not unlike what happened frequently in Keystone comedies. In fact, Chaplin would frequently draw from the experiences in his Keystone productions.

The box office success of *His Trysting Places* aided Chaplin's continuous progress from a financial perspective. However, according to Chaplin, he was unaware that other studios increased their interest in the most popular comedian in movies around the time *His Trysting Places* was released and his contract with Keystone was about to conclude. Chaplin recalled in his autobiography:

> I had a month to go with Keystone, and so far no other company had made me an offer. I was getting nervous and I fancy Sennett knew it and was biding his time. Usually he came to me at the end of a picture and jokingly hustled me up about starting another. Now, he kept away from me. He was polite, but aloof. In spite of the fact, my confidence never left me. If nobody made me an offer, I would go into business for myself. Why not? I was confident and self-reliant.

# CHAPTER 37

# *Getting Acquainted*

**Alternate titles: *A Fair Exchange; Exchange Is No Robbery; Hello Everybody***

Running Time: One Reel
Filmed November 13–14, 1914
Released December 5, 1914

**Credits**
Written and directed by Charlie Chaplin

**Cast**
Charlie Chaplin (Charlie), Mabel Normand (Mabel), Mack Swain (Ambrose), Phyllis Allen (Charlie's Wife), Harry McCoy (Flirt), Edgar Kennedy (Cop), Cecile Arnold (Flirt), Glen Cavender (Turk), Joe Bordeaux (Motorist), Peggy Page (Girl in Park)

Significant as the last film Charlie Chaplin shot for Keystone (but not the final one released), this one-reeler is yet another slapstick park comedy with flirtations and dalliances among its principal cast of Mack Swain, Mabel Normand, Phyllis Allen, and Chaplin. As with the second half of *His Trysting Places*, Chaplin deftly handles the intricacies of the different relationships and romantic tangents, causing each character to somehow become connected before the reel concludes. It is briskly paced, is filled with top performances, and has some clever sight gags. But it does not match the lofty level Chaplin had established with his better Keystone films by this time, including the two-reel *Dough and Dynamite* or *His Trysting Places*, as well as the one-reel *The New Janitor* or *Gentlemen of Nerve*.

Charlie is married to Phyllis; Mack is with Mabel. Using the same actors he had enjoyed in previous outings, Chaplin again overrules the physical appearances of the various players. Mabel and Charlie are attractive; Mack and Phyllis are not.

*Getting Acquainted* opens with a close-up of Charlie and Phyllis on a park bench. Phyllis is blowing her nose, and Charlie acknowledges the sound by pantomiming a trombone slide. While she is often cast in battle-axe roles, Phyllis Allen would frequently be used by Chaplin as an offbeat mate for himself, or even an object of attraction. In *Getting Acquainted*, with her frumpy look, unsmiling expression, and sloppy nose blowing, Allen is particularly unattractive.

Ambrose, however, is shown as sweet, playful, and friendly. While Charlie and Phyllis sit idly on the bench with little interaction and no discernible affection, Ambrose and Mabel enter the park very happily responding to each other with smiling and cooing. Mabel seems enamored with Ambrose. Ambrose responds in kind but is easily distracted. When a motorist with a fancy car needs help cranking the starter in front, Ambrose is happy to oblige. Chaplin allows Mack Swain to riff, presenting his Ambrose character's dutiful nature as ineffective as he struggles to twist the starter. Chaplin shoots this from behind, with Swain's posterior facing the camera, wriggling and wrenching as the big man unsuccessfully attempts to turn the car's ignition crank.

While Ambrose is preoccupied, Charlie wanders off and discovers cute Mabel. He uses his cane to lift her dress, and when she responds with an appalled reaction, he scolds his cane and spanks it. This silliness does not endear him to Mabel. She shouts out to her distracted husband, who has accepted the motorist's offer for a ride, now that the car has started. Mabel then yells for the park cop. The cop chases Charlie around an evergreen bush while Mabel scratches her head in confusion. When Ambrose returns from his ride, he notices Phyllis, sitting alone, and goes over to her. He pokes at the large black birthmark on her chin and giggles merrily. She also cries for the police.

The situations are typical for Chaplin's Keystone comedies, which often examined the possibilities among different couples with roving eyes. The comedy here is how cohesively Charlie and Mabel seem to match on a purely physical level, while the homely Swain and Allen also seem rather right for each other. Chaplin does not prefer such stereotyping and appears to believe a more offbeat, surreal approach would be funnier.

The way Chaplin ties the characters together this time is to have Mabel and Phyllis eventually find each other in the park and commiserate as to how they are being treated by their men. When each woman introduces the other to her husband, the reaction from all is initially a series of Keystone-style double takes. When the cop prepares to remove Charlie and Ambrose from the park for disruptive behavior, the wives come to their rescue. The cop, angered by the hassle, sees another man innocently flirting with a young woman and soundly beats him with his billy club. Finally, the situations among the couples are worked out, all is forgiven, and the four of them wander off happily—until Charlie accidentally taps Phyllis on the backside. She angrily accuses Ambrose and then simply grabs Charlie by the seat of the pants and drags him away as Mabel and Ambrose stand giggling.

The physical contrasts between Swain and Chaplin, Swain and Normand, Allen and Chaplin, and Allen and Normand are all used to good advantage here.

Clockwise from left: Alice Davenport, Mack Swain, Charlie, and Mabel Normand.

The fact that Charlie is not the victor this time, and does not get the happy-faced fade-out as he had in *Gentlemen of Nerve* or *His Trysting Places*, makes *Getting Acquainted* seem like more of an experiment than the typical Keystone or the typical Chaplin structure.

*Getting Acquainted* was another fast-paced, breezy one-reel slapstick comedy for the Keystone studio, but by this time, Chaplin's stardom had reached the point where he was ready to negotiate his contract with Sennett or, better still, look for an opportunity where his creative freedom did not have to follow any semblance of an established structure or style. His Keystone contract concluding, Sennett initially offered Chaplin $450 per week. Chaplin recalled in his autobiography:

> About this time, Sennett began to talk of renewing my contract and wanted to know my terms. I knew to some degree the extent of my popularity, but I also knew the ephemera of it, and believed that, at the rate I was going, within a year I would be all dried up, so I had to make hay while the sun shone. "I want a thousand dollars a week," I

said, deliberately. Sennett was appalled. "But I don't make that," he said. "I know it," I answered, "but the public does not line up outside the box office when your name appears as they do mine."

Sennett tried to reason with Chaplin, pointing out Ford Sterling's lack of success after venturing from his Keystone success (Sterling would be back working at Keystone by the next year). Chaplin argued that all he needed to make a good comedy was a park, a policeman, and a pretty girl: "in fact I made some of my most successful pictures with just that assembly." Sennett offered $500 per week for the first year, $700 for the next, and $1,500 for the following. Chaplin agreed, only on the condition that the payments be reversed, with him getting $1,500 the first year, $700 the second, and then $500 per week. Sennett refused.

Chaplin received an offer from Carl Laemmle at Universal studios, who offered to pay him the unusual fee of twelve cents per foot of film, and finance the productions. But he also refused Chaplin's request for $1,000 per week. A rumor had begun that Chaplin wanted a $10,000 signing bonus upon joining another production company. Chaplin would later claim that he did not start the rumor and had no idea how it got around. But he was quite pleased when Jess Robbins, a representative of the Essanay company, was prepared to offer just that, along with $1,250 per week.

In the period when his future was uncertain, Chaplin found it a strain to concentrate on his last films at Keystone. Under those circumstances, it is fairly easy to see why he relied on something as easily produced as a typical Keystone park comedy with a small ensemble cast with whom he enjoyed working. Some of the characters seem unnecessary (Cecile Arnold and Glen Cavender as a flirt and her knife-wielding turk boyfriend), but the central two couples are turning in the usual committed, creative performances.

While Mabel Normand's life took some tragic turns and she never worked with Chaplin again, Swain and Allen were among the Keystone players who showed up in the comedian's later films. Allen would make appearances with Chaplin at Essanay, Mutual, and First National, last appearing with him in his 1922 featurette *The Pilgrim*. Swain would make a lasting impression as Big Jim in Chaplin's brilliant 1925 United Artists feature *The Gold Rush*.

*Getting Acquainted* is by no means a culmination of Chaplin's Keystone tenure. Funny though it is, *Getting Acquainted* is not the comedian's best work and does not present a compendium of all he had learned at Keystone. But because it is the last film he produced for the company, it is interesting in that it shows how Chaplin reimagined the standard Keystone park comedy through his own comic vision.

Characters are more effectively established with nuance, such as Phyllis's nose blowing and Ambrose's giggly demeanor. There is some level of complexity as to how Ambrose is so easily distracted by the fancy car that he forgets his cute girlfriend and wanders over to the auto and its owner. Charlie is a scamp in this picture, flirting with Cecile, flirting with Mabel, and doing so in the sort of aggressive manner he had exhibited in earlier Keystone subjects. But unlike the former films, *Getting Acquainted* is not a random series of aggressive behaviors that lead into a chase or a free-for-all. The chases are incorporated within the film's plot structure once the cop character has been introduced, and they last only briefly.

Naturally, the release of *Getting Acquainted* was met with the usual critical reaction. *The Cinema* stated in their review: "Yet another fine Charles Chaplin number, including the celebrated Mabel Normand."

While its park setting and flirtatious philanderings constitute a standard Keystone premise, *Getting Acquainted* features no brick throwing or spills in the lake. Chaplin's more refined vision set the film apart from the typical Keystone production with the same setting and a similar premise. While not a culmination, *Getting Acquainted* stands out as presenting some level of how much Chaplin learned as a comedian and filmmaker, eschewing the more blatant slapstick that was so much a part of the Keystone formula, and presenting a greater level of refinement, not only in his cinematic structure and his own performance, but in the performances of his supporting players. Chaplin's choosing to use the actors he does would likely suggest that their response to his direction was positive. After he left Keystone, there were actors who found his exacting style of direction too limiting, including Marlon Brando decades later. While not among his very best Keystone comedies, *Getting Acquainted* is among his most interesting, partly for its being his final production for the studio, and also for how it shows his development at the apex of his Keystone period.

Chaplin later stated that he left Keystone only a day or so after finishing the editing on his final production for the studio, but there seems to be no haste with the editing. While the film itself does not reach the level of the comedian's best work for Sennett, it is edited and structured in a manner that would indicate Chaplin intended that his final film for Keystone was going to receive the same attention and care as any of his previous productions.

There would be two more Keystone films to be released before Chaplin began producing exclusively for Essanay. One is a two-reel comedy set in prehistoric times in which Chaplin once again investigated a different setting, while the other is Mack Sennett's lofty feature production *Tillie's Punctured Romance*, which had been filmed while Chaplin was working on earlier comedies like *The Fatal Mallet* and *A Busy Day* but was not released until December 14, 1914.

# CHAPTER 38

# *His Prehistoric Past*

**Alternate titles: *A Dream; The Hula Hula Dance; King Charlie; I Am King; The Caveman; Caveman Charlie; Happy Dreams; Hoola Hoola Dance***

Running Time: Two Reels
Filmed October 14–27, 1914
Released December 7, 1914

**Credits**
Written and directed by Charlie Chaplin

**Cast**
Charlie Chaplin (Charlie), Mack Swain (King), Fritz Schade (Medicine Man), Peggy Page (Queen), Gene Marsh, Cecile Arnold, Vivian Edwards (King's Other Wives), Grover Ligon, Charles Lakin, Billy Gilbert (Cavemen), Sydney Chaplin (Cop in Park)

The last of Charlie Chaplin's Keystone short comedies to be released (his first film for Essanay studios would come out only two months later), *His Prehistoric Past* is unfortunately one of his less effective two-reelers. Chaplin appears to be enjoying exploring the Stone Age setting, but it comes off as little more than a disjointed version of a Keystone park comedy with a different setting and costumes.

Charlie decides to take an afternoon nap on a cramped park bench, and upon falling asleep, he dreams himself into the Stone Age. In his autobiography, Chaplin fondly recalled his first entrance as a caveman:

> I appeared dressed as a prehistoric man wearing a bearskin and, as I scanned the landscape, I began pulling the hair from the bearskin to fill my pipe. This was enough of an idea to stimulate a prehistoric story, introducing love, rivalry, combat, and chase. This was the method by which we all worked at Keystone.

While Chaplin pretty much admits *His Prehistoric Past* is little more than the Keystone formula, he seems to also be stating that this was the standard working method at the studio and the parameters within which he had to work. It is evident by such films as *The New Janitor*, *The Face on the Bar Room Floor*, and *His Trysting Places*, however, that Chaplin was given the freedom to creatively extend beyond those parameters.

There is some semblance of composition in the scene that introduces Mack Swain as the caveman king. Swain, a very big man, is surrounded by several attractive, slender women: his harem. The large man surrounded by small women carefully stationed around him is nicely composed and frames the sequence effectively by accenting the king's success with female underlings, and his enormous presence. Charlie raises the big man's ire when he throws a rock at a rival and it hits the king. Sending an underling to chase Charlie around a large boulder, the king eventually enters the action himself, but he appears to admire Charlie's gall and befriends him.

The most interesting thing about this rather uneven transitory sequence is the way Swain approaches his role as the king. Chaplin instructs him to play against type, something Swain did effortlessly, and thus the big man comes off as delicate and effete, with mincing and prancing mannerisms. Chaplin would present bigger men in this same manner later in his career, most notably Bud Jamison in his later Essanay comedy *By the Sea* (1915). Chaplin's exacting direction would often include acting out the part and expecting the supporting player to follow it closely, but Swain's committed enthusiasm is evident. When he needs to present his stature as commanding, he does so with equal aplomb.

As *His Prehistoric Past* continues, no real plot develops. It is merely a series of sequences, either funny or pointed. When Charlie enters the king's royal quarters, he is instructed to wipe his feet on the back of a slave. The women surrounding the king are merely pretty objects to play with. Here Chaplin looks at caste systems and makes fun of the different status levels in society.

When Charlie leaves the king's cave, he is surrounded by the women. Their fickleness is further presented when another man comes along and they divert their attentions to him. Charlie, however, appears to have most interest in the queen, much to the king's chagrin. A duel is necessary, and Charlie outsmarts the king into falling over a cliff. At that point, Charlie proclaims himself king and intends to partake in all benefits and luxuries. The true king has survived, however, and crawls up the mountain to reclaim his throne. Just as he is hitting Charlie on the head with a rock, the scene fades into one of Charlie on the park bench being clubbed by a policeman.

*His Prehistoric Past* not only is uneven and meandering but also features scenes that do not appear to fit comfortably into the rest of the film. For instance, a scene in the water with Charlie and the queen battling rough waves seems to be placed there with no substantial connection to the rest of the material. There are other scenes that do not effectively flow into each other with the cohesion we had now come to expect from Chaplin's direction.

There are some minor nuances that are amusing. When Charlie is shot in the backside with an arrow, he is so taken by the woman he is flirting with, he doesn't notice. When he becomes the new king, he shows his strength by pulling a tiny twig from a massive tree, flexing his muscles and using the stick to pick his teeth. There is also a neat gag where the king and Charlie go hunting. Charlie finds a hen up in a tree, shoots at the nest, and several eggs drop onto the king's head.

The idea of putting comedians in a Stone Age setting would be used several more times, most notably by Buster Keaton in *The Three Ages* (1923), Laurel and Hardy in *Flying Elephants* (1927), and the Three Stooges in *I'm a Monkey's Uncle* (1948). The Laurel and Hardy film was made before the duo had established their onscreen relationship, and the Keaton film is his first attempt at a feature. The Stooges comedy, made while Shemp Howard was part of the act, can be considered one of the better films from that period in the trio's career.

*Charlie as a caveman.*

*His Prehistoric Past* appears to be a fairly close parody of D. W. Griffith's 1912 one-reeler *Man's Genesis*, which explores prehistoric times in a more melodramatic fashion. The plot of *Man's Genesis* features a weaker man conquering a larger man to win the hand of a woman by inventing the club as a weapon. As primitive filmmaking about a more primitive era, *Man's Genesis* is interesting. It also is a harbinger for the Stone Age setting Griffith would use in his mammoth feature-length epic *Intolerance* (1915). The Buster Keaton feature *The Three Ages* draws from both *Man's Genesis* and *Intolerance* for its satire.

*His Prehistoric Past* is also, as was *Man's Genesis*, in response to paleontological discoveries that were in the news during this period. In 1912, when bone fragments were discovered in a gravel pit at Piltdown, East Sussex, England, they were presented as the fossilized remains of a previously unknown early human, called the Piltdown Man after the site of the discovery. (The Piltdown Man was revealed as a hoax in 1953 and is considered one of the most elaborate paleontological hoaxes of all time.) These sorts of discoveries aroused public interest, so popular culture responded via movies, comic strips, and other forms of entertainment. Despite its inspiration and its influence, *His Prehistoric Past* remains a pedestrian affair, our disappointment heightened in that it came along at a time when Chaplin had already proven how much he had learned about screen comedy and the cinematic process. Little in this two-reeler is noteworthy, and it is not as effective as some of the earlier Chaplin films directed by others, including *A Film Johnnie* and *Caught in a Cabaret*.

It is interesting that the cop who accosts Charlie upon awakening at the end of this film is his real-life half-brother, Sydney. Sydney Chaplin had been recommended by Chaplin to Mack Sennett and hired as a Keystone comedian in October 1914. Sydney would perform in several short comedies as the character Gussle, and he would especially shine in Sennett's 1915 feature *A Submarine Pirate*. Sennett hired Sydney Chaplin at a salary of $200 per week. Chaplin recalled in his autobiography:

> After Sydney joined the Keystone company he made several successful films. As he was so successful, I approached him about joining me and starting our own company. "All we need is a camera and a back lot," I said. But Sydney was conservative. He thought it was taking too much of a chance. "Besides," he added, "I don't feel like giving up a salary which is more than I have ever earned in my life." So he continued with Keystone for another year.

By the end of 1915, Sydney would leave Keystone and concentrate on being his half-brother's business manager.

Like *Getting Acquainted*, the final film Chaplin shot at Keystone, *His Prehistoric Past*, the final Chaplin Keystone release, is not a culmination of what he had learned at the studio. However, it is quite clear that Chaplin benefited tremendously from his apprenticeship with Mack Sennett's Keystone Studios. Chaplin learned the studio's established method of making slapstick comedies, then investigated possibilities to extend this practice and ultimately challenge its structure. The better films Chaplin supervised remain among the finest productions in the studio's history. Period critics were, however, completely satisfied with *His Prehistoric Past*. The *San Francisco Call and Post* stated: "Charlie Chaplin and other members of Keystone company have outdone all of their previous fun-provoking efforts."

In his autobiography, Chaplin mentions *His Prehistoric Past* as a film on which he had been distracted by offers from other studios. *His Prehistoric Past* was filmed weeks earlier than *Getting Acquainted*, although released two days later. Chaplin recalled that finishing *His Prehistoric Past* was "a strain, because it was hard to concentrate with so many business propositions dangling before me. Nevertheless, the picture was eventually completed." This would be a feasible excuse for the disjoined nature of the two-reeler and would also mean *Getting Acquainted* was produced in similar haste.

Chaplin did attend a motion picture industry ball in November 1914, shortly after having completed *Getting Acquainted*, and this is when the offers appear to have been coming from other studios. Initially, it appears Chaplin would have remained with Keystone had Sennett agreed to the $1,000 per week salary. When Jess Robbins at Essanay made the $1,250 per week offer, along with the $10,000 signing bonus and full creative control of each production, Chaplin and business manager Sydney agreed to the terms.

The *Washington Press* on December 19, 1914, stated: "Members of the Essanay Film Company at Niles are jubilant over the addition to their staff of Charles Chaplin, comedian. Chaplin was with the Keystone company, and is by far one of the most popular comedy artists in the motion picture industry." Chaplin recalled in his autobiography: "It was a wrench leaving Keystone, for I had grown fond of Sennett and everyone there. I never said goodbye to anyone; I couldn't. I finished cutting my film on Saturday night and left the following Monday."

The absolute final Keystone release to feature Charlie Chaplin in the cast would be *Tillie's Punctured Romance*, which came out on December 21, 1914, after Chaplin had left the studio. This ambitious first feature film was intended to be a spotlight for stage actress Marie Dressler, who has the title role and received star billing. But while Dressler would eventually become one of the most beloved stars on the Metro Goldwyn Mayer lot by 1930, in 1914 she was a stage actress with blatant gestures in a Keystone feature. When the film was released, it was Charlie Chaplin who was singled out as the most effective performer in the feature, only increasing his stardom. Essanay, about to go into production on their first Chaplin film, was the studio that most benefited from Mack Sennett's lofty feature-length project.

# CHAPTER 39

# *Tillie's Punctured Romance*

---

Running Time: Six Reels
Filmed April 14–June 9, 1914
Released December 21, 1914 (initially offered on a state rights basis in November 1914)

**Credits**
Produced and directed by Mack Sennett (and an uncredited Charles Bennett)
Written by Hampton Del Ruth and Craig Hutchinson
Based on the play *Tillie's Nightmare* by Edgar Smith

**Cast**
Marie Dressler (Tillie), Charlie Chaplin (City Slicker), Mabel Normand (City Slicker's Girl), Mack Swain (Tillie's Father), Charlie Bennett (Mortgage Holder, Restaurant Manager), Douglas Banks (Tillie's Uncle), Chester Conklin (Waiter, Party Guest, Diner), Edgar Kennedy (Butler, Restaurant Manager), Glen Cavender (Policeman, Pianist, Diner), Charles Parrott (Detective in Movie Theater), Harry McCoy (Singer, Pianist, Jailbird, Servant, Diner), Phyllis Allen (Party Guest), Gordon Griffith (Newsboy), Billie Bennett (Maid, Party Guest), Frank Thompson (Reverend), Fritz Schade (Waiter, Cop, Jailbird, Diner, Cook), Morgan Wallace (Thief in Film at Theater), Minta Durfee (Thief's Accomplice in Film at Theater), Hampton Del Ruth, Hugh Saxon (Secretary), Fred Fishback (Servant), Ted Edwards (Waiter, Cop), Slim Summerville (Diner, Cop), Hank Mann, Al St. John, Dan Albert, Grover Ligon, Billy Gilbert, Robert Kerr (Cops), Alice Howell (Diner), Eva Nelson, Dixie Chene, Wallace MacDonald, Alice Davenport (Guests), Meiklejohn and Hazel Allen (Dancers), Peggy Page (Maid, Waitress) Dick Smith, Rube Miller (Bits). (The newsboy role was not played by Milton Berle as the comedian claimed and has been widely reported.)

---

Sennett's decision to produce a six-reel comedy in 1914 was ambitious and impressive, but at the time, it was a bit of a gamble. Feature-length films were comparatively rare. This is before D. W. Griffith redefined feature films with the epics *Birth of a Nation* (1915) and *Intolerance* (1916). For the most part, any longer film produced this early in cinema's evolution was usually a drama with a statement, such as George Loane Tucker's story of white slavery, *Traffic in Souls* (1913), or was of a historical nature, like Thomas Ince's *The Battle of Gettysburg* (1913). Sennett's choice to extend his knockabout comedies to feature length was daunting in theory. Could such humor sustain an entire hour of footage? Some Keystone films seem protracted at 20 minutes.

Sennett realized that film actors did not enjoy the notoriety and stardom of those from the theater, and comedians were especially dismissed by the upper classes, who also looked down on overtly physical comedy. The working class was fine with slapstick short comedies, but would they sit through an entire feature film of this nature? Sennett knew that if he was going to introduce his bombastic comedy style to feature-length production, he would need a star from the theater that was a noted name, as well as willing and able to engage in Keystone's method of comedy. Marie Dressler, then the popular star of the stage success *Tillie's Nightmare* on which this film is based, was the star Sennett needed, and she was quite willing to perform a bombastic slapstick version of her most noted theatrical role. The principal cast was filled out by Charlie Chaplin and Mabel Normand, while virtually every comedian on the Keystone lot appeared in smaller roles. One exception was Roscoe Arbuckle, who was nixed by Dressler because she wanted to be the only fat comedian in the cast. This does not explain the appearance of Mack Swain as her father, however.

Sennett paid Dressler the then-enormous amount of $35,000. Since the entire budget of the film was only $50,000, it can be imagined how much more she was paid than the other players. Despite her lofty status and high salary, Dressler is quite game throughout this raucous slapstick comedy, shrugging off any legitimate theater superiority and engaging in the kicks and pratfalls that would be expected of a Keystone comedian.

Originally slated for a two-week shoot, the film took nearly two months to complete, mostly due to the cast of nearly every Keystone player still being active in short films being produced at the same time. Chaplin himself completed *A Busy Day*, *The Fatal Mallet*, *Her Friend the Bandit*, *The Knockout*, *Mabel's Busy Day*, and *Mabel's Married Life* while acting as the male lead in *Tillie's Punctured Romance*. According to Chaplin's autobiography, "It was pleasant working with Marie, but I didn't think the film had much merit. I was eager to get back to directing myself." Chaplin's very next film after completing *Tillie's Punctured Romance* would be *Laughing Gas*, and from that point on he would be exclusively directing his own films while his popularity continued to skyrocket.

Sennett's approach to directing *Tillie's Punctured Romance* wavers between his carefully keeping the action in the frame and making discernible choices as to the composition of the shot. There are several different settings in this feature. It is not simply limited to a park, nor was it filmed at an actual event. A stronger plot, more character development, and greater substance were necessary to sustain a full-length feature over the one- and two-reel films that remained Sennett's bread and butter, so as director, he proceeded accordingly.

The story is as old as melodrama. Tillie is a farm girl. Charlie is a city slicker who dupes her into coming to the big city. Once there, he and Mabel, his girl-friend, abscond with her money. Penniless and alone in the big city, Tillie takes a job as a waitress. When Charlie reads in the paper that she is heiress to her uncle's millions, he hurriedly returns to her, whisks her off to the justice of the peace, and prepares to share in her wealth. When Tillie catches him with Mabel at their wedding party, Charlie must retreat, with Tillie chasing him and firing a pistol. After a wild slapstick finale featuring the Keystone Cops, Tillie and Mabel decide that Charlie is not good enough for either of them. They tearfully embrace as the film ends.

The general plot for *Tillie's Punctured Romance*, essentially a melodramatic narrative structure, is augmented by Sennett for comedy. The elements are ste-reotypes, but rather than overplay them for dramatic emotion, Sennett has his actors overplay them in the grand Keystone tradition of broad comedy. In Marie Dressler's first moments as Tillie, she is kicked in the behind by her father, who is played by big, burly Keystone regular Mack Swain. Chaplin liked using the enormous Swain as a physical contrast to his own diminutive frame. Dressler, however, is a big woman, and is not dwarfed by Swain. In fact, there is little con-trast between the father and daughter rube farmers. And naturally, in a Keystone picture, a father would discipline his errant daughter in such a silly manner.

Charlie first appears shortly after a brief opening scene that introduces the title character. This time he is not a tramp but a wily city slicker. Chaplin ex-pertly projects his character's manner—standing about, tweaking his mustache, looking askance at his surroundings, wickedly imagining how he can achieve some sort of monetary benefit from the rural types who inhabit this rustic area. He meets Tillie due to a bombastic Keystone gag. The farm girl is playing fetch with her dog, using a brick instead of a stick or a ball. She throws the brick and it smacks Charlie in the face, knocking him down on the dirt road.

Brick throwing is something of a constant in Keystone comedies, including Chaplin's films. The earlier, more raucous Keystones, before Chaplin began ex-perimenting with different ideas, can pretty much be counted on for a few bricks being thrown. That Charlie and Tillie's meeting hinges on the former being hit by a thrown brick seems like the perfect harbinger for the first feature-length comedy film.

Chaplin's city slicker has little in common with his noted tramp character. He is nattily dressed, sporting a straw hat and a trimmed mustache, but he does have a cane. He carries himself in a much more haughty fashion. Flirting with the homely Tillie, cajoling her naive bumpkin father, Charlie's city slicker is a con man in the same way as his character in his first Keystone, *Making a Living*. Only this time, the established Chaplin is able to exhibit the creative ideas that were ignored by the earlier film's director, Henry Lehrman. For his part, Mack Swain as the father exhibits paternal concern, friendly acceptance, and seething suspicion during the entire time Charlie is speaking to him. Tillie's rustic manner manifests itself with more brick throwing, this time in a coy, playful fashion. It is not long before she is talked into leaving her rural surroundings for city life with her new beau.

With the opening scenes, it is quite evident that this is Sennett's film and not Chaplin's. There is no subtlety to the action, except when exhibited by the actors. For example, Swain and Chaplin's facial expressions convey thoughts or feelings that could be considered comparatively subtle. Sennett appears to be pacing himself. He seems to know that exploding with gags in a six-reel feature

*Chaplin and Marie Dressler made a good team in the landmark feature* Tillie's Punctured Romance.

would not be sustainable as it would in a one-reeler. But the comedy that happens along the way is the sort of Keystone bombast that is to be expected of the boss's direction.

While Dressler chews the scenery with gusto from the very outset, Chaplin's city slicker seems comparatively more poised and with greater depth, despite also playing on stereotypes. We might wonder why the city slicker would be interested at all in Tillie's money, why he would assume she had any. This, in fact, establishes Chaplin's character as the ultimate smalltimer. He goes after one who is easy prey rather than one who may have a greater amount of money.

Once Charlie gets Tillie to the big city and hooks up with Mabel, there is another factor in the ensemble. Mabel Normand is a formidable comic and a veteran of the movies whose capable performance is further enhanced by her cuteness. The viewer almost wants the more attractive city cons to successfully dupe the bombastic farm girl, clad in a gaudy dress and a ridiculous hat with a large bird replica on top. Dressler is the same sort of homely comic character that Phyllis Allen had been in so many Keystone productions. Only Allen was a formidable supporting player, while Marie Dressler is the central figure and essays the title role. Mabel, at first not understanding what Charlie is doing with this woman, plays spurned, vengeful, tough, and demure all at once, and most effectively. Dressler merely hams it up in comic fashion. It is funny, but not with the impressive depth provided by the likes of Chaplin or Normand.

Before the narrative progresses any further, Sennett takes what has already been established and tries to get laughs from the fish-out-of-water premise of Tillie in the big city. He stages a restaurant scene with Charlie and Tillie in the foreground as the activity of dancing, movement of the wait staff, and customers eating all swirl about them. Sennett goes for obvious yet funny gags, such as Tillie reacting to taking her first drink by spitting out its contents in Charlie's face. As Tillie easily becomes inebriated, she dances about the restaurant, her large body becoming intrusive as it knocks into other dancers, waiters, and customers. The activity that had surrounded Tillie and Charlie must now accommodate her as she enters it in a most overbearing manner.

Meanwhile Charlie and Mabel are seated nearby, laughing derisively at the naive farm girl they are about to dupe. Charlie has been instructed to hold Tillie's purse. He and Mabel leave with the money. Tillie is a complete stereotype—a homely, overweight farm girl who is happy to receive the affections of any man, especially one so superficially charismatic and slick. But upon being duped, she appears to be more victimized by an empty purse than a broken heart.

Sennett appears to think that the spectacle of big Tillie dancing about is a particularly amusing image, as he has her continue to do so even after being arrested by police for drunkenness and taken to the station. She remains playful, biting at pointing fingers and bumping the officers around by dancing in their personal space. Her naiveté is such that she appears to have no idea she is being arrested. Even after she is bailed out by a rich uncle (a convenient plot device that ends up being the axis to the film's conclusion), Tillie remains playfully sloshed. Arriving at the uncle's mansion, she tickles his stoic servants, who are clad in uniforms and powdered wigs. Sennett lingers on the antics of drunken Tillie beyond their capacity to be amusing, but this does play further into her inability to adapt to areas that are far removed from her rural background.

Sennett next chooses to investigate the more melodramatic elements of his narrative. Tillie, homeless and penniless, must find a job. She waitresses in a seedy diner where the proprietor treats her in the same rough manner as her father had. Charlie and Mabel attend a movie about two people duping another, and they have an attack of conscience. While the three-shot of the two of them and actor Charles Parrott as a suspicious detective yields some great reaction shots to the movie they are watching, this is perhaps the flattest scene in the feature. It seems incongruous that Mabel and Charlie would feel any remorse for what they have done, as it seemed to be the sort of thing they engaged in fairly regularly. The three-shot is rewarding, though, especially since negative space

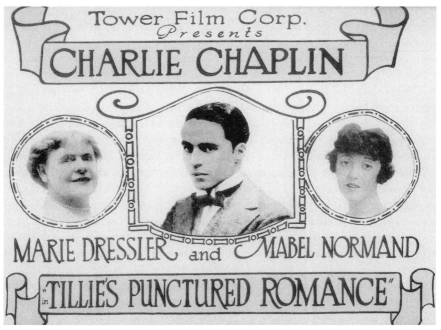

*One of the many rereleases featured Chaplin with star billing instead of Marie Dressler.*

is filled with other patrons, composing the shot with the sort of effectiveness that Sennett usually overlooked in an effort to finish a picture as quickly and inexpensively as possible.

The slapstick spirit returns when Charlie and Mabel happen to be customers at the restaurant in which Tillie is employed. Tillie sees them and faints, dropping a tray of food on Charlie, who flees with Mabel before Tillie is revived. While seated on a park bench, Charlie buys a paper (slapping away the paperboy) and reads that Tillie's rich uncle has been killed in a hiking accident and she is to inherit his fortune. He sneaks away from Mabel without her realizing it, returns to the diner, and tearfully proclaims his love for Tillie just before officials enter the establishment to inform her of the inheritance. Since Charlie arrived before these officials, Tillie does not realize he knew about the money ahead of time, and she believes his sob story. Perhaps not in love, but still desperate for some level of companionship, Tillie hurries off with Charlie to the justice of the peace.

In examining the Keystone Chaplins in release order, we have already discussed in the text how the comedian modified his screen character over several films, especially once he began directing himself. The shooting of *Tillie's Punctured Romance* occurred over a period when Chaplin made several of his short films, so his character development was happening during the time he acted in this feature. At this point in the film, we can see how aspects of Chaplin's earlier character are utilized in this context. The sly rascal that moviegoers enjoyed was incorporated into the wily city slicker, with behaviors that were again oddly forgivable. He cons a naive farm girl, takes advantage of her, and leaves her penniless, then rushes back to her once she has acquired a fortune. Her naiveté causes her to trust him once again. Thus, Charlie is the villain of this story, the one the viewers should hiss. Still, in the same manner as the abject brutality in *The Property Man*, Charlie comes off as amusingly sneaky rather than reprehensibly crooked. Tillie's boorishness is often funny, but we frequently laugh in a derisive manner. This may or may not have been Sennett's approach and ultimate vision (and judging by the ending of the feature, it was not), but Chaplin's creative performance and Mabel Normand's equally strong support carry the fringe of the narrative more effectively than Dressler's anchoring its center.

Sennett next dwells on rustic Tillie's attempt to fit into the world of the very wealthy. The decor of the mansion is vast, and Sennett does a nice job of keeping Tillie's imposing presence somewhere near the center of the frame in order to present the largeness of her surroundings. Sennett is especially impressive during the wedding party sequences on the mansion set, as he surrounds the action of the central characters in the foreground with constant background movement. But the balance is what is most interesting. The background movement is noticeable but reserved. It does not distract from what is taking place in the foreground, where we must focus. The background simply frames the immediate action by the central characters.

Normand is at her best during the wedding party sequences. Following Charlie in an attempt to confront him, she gets a job as a servant and must maintain that status without being spotted by Tillie. This is, on the surface, not difficult in that the large building and amount of people would help with avoiding the bride. But what makes Normand's performance so delightful is her city sharpster character attempting to fit in as a servant, having no idea how to conduct herself. She maneuvers about the large mansion in a search for Charlie, but at the same time she has to maintain her servant status, so she curtsies at anyone who looks her way.

The narrative is on hold during the wedding party sequences, but Sennett does not turn them into a constant gag fest. There are little bits of business that run through and maintain the film's comic rhythm and pace. Charlie develops a meaningless rivalry with another guest (Chester Conklin) whom he dislikes and finds to be in the way. Mabel continues to scurry about in her disguise, attempting to reach Charlie. Tillie displays her characteristic boorishness among higher-level members of society. There is a dance sequence done by professionals, after which Charlie and Tillie attempt to do the same. This is possibly Sennett's attempt to protract his film to feature length, but it works. The initial dance is uninteresting but works as a setup for Charlie and Tillie, presenting physical contrast with each other, stumbling about the dance floor in a most amusing fashion. Tillie bumps Charlie and he flies into another room. Charlie sneaks away and the drunken Tillie keeps dancing, oblivious to being alone (a throwback to her drunkenness established earlier in the picture).

Sennett appears to truly be in his element with the slapstick conclusion. Mabel finds Charlie, he is discovered with her by Tillie, and the uncle, who has been found alive, returns home to find a wedding reception taking place. He contacts the police and angrily throws everyone out, while the rejected Tillie finally reaches her boiling point. Finding a handgun, she angrily fires random shots in the air as the others flee. Charlie and Mabel are chased to a pier by Tillie upon the arrival of the Keystone Cops. The wild slapstick free-for-all includes tumbles off the pier, speedboats zipping through the ocean and capsizing, and a car full of cops screeching about the pier after Charlie and Mabel. This all adds up to a definite comfort zone for the director. Charlie the con is taken away. Mabel and Tillie embrace in alliance against the man who duped them both.

The film ends with a curtain closing and then Dressler, Chaplin, and Normand each taking bows. Perhaps it is because this is a major production and not a short comedy. Maybe it is in relation to Dressler's stage stardom. Whatever the reason, it is an interesting way to conclude.

As has been discussed throughout this study, Sennett's direction concentrated on gags and gag situations, resting on the most exaggerated slapstick sequences and comic violence. His approach to *Tillie's Punctured Romance*, a six-reel feature, is more studied and far more structured. There is certainly plenty of characteristic slapstick, and the ending is indeed pure Sennett, but the director seems to take great care in pacing his film so that it builds to the obligatory chase that was Sennett's concluding specialty.

While he had yet to fully develop to the level of character that could be found in *His Trysting Place* or *Dough and Dynamite*, Chaplin appears to be allowed some nuance with his character. Working within the parameters of his city slicker role, Chaplin maintains this character effectively within the narrative. Going beyond Sennett's basic direction, Chaplin peers at Tillie and Mabel in much the same manner, telling us that he has no real affection for either. He responds occasionally with a glance to the audience as if he realizes we are watching and know what he is up to. He carries himself with confidence, and he devilishly reacts with delight when about to come into more money. Mabel Normand balances her character's cuteness and trustworthiness with a sense of conniving that is clearly manipulated by Charlie's dominance. Marie Dressler loses all inhibition and dives into the Keystone slapstick bombast, which works with her rustic character.

Despite working from stereotypical melodrama, *Tillie's Punctured Romance* maintains the sense of fun that permeates all of the Keystone comedies. Chaplin expert Phil Posner summed up the Keystone films by referring to them as "actors with steady work being paid to do crazy shit day after day, largely improvising comic business. It must have been a riot for them." Chaplin might have had fun but was far too serious about the creative process to simply relegate himself to a good time playing silly for the camera. However, he appears to be having fun as the city slicker, perhaps his most offbeat role since *Cruel, Cruel Love* earlier in his Keystone tenure.

Most of the drama regarding *Tillie's Punctured Romance* occurred after the film was completed and was being prepared for distribution. According to Brent Walker, in his book *Mack Sennett's Fun Factory*:

> The feature was initially offered in trades in November on a states rights basis—a process in which a producer leased the rights of his film to several independent film exchanges covering different regional territories, rather than retaining a single national distributor who handled the film throughout the country. Sennett and his partners Kessel and Bauman then worked out an agreement with Al Lichtman, called the Alco Film Company to distribute *Tillie's Punctured Romance*. Alco was to pay Kessel and Baumann $100,000 for the negative, while being responsible for the cost of striking their own

release prints, and it was given an official Alco release date of December 21, 1914, which was the date it opened at the Republic Theater in Los Angeles, with Sennett, Normand, and Chaplin in attendance. The Alco Film Corporation would dissolve into bankruptcy a few months later, while a legal battle would take place over the rights. Marie Dressler and (husband) James Dalton would file suit against Sennett and Kessel and Baumann because they felt their initial agreement (part of Dressler's initial agreement was to allow her husband to be involved in the film's distribution) had been reneged upon; a litigation that lasted well into 1915 until a court-ordered opening of the books by Sennett satisfied the Daltons with regard to their percentage of the profits. Despite all this, *Tillie* did well at the box office, although exact figures are not known. This endeavor forever whetted Sennett's appetite to leave short films behind altogether and become a feature-length producer.

The review in *Variety* stated: "Mack Sennett directs the picture right well. Dressler wears clothes that make her appear ridiculous. Furthermore she makes gestures and distorts her face in all directions, which help all the more. The picture runs a trifle too long, but the hilarious, hip-hurrah comedy finale is worth waiting for." *Motion Picture Herald* stated: "Marie Dressler breaks into the story at the first jump. She fits into the Keystone style of work as to the manner born. Charlie Chaplin plays opposite Marie Dressler. The two constitute a rare team of funmakers. Chaplin outdoes Chaplin; that is all there is to it. Mack Sennett has done well."

*Tillie's Punctured Romance* remained in circulation for many years under different titles and frequently reedited. One particularly notorious 38-minute version was released by the low-budget Monogram Pictures in 1941 and rereleased by a distribution outfit called Burwood Pictures in 1950. This edit, with music and obtrusive narration, is often found on Chaplin DVD collections that haphazardly gather public domain versions of his early films and offer no support for the brilliance of his legacy.

One of the more interesting footnotes regarding Sennett's landmark feature involved an in-name-only remake. In 1928, producer Al Christie, who presided over some interesting comedies during the silent era, reworked *Tillie's Punctured Romance* as a circus comedy, keeping the original title. Tillie was played by Louise Fazenda, and W. C. Fields co-starred as a ringmaster. Sadly, this intriguing remake is one of the numerous films produced during the silent era that are now lost. History tells us that the 1928 *Tillie's Punctured Romance* was a box office flop that received scathing reviews. It is unfortunate that the later effort is now unavailable for assessment. Mack Swain plays Tillie's father in this remake as well. Chester Conklin is another Keystone actor who appears in a smaller role, and not the same one he had essayed in the Sennett feature.

Despite Sennett's misgivings as to the bankability of his own stock company, *Tillie's Punctured Romance* actually benefited co-star Charlie Chaplin more so than it did Marie Dressler, despite her status as a popular stage actress. When it was released near the Christmas season of 1914, critical notices and audience reaction cited Chaplin as the movie's nominal star, while Marie Dressler would have to wait nearly 15 years before she finally enjoyed recognition as a beloved, award-winning movie performer.

Of course while Chaplin was popular during the filming of *Tillie's Punctured Romance* due to the successful short films he had been making and continued to make during this feature's production, he had reached his height by the time the film was released. Had Sennett begun filming as late as the movie's eventual December 1914 release date, perhaps he would not have felt Marie Dressler was necessary for box office clout. Chaplin could have maintained box office for a feature production based on his own popularity. Dressler's willingness and cooperation made her quite popular with the director and her supporting cast, including Chaplin.

Attempting to play off this film's success, Dressler made two more Tillie movies for other producers. *Tillie's Tomato Surprise* (Howell Hansel, 1915) is only survived by one existing reel of its six-reel length and cannot be assessed, but period reviews dismissed it as a failure, and it did not enjoy any box office success. *Tillie Wakes Up* (Harry Davenport, 1917) seems promising in that it was written by Francis Marion, who would pen many of Dressler's most popular films of the 1930s. This film, however, is a rather dull, pedestrian affair that tries to trade on the slapstick and boorish facial expressions of Tillie (who leaves her dull husband to have fun at Coney Island with a neighbor, played by Johnny Hines). It is interesting especially for those who are familiar with and appreciate the Sennett film, and Dressler works hard. But success in silent pictures was not to be had, and Marie Dressler returned to the stage. It was talking pictures that made her a star. By the time she succumbed to breast cancer in 1934, Marie Dressler was one of the biggest stars in movies. (For more on Marie Dressler, see the bio in appendix A.)

At the time *Tillie's Punctured Romance* was released, Chaplin was prepared to begin employment at the Essanay film company in Chicago, in order to enjoy greater creative control and more time to work out his comic ideas than the budget-minded Sennett would allow. His success in this popular feature helped solidify his reputation shortly after signing with the company. Having just signed the most popular star in movies, Essanay owners G. M. Anderson and George Spoor were quite pleased that their new star acquisition was enjoying accolades in a major feature-length production. They wanted Chaplin to immediately begin production on his first Essanay comedy, appropriately titled *His New Job*.

# CHAPTER 40

# Chaplin after Keystone

In the course of a year, Chaplin had completed 36 films at Keystone, including one- and two-reel subjects as well as the feature-length *Tillie's Punctured Romance*. Chaplin refined the slapstick methods of this studio while honing his character and investigating other possibilities for comedy on film. By the end of 1914, Chaplin's popularity was magnificent.

The popularity of Chaplin's films was certainly noticed by other movie producers, who made offers to lure him away from Keystone. A story in the December 23, 1914, issue of the *New York Daily Mirror* discussed Chaplin's stardom as well as his rumored position for a new studio:

> Charlie Chaplin, the comedian who has created such a following since his advent into pictures a comparatively short time since, announces that he will leave the Keystone studio. Rumor sends him to various studios, the Essanay being the latest whisper.

Only three days later, *Moving Picture World* had this to say:

> The announcement was made in New York on Monday evening December 14 by George K. Spoor, president of Essanay Film Manufacturing that Charles Chaplin, famous screen comedian, had signed with his company. The information was contained in a telegram from G.M. Anderson from Niles Calif. Mr. Chaplin in a remarkably short time has created for himself a unique position in the film world. He is a man who seldom gives one an opportunity to laugh with him; at the same time he gives occasion aplenty to laugh at him. The name of the director under whom he will work has not been announced, but it is assumed that he will be under the general direction of Mr. Anderson at the Niles studio situated near San Francisco.

For Sennett's part, he took the loss of Chaplin in stride. He survived losing both Fred Mace and Ford Sterling, and he would eventually handle the loss of Roscoe Arbuckle and Al St. John when Arbuckle accepted a lucrative offer from Joseph Schenck and took nephew St. John with him. Sennett would later acquire such comedians as Ben Turpin and Harry Langdon in their wake. Even Charley Chase and Harold Lloyd had some Keystone experience before embarking on more successful careers elsewhere. Buster Keaton is the only giant of silent screen comedy never to have worked at the Mack Sennett studios. Keaton began his career with Roscoe Arbuckle, after Arbuckle left Sennett for Schenck, but did not work with Sennett until Mack directed Buster's 1935 talkie *The Timid Young Man*.

The Essanay company began in 1907, the name formed from the first initials of its founders' last names—George Spoor and Gilbert Anderson. An actor whose career dates back to the beginning of movies, Anderson appeared in director Edwin S. Porter's milestone *The Great Train Robbery* (1903), the first to establish western action drama, using crosscut editing to increase suspense. By 1906, Anderson was directing his first westerns for the Selig Polyscope Company.

Anderson met George K. Spoor in early 1907. Spoor was already managing an opera house in Waukegan, Illinois, by the time he was 22. Fascinated when he saw his first moving picture in the late 1890s, Spoor partnered with inventor Edward Amet, who made movie projectors, while Spoor found vaudeville houses at which the movies could be presented. Spoor was impressed with Anderson's successful film career, and the two formed a partnership. Most of Essanay's first successes were films starring Anderson as the cinema's first cowboy hero, Broncho Billy.

Chaplin's contract with Keystone was about a month away from concluding when he attended a motion picture industry ball in November 1914. Essanay representative Jess Robbins, along with Anderson, met with Chaplin and his brother Sydney, now acting as business manager, and a deal was reached for a salary of $1,250 per week and a signing bonus of $10,000.

An article in the *Washington Press* on December 19, 1914, celebrated Chaplin's signing with Essanay: "Members of the Essanay Film Company at Niles are jubilant over the addition to their staff of Charles Chaplin, comedian. Chaplin was with the Keystone company for some time, and is by far one of the most popular comedy artists in the motion picture industry." In the January 16, 1915, issue of *Motography*, writer Clarence J. Cane covered Chaplin's arrival at Essanay as a major news story:

> He arrived in Chicago the latter part of last week, in company with
> Broncho Billy Anderson, and will remain at the Essanay studios in

that city indefinitely, producing his inimitable farce comedies which have proved such a drawing card for exhibitors in all parts of the world. He seldom moved as fast while on the screen as he did during the first few days of his stay in the Windy City. Charlie was wanted here and Charlie was wanted there, from the time he arrived in the morning until he left at night. Therefore it was a rather difficult task to catch him, but I finally managed to corner him in the advertising department of the big studio on Argyle street for an interview.

An indication as to how Chaplin was planning on refining his comedy in his films for the new studio was also evident in his interview for the Cane story:

> "I have a distinct theory regarding farces, and one which, to my mind, meets with public favor. I believe that a plot which could easily become a dramatic subject, but which is treated in an amusing manner and which burlesques events of daily life, with which the average person is familiar, depending principally upon its humorous action for laughs, is the one to make a successful farce comedy. Many persons see a subject on the screen and say that such-and-such a thing should be done this way or that. They do not realize that we do things on the spur of the moment and that our minds are under a constant strain, for we must concentrate on our work from morning till night."

Chaplin added: "Just say that I am doing my best to please them and that I hope my releases under the Essanay banner will be as agreeable to them as my past work. And say! Tell them I'm just a fellow, a human being like they are and that I enjoy almost everything that is enjoyable."

Chaplin's first few Essanay efforts appeared to be refined versions of films he had done for Sennett. *His New Job* (1915) used movie set ideas established in the Keystone film *The Masquerader* (1914). *A Night Out* (1915) was similar to *The Rounders* (1914). Chaplin even revisited the park setting for *In the Park* (1915).

While the Keystone comedies did not advertise actors by name, once Chaplin went to Essanay, and his name started appearing in movie advertisements and subsequently became known, Keystone films he had made would do likewise. Ads for films like *Laughing Gas* and *Mabel's Married Life* show Chaplin's name as the featured star when these appeared in theaters just after Chaplin's first Essanay release.

Perhaps *A Jitney Elopement* (1915) truly shows Chaplin's idea for a more refined approach to his comedy. His manner is much more subtle, the comedy much gentler. There is a nicely choreographed car chase to conclude the piece that appears to be Chaplin showing up Keystone on one of its tried and true ideas for a handy conclusion.

The Essanay film that is considered a real milestone is *The Tramp* (1915), which incorporates the pathos that would soon become an integral part of Chaplin's work. From this point, Chaplin would explore different levels of dramatic depth on many of his films, and his central Charlie character became a warmer, deeper character. One of his final Essanay productions was *Burlesque on Carmen* (1916), which cleverly satirizes the classic story in a smart production filled with interesting ideas.

As had happened at Keystone, Chaplin once again showed amazing growth as a comedian and filmmaker in the span of only a year at Essanay. As his artistry grew, so did his exacting method of direction. It had already been established at Keystone that he would act out parts for his supporting cast and expect them to mimic his gestures. The greater freedom he was allowed at Essanay caused him to retake scenes until his perfectionism was sated. This ran into money, worrying the studio heads, but Chaplin's films always made money.

Chaplin left Essanay and joined the Mutual Corporation in 1916 for even more money and a level of creative freedom that is still mind boggling. He would film entire scenes and then choose not to use them. He would have enormous sets built rather than use location filming. His retakes became even more constant and his direction more demanding. The result? The 12 short films produced for this company are perhaps the greatest films of his career. Of course his later feature-length productions would endure as classics, but the best of these were only as good as his Mutuals. Chaplin was later to call the Mutual period the happiest days of his life.

*The Floorwalker*, Chaplin's first Mutual picture, had Charlie working in a large department store. Throughout the film, we see the slapstick learned at Keystone and the character refinement developed at Essanay. With unlimited time to indulge in several takes and changed ideas, Chaplin's gags were more creative in *The Floorwalker*. Chaplin extends the Keystone chase scene by incorporating an escalator. Running up as the stairs go down, Chaplin gets a great deal of mileage out of his big, electronic prop, which prompted Sennett to wonder, "Why didn't I think of that?"

Mutual is where Chaplin wavered between straight-up comedies like *Behind the Screen* (1916), *The Fireman* (1916), and *The Adventurer* (1917) and a film with a more dramatic structure like *The Vagabond* (1916). Experimenting with different ideas, Chaplin engaged in a veritable one-man show with *One A.M.* (1916). Charlie is an inebriated society man coming home to his mansion and confronting the household's inanimate objects from a stairway to a bed to a bearskin rug. Chaplin's comic creativity is at its most clever and interesting.

Perhaps Chaplin's masterpiece at Mutual was *Easy Street* (1916), in which Charlie plays an officer who cleans up the roughest neighborhood in town. How far he had come as both a comedian and filmmaker since his Keystone period is most evident in this brilliantly funny comedy that confronts the basics of good and evil with the innocent, diminutive Charlie subduing an enormous bully with his wits and, thereafter, gaining the quivering respect of the other toughs on the street.

Once Chaplin had completed the brilliant Mutual shorts, he ventured to First National Pictures in 1918. This is where Chaplin investigated longer-form cinema such as the four-reeler *The Pilgrim* (1922) and the six-reel feature *The Kid* (1920), the first feature in which Chaplin had appeared since *Tillie's Punctured Romance* at Keystone. Charlie caring for an abandoned child with loving tenderness is a far cry from his carrying around a baby by the scruff of its diaper in the Keystone picture *His Trysting Places* (1914). *The Kid* is as much a drama as it is a comedy. Just as Mack Sennett had to augment his style when directing his first feature-length film, *Tillie's Punctured Romance*, so did Chaplin. But while Sennett merely rested his usual slapstick on a stronger narrative and paced his gags more carefully, Chaplin went for a straight dramatic narrative with comedy highlights.

Chaplin's greatest level of creative control came when he joined with Douglas Fairbanks and Mary Pickford to form United Artists, a studio for independent filmmakers to supervise productions in which they appear. Here Chaplin made his most famous feature-length films, including *The Gold Rush* (1925) and the wonderfully funny *The Circus* (1928).

*The Gold Rush* was Chaplin's most ambitious film up to that time, featuring Charlie surviving in the frozen tundra in a search for gold, with the welcome addition of old Keystone supporting player Mack Swain turning in a career defining performance. *The Circus* is often unfairly overlooked because it is funny without pretense.

Chaplin had been working on *City Lights* since 1929, and by the time it was ready for release in 1931, the talking picture revolution had occurred. While Harold Lloyd hastily added sound effects and dialog to his completed silent *Welcome Danger* (1929), Chaplin refused to add dialog to *City Lights* and decided to release it as a silent. The story of Charlie working to help a blind girl who desperately needs money was a far more dramatic comedy than even *The Kid* had been. Recalling how Keystone Charlie responded to infirmity (e.g., the wheelchair-bound man in *His New Profession*), it is interesting to see how the screen character of Charlie has evolved by the time he made his brilliant feature.

Theater critic Alexander Woollcott reviewed *City Lights* in his book *While Rome Burns* and had this to say about the talking picture revolution:

> I suppose I should break down at this point and admit that if there is one thing I cannot abide in this raucous age it is the transitory monstrosity known as the talkie. This aversion is essentially undebatable, just as I could never explain to the manufacturer who put out

a Venus de Milo with a clock in her stomach that he had, to my no-
tion, got hold of a bad idea. The fact that the public has clasped to
its multitudinous bosom this movie without a single spoken syllable
in all its crowded length is no proof that the talkie is doomed or even
on the wane, and no proof that any other player would be accepted
at his face value.

Many believed that sound pictures were a novelty, and that silents would
continue to be produced. However, by the 1930s, it was obvious that talking
pictures had eclipsed the silent cinema. People like Alexander Woollcott (and
Chaplin) insisted that silent films from any country could be shown without
a language barrier, simply by changing the intertitles. The idea of talkies with
subtitles or dubbed was not considered. Talking pictures did have their share
of casualties. Many top stars of the silent era did not have the right voice for
sound films (too high pitched, low pitched, accents, etc). By the time Chaplin
produced *Modern Times* in 1936, silent movies were already considered archaic.
However, this film's lack of dialog did not hurt its success, proving Chaplin's
continued popularity.

Chaplin finally conceded his battle with talking pictures by 1940 with *The
Great Dictator*. Playing two roles—an innocent Jewish barber and fascist dictator
Adenoid Hynkel, a variation on Adolf Hitler, Chaplin created a very funny satire
in what may be his last truly great movie. His subsequent films were interesting
artistic failures. *Monsieur Verdoux, Limelight,* and *A King in New York* all have
worthwhile moments, but Chaplin's indulgence had, by this time, become intrusive to his achievement. In these later films, the silent-screen veteran embraces
dialog a bit too much, as he talks (and talks) his way through these roles. There
is still a lot of humor, and a great deal of heart, but Chaplin also felt the need to
be preachy, overlong, and self-gratifying.

Chaplin made *A Countess from Hong Kong* in 1967, with Marlon Brando
and Sophia Loren in the leading roles. In an era where cinema was being challenged by the likes of *Bonnie and Clyde* and *The Graduate*, Chaplin's quiet
simplicity seemed quaint at best. Penning his autobiography, hoping to some-
day make another film, Chaplin kept his fertile mind busy until his death on
Christmas Day in 1977.

As a true icon of film and the most noted representation of the silent era,
Charlie Chaplin is important enough to be studied at all levels. This brilliant career, featuring some of the most important films in movie history, had its genesis
at Mack Sennett's Keystone studio. Some of the best Keystone films, including
*His Trysting Places* and *Dough and Dynamite*, can hold their own against any of
the films Chaplin produced in his long career. There are often two schools of
thought on Chaplin. Some dismiss the groundbreaking short films for Keystone,
Essanay, and Mutual, reserving their enthusiasm for the likes of such features

as *The Kid*, *The Gold Rush*, *City Lights*, and *Modern Times*. The talkies are uniformly perceived as interesting but dismissible, as unrewarding a culmination to his career as the silent shorts are at its genesis.

However, Chaplin's early films are often among his strongest, and the importance of his Keystone work should not be dismissed. The raw, primitive, early experiments with his character and his perception of comedy on film reveal some of the most creative, innovative ideas of their time. The Keystone films featuring Charlie Chaplin are the foundation of virtually any comedy movie made since.

# Appendix A: Supporting Players in Chaplin Keystone Comedies

**Phyllis Allen (1861–1938)**

Allen was the prototypical homely battle axe in such Chaplin films as *The Rounders* and *Getting Acquainted*, specializing in such roles throughout her Keystone career. Having started in vaudeville, she continued in films until her retirement in 1928. Chaplin would use her in his post-Keystone films such as *The Vagabond* (Mutual, 1916), *Pay Day* (First National, 1921), and *The Pilgrim* (First National, 1922).

**Roscoe "Fatty" Arbuckle (1887–1933)**

One of the leading comedians of the silent era, Arbuckle showed his cleverness and creativity in his work for Keystone and later in Joseph Schenck's Comique productions. His career was ruined in 1921 when he went through a very public trial for the rape and murder of actress Virginia Rappe. Although acquitted, Arbuckle could only sustain employment by directing under the pseudonym William Goodrich. He later made a comeback in sound two-reelers at Warner Brothers in 1932 but died the following year. Throughout the trial, Chaplin remained vocally supportive of Arbuckle's innocence in the press. Appearing in such Chaplin Keystones as *His New Profession* and *A Film Johnnie*, Arbuckle was Chaplin's co-star in *The Rounders*. He also appeared opposite Mabel Normand in several popular films. Later at Comique, he introduced Buster Keaton to the screen. He frequently directed his own subjects.

**Cecile Arnold (1893–1931)**

Flirty, blonde, and attractive, Arnold appeared with Chaplin in many Keystones, including *The Property Man*, *Those Love Pangs*, *The Face on the Bar Room Floor*, and *Gentlemen of Nerve*. She left Keystone in 1914 but returned for a stint in 1917.

## Glen Cavendar (1883–1962)

Chaplin's assistant director, Cavendar also acted in several Keystones, including the Chaplin films *Cruel, Cruel Love* and *Tillie's Punctured Romance*.

## Charley Chase (see Charles Parrott).

## Chester Conklin (1886–1971)

Chaplin's nemesis on screen and dear friend off screen, Conklin had a formidable career from silent comedies to sound films through the 1960s. Billed as Walrus because of his mustache, Conklin would often be at odds with Charlie, including in such films as *Dough and Dynamite* and *Tillie's Punctured Romance*. Chaplin would continue to use Conklin's services as late as his first talkie, *The Great Dictator* (1940). Conklin would later appear with such comedians as the Three Stooges and Jerry Lewis.

## Jess Dandy (1874–1923)

A heavyset actor, Dandy appeared in many Chaplin Keystones, including *The Property Man*, *The Face on the Bar Room Floor*, and *His New Profession*. Initially a stage performer, Dandy returned to Broadway after his 1914 Keystone stint. He died while appearing in the play *Just Married in Boston*.

## Marie Dressler (1869–1934)

Famous in the Chaplin legacy by starring in Mack Sennett's groundbreaking feature *Tillie's Punctured Romance*, stage actress Dressler could not parlay that film's success into a movie career during the silent era. Her big break came when she appeared in Greta Garbo's first talkie, *Anna Christie* (1930), in a role that earned her great recognition. She won a Best Actress Oscar for *Min and Bill* that same year. Appearing in many more films and enjoying major movie stardom, Dressler succumbed to breast cancer in 1934, still among the most popular performers in cinema.

## Minta Durfee (1889–1975)

Married to Roscoe Arbuckle, Durfee was a Keystone regular, appearing in many of the studio's films, including such Chaplin comedies as *Cruel, Cruel Love*, *The Star Boarder*, and *Twenty Minutes of Love*. Durfee remained active as late as 1971, appearing in the film *Willard* that year.

## Ted Edwards (1883–1945)

Edwards had small bit parts in several Chaplin Keystones, usually as a cop, a bystander, or a customer in a diner. He would later appear with Chaplin in *A Dog's Life* (1921) in a small role. He left movies in 1922 and became a woodworker and contractor.

**Billy Gilbert (1891–1961)**
Spending three years at Keystone, the diminutive Gilbert appeared often with Chaplin, including in such films as *Cruel, Cruel Love*, *The Star Boarder*, *His Trysting Places*, and *Tillie's Punctured Romance*, usually in small roles. After leaving Keystone in 1916, he would return to Sennett in 1918 and then again in the 1920s. Often Gilbert would play several small roles in one film. He is not to be confused with comedy actor Billy Gilbert (1894–1971) who appeared in such film's as Laurel and Hardy's *The Music Box* (1932) or *His Girl Friday* (1940). However, when the Keystone Billy Gilbert died, the wife of the other Gilbert (then still active in films and TV) received several sympathy cards.

**Gordon Griffith (1907–1958)**
As a child actor, Griffith appeared in many Keystones over a 14-month period, including with Chaplin in *The Star Boarder*, *Caught in a Cabaret*, and *Tillie's Punctured Romance* (in a role comedian Milton Berle always claimed to have played). His other films include *Tarzan of the Apes* (1918), *Huckleberry Finn* (1920), and *Little Annie Rooney* (1925). He later worked as a producer.

**Bill Hauber (1891–1929)**
Hauber appeared in Keystone films between 1912 and 1916, including with Chaplin in such films as *Cruel, Cruel Love*, *The Thief Catcher*, and *His New Profession*. He later acted as comedian Larry Semon's stunt double. He was killed in an airplane crash while scouting locations for the 1929 film *The Aviator*.

**Alice Howell (1888–1961)**
Howell appeared in bit parts in some Chaplin Keystones, her biggest role probably as the dentist's wife in *Laughing Gas*. She later worked for Keystone alumnus Henry Lehrman in his LKO comedies before establishing her own production company. After her company went bankrupt, she appeared in a few character roles in features into the mid-1920s, eventually going into real estate.

**George Jeske (1891–1951)**
A bit player in a handful of Chaplin Keystones, Jeske appeared in such films as *The Thief Catcher*, *Tango Tangles*, and *The Property Man*. He later became a writer and director for films and radio. When his health began to fail, he left movie work and managed a theater in Indigo, California, until his death.

**Edgar Kennedy (1890–1948)**
One of the original Keystone Cops, Kennedy had a long, illustrious career in movie comedies from the silent era through the 1940s. Appearing often with Chaplin in such films as *His Favorite Pastime*, *Caught in a Cabaret*, *Cruel,*

*Cruel Love*, and *Tillie's Punctured Romance*, Kennedy later worked at the Hal Roach studios as an actor and sometimes director. He then starred in his own series of two-reel comedies at RKO. He remained active with this series until his death.

### Virginia Kirtley (1883–1956)
Noted as being Chaplin's first leading lady, playing the female lead in *Making a Living*, Kirtley was to appear in no other Chaplin films. (She did not play the object of his affection in *A Film Johnnie* as has been erroneously reported.) She kept working in silent films until 1928. She was married to comedian Eddie Lyons, then married actor Eddie Fetherston after Lyons died in 1926.

### Grover Ligon (1885–1965)
Appearing in small roles in many Keystone films, including with Chaplin in such shorts as *Mabel's Married Life*, *Caught in a Cabaret*, *The Masquerader*, *Those Love Pangs*, and *Mabel at the Wheel*, Ligon was frequently in demand as a stuntman. Like many actors who came to Hollywood when it was in the early stages of growth, he went into real estate with some measure of success. He retired from films in 1938 to concentrate on his real estate business.

### Wallace MacDonald (1891–1978)
Playing bit roles in such Chaplin Keystones as *The Star Boarder*, *Caught in a Cabaret*, *Mabel's Married Life*, and *The Face on the Bar Room Floor*, MacDonald continued to act into the talking picture era. He later became a writer, director, and producer. He produced many films for Columbia Pictures' B-movie unit, remaining active to the end of the 1950s.

### Hank Mann (1887–1971)
A veteran Keystone Cop, Mann had a long and distinguished career in films that lasted into the 1960s. He appeared with performers ranging from Abbott and Costello to the Three Stooges to Jerry Lewis. Having only tiny bit roles and extra work in such Chaplin Keystones as *Caught in a Cabaret*, *Mabel's Married Life*, and *Tillie's Punctured Romance*, Mann made a greater impression appearing in the comedian's later films in roles such as the tough fighter Charlie must face in *City Lights* (1931).

### Harry McCoy (1889–1937)
Appearing in many silent comedies for various studios, McCoy had a stint at Keystone in such Chaplin films as *Mabel at the Wheel*, *His New Profession*, *The Masquerader*, and *Tillie's Punctured Romance*. He was working as a writer and gag man for the Walt Disney studios when he died at age 47.

### Charlie Murray (1872–1941)

A star in his own right at Keystone, Murray appeared with Chaplin in such films as *The Masquerader, His New Profession*, and *Tillie's Punctured Romance*. Murray remained active in films until the end of the 1930s. He achieved some of his biggest success in a series opposite George Sidney called *The Cohens and the Kellys*, which ran from the late silent into the early talkie era.

### Norma Nichols (1894–1989)

Appearing with Chaplin at Keystone in *The Property Man* and *Dough and Dynamite*, Nichols remained active in films until the mid-1920s, supporting such comedians as Ham and Bud (Lloyd Hamilton and Bud Duncan) at Kalem studios and Larry Semon at Vitagraph. She was still living in Los Angeles when she died at age 95.

### Eddie Nolan (1888–1943)

A supporting player and assistant director at Keystone, Nolan appeared with Chaplin as the bartender in *The Face on the Bar Room Floor* and reportedly essayed four different roles in *Tillie's Punctured Romance*. Sustaining a serious head injury as a child that affected his mental state, Nolan was noted for succumbing to violent rages. In 1931, he was arrested for beating a girlfriend to death. He was sentenced to life in prison, was paroled in 1942, and died a year later.

### Mabel Normand (1892–1930)

One of the true shining lights of the Keystone studio, Normand was already something of a movie veteran when Chaplin arrived at Sennett's production company in 1914. However, Chaplin's enormous popularity eclipsed hers, causing her to be referred to as the Female Chaplin. In her films, she displays amazing prowess as an actress. She is also one of the very first women to direct films, helping Chaplin learn the rudiments of the process when he became interested in directing. Appearing in many Chaplin Keystones, often as his co-star, and directing a few of them herself, Normand was even better known for her co-starring stints opposite Roscoe Arbuckle, including in the classic *Fatty and Mabel Adrift* (1916). Beset by scandal in her private life, she had problems with drugs and alcohol. Normand and Sennett never married but remained a couple for many years; she married actor Lew Cody in 1926. She only lived to be 37.

### Frank Opperman (1861–1922)

Playing in some of the first Keystones as far back as 1912, Opperman essayed several roles in *Tillie's Punctured Romance*, including the justice of the peace. He appeared in small roles in such Chaplin Keystones as *Mabel's Busy Day, The Property Man, The Face on the Bar Room Floor*, and *Gentlemen of Nerve*.

## Peggy Page

A supporting performer in a number of Chaplin films, Page was for a long time lost to history. Page's identity was discovered by film historian Steve Rydzewski in 2011 after years of research; she had previously been incorrectly identified as Helen Carruthers. Probably her best role in Chaplin Keystones was as the innocent dental patient Charlie flirts with in *Laughing Gas*. She also appeared with him as the secretary in *The New Janitor* and as Clarice in *His Trysting Places*, and she had several smaller roles in films such as *Recreation*, *Mabel's Busy Day*, *Gentlemen of Nerve*, and *His New Profession*.

## Charles Parrott (Charley Chase) (1893–1940)

Starting out as a comedian at Keystone, the talented Parrott later did his first directing at the studio. Appearing with Chaplin in such films as *His New Profession* and *Gentlemen of Nerve*, Parrott later went to the Hal Roach studios and, as Charley Chase, became the star of a long-running series of short comedies that extended into the 1930s. Chase left Roach for Columbia in 1936, appearing in comedies for that studio until his death. While at Columbia, Chase also directed several films, including some of the noted Three Stooges comedies such as *Mutts to You* and *Violent Is the Word for Curly* (both 1938). When he died in 1940, movie theater owners throughout the United States sent notes to the periodical *Motion Picture Herald* expressing their sadness that his popular short comedies would no longer be.

## Peggy Pearce (1894–1975)

In his autobiography, Chaplin said Pearce was his first big Hollywood romance. She appeared as the object of his affection in *A Film Johnnie* and was in a few more of his Keystone efforts. Pearce left acting at the end of the 1910s but worked in the Warner Brothers wardrobe department.

## Al St. John (1893–1963)

An acrobatic comedy actor, and nephew to Roscoe Arbuckle, St. John appeared with Chaplin in very small roles at Keystone in such films as *His Prehistoric Past* and *Tillie's Punctured Romance*. He did perhaps his best work when he left Sennett's studio with Arbuckle for the Comique shorts. St. John became a popular western sidekick in low-budget cowboy films featuring Buster Crabbe and Lash LaRue. Crabbe told this author in 1980, "The only good thing about those western quickies I did was having the best sidekick in the business." St. John left films at the end of the 1940s but remained active in rodeos doing bicycle tricks and other stunts. He was on tour when he died.

### Fritz Schade (1879–1926)

The rotund Schade supported Chaplin in such Keystones as *Laughing Gas* and *The Property Man*. He is not the father of actress Betty Schade, although her father did have the same name.

### Ford Sterling (1880–1939)

One of the top comedians of cinema's early years, Sterling came with Sennett from Biograph and quickly became the new Keystone company's biggest comedy star. He left Keystone for Henry Lehrman's LKO production company in 1914 but returned to Sennett two more times (1915–1917 and 1918–1920). Having had stage experience before entering films in 1912, Sterling eventually began freelancing in top-level features during the 1920s, doing an especially fine job in the title role of *The Show Off* (1926). He made some appearances in talkies during the 1930s, re-creating his famous Keystone Cop role as police chief in *Keystone Hotel* (1935), a Warner Brothers short comedy re-creating the Sennett slapstick with old favorites like Sterling, Ben Turpin, Chester Conklin, and Marie Prevost. Suffering from myriad health problems in the later 1930s, Sterling had a leg amputated due to thrombosis in 1939 and died later that year.

### George "Slim" Summerville (1892–1946)

Appearing in bit roles in several Chaplin Keystones (usually as a cop, a spectator, man on the street, etc.), Summerville graduated to starring roles in Keystone comedies by 1916. He left Keystone for Fox Sunshine comedies in 1918, where he acted and, beginning in 1920, directed. He remained very active in silent comedies and later in more dramatic roles in sound feature films such as *All Quiet on the Western Front* (1930) and with Shirley Temple in *Captain January* (1936).

### Mack Swain (1876–1935)

Swain, at 6 feet 2 inches and with a 240-pound frame, seemed gargantuan opposite the diminutive Charlie in numerous Chaplin Keystones. Chaplin liked this contrast and used Swain frequently. He became famous for playing Ambrose in his own starring series of Keystone comedies. Swain's most noted performance would come after Chaplin left Keystone and hired him for a major role in his United Artists feature *The Gold Rush* (1925). Swain was traveling with his wife, visiting friends, when he died of an internal hemorrhage at the age of 59.

### Josef Swickard (1866–1940)

Perhaps best known by silent film buffs as having played Rudolph Valentino's father in *Four Horsemen of the Apocalypse* (1921), Swickard also appeared in several Chaplin Keystones, most notably as Mabel's father in *Caught in a Cabaret* and Charlie's abused assistant in *The Property Man*.

# Appendix B: Chaplin's Post-Keystone Films

## Essanay Productions

Written and directed by Chaplin. All two reels in length unless noted.

### 1915

*His New Job* (released February 1): Ben Turpin, Leo White, Charlotte Mineau

*A Night Out* (released February 15): Ben Turpin, Bud Jamison, Edna Purviance, Leo White

*The Champion* (released March 11): Edna Purviance, Ernest Van Pelt, Bud Jamison, Leo White, Ben Turpin

*In the Park* (released March 18—one reel): Edna Purviance, Bud Jamison, Leo White, Leona Anderson

*A Jitney Elopement* (released April 1): Edna Purviance, Ernest Van Pelt, Leo White, Lloyd Bacon, Paddy McGuire

*The Tramp* (released April 11): Edna Purviance, Ernest Van Pelt, Lloyd Bacon, Paddy McGuire, Leo White, Bud Jamison

*By the Sea* (released April 29—one reel): Billy Armstrong, Margie Reiger, Edna Purviance, Bud Jamison, Snub Pollard

*Work* (released June 21): Edna Purviance, Charles Inslee, Marta Golden, Billy Armstrong, Leo White

*A Woman* (released July 12): Edna Purviance, Charles Inslee, Marta Golden, Margie Reiger, Billy Armstrong

*The Bank* (released August 9): Edna Purviance, Charles Inslee, Carl Stockdale, Billy Armstrong

*Shanghaied* (released October 4): Edna Purviance, Billy Armstrong, Fred Goodwins, Paddy McGuire

*A Night at the Show* (released November 20): Fred Goodwins, Paddy McGuire, James T. Kelley, Dee Lampton

## 1916

*Police* (released March 27): Edna Purviance, Bud Jamison, Paddy McGuire, Snub Pollard

*Burlesque on Carmen* (released April 16—a four-reel version was released with added scenes): Edna Purviance, John Rand, Ben Turpin, Leo White, Jack Henderson

*Triple Trouble:* Film put together by Essanay from Chaplin outtakes and new footage

# Mutual Studios

Written and directed by Chaplin, all two reels in length.

## 1916

*The Floorwalker* (released May 15): Edna Purviance, Eric Campbell, Charlotte Mineau

*The Fireman* (released June 12): Edna Purviance, Eric Campbell, Albert Austin, Leo White

*The Vagabond* (released July 10): Edna Purviance, Eric Campbell

*One A.M.* (released August 7): Albert Austin

*The Count* (released September 4): Edna Purviance, Eric Campbell

*The Pawnshop* (released October 2): Edna Purviance, Albert Austin, Eric Campbell

*Behind the Screen* (released November 13): Edna Purviance, Eric Campbell

*The Rink* (released December 4): Edna Purviance, Eric Campbell, Henry Bergman

## 1917

*Easy Street* (released January 22): Edna Purviance, Eric Campbell

*The Cure* (released April 16): Edna Purviance, Eric Campbell, Henry Bergman

*The Immigrant* (released June 17): Edna Purviance, Eric Campbell

*The Adventurer* (released October 23): Edna Purviance, Eric Campbell

# First National Films

Written and directed by Chaplin.

## 1918

*A Dog's Life* (released April 14—three reels): Albert Austin, Sydney Chaplin, Henry Bergman

*Shoulder Arms* (released October 20—three reels): Edna Purviance, Syd Chaplin, Henry Bergman, Albert Auston

## 1919

*Sunnyside* (released June 15—two reels): Edna Purviance, Tom Wilson, Henry Bergman, Loyal Underwood

*A Day's Pleasure* (released December 7—two reels): Edna Purviance, Jackie Coogan

## 1921

*The Kid* (released February 6—six reels): Jackie Coogan, Edna Purviance, Carl Miller, Lita Grey

*The Idle Class* (released September 25—two reels): Edna Purviance, Mack Swain, Henry Bergman, Lita Grey

## 1922

*Pay Day* (released April 2—two reels): Phyllis Allen, Mack Swain, Edna Purviance

## 1923

*The Pilgrim* (released February 25—four reels): Edna Purviance, Syd Chaplin, Mack Swain

# United Artists

Written and directed by Chaplin.

*A Woman of Paris* (1923; released October 1—84 minutes): Adolphe Menjou, Edna Purviance

*The Gold Rush* (1925; released August 16—82 minutes): Georgia Hale, Mack Swain

*The Circus* (1928; released January 7—71 minutes): Merna Kennedy, Allen Garci

*City Lights* (1931; released February 6—87 minutes): Virginia Cherrill, Harry Myers

*Modern Times* (1936; released February 5—87 minutes): Paulette Goddard

*The Great Dictator* (1940; released October 15—126 minutes): Paulette Goddard, Reginald Gardner

*Monsieur Verdoux* (1947; released April 11—123 minutes): Martha Raye, Marilyn Nash

*Limelight* (1952; released October 23—143 minutes): Claire Bloom, Buster Keaton

*A King in New York* (1957; released September 12, but not seen in the United States until 1973—110 minutes): Dawn Addams, Michael Chaplin

*A Countess from Hong Kong* (1967; released January 5—108 minutes): Marlon Brando, Sophia Loren

Chaplin also made guest appearances in the films *The Nut* (United Artists, 1921), *Hollywood* (Paramount, 1923), and *Show People* (MGM, 1928). He appeared in the half-reel subject *The Bond for the Liberty Loan Committee* in 1918, having also written and directed the film.

# Bibliography

## Books

Agee, James. *Agee on Film: Reviews and Comments.* Boston: Beacon, 1964.

Ankerich, Michael G. *Broken Silence.* Jefferson, N.C.: McFarland, 1993.

Arvidson, Linda. *When the Movies Were Young.* New York: Benjamin Blom, 1925.

Asplund, Uno. *Chaplin's Films.* New York: A.S. Barnes, 1976.

Bengston, John. *Silent Traces: Discovering Early Hollywood through the Films of Charlie Chaplin.* Santa Monica, Calif.: Santa Monica Press, 2006.

Blum, Daniel. *A Pictorial History of the Silent Screen.* New York: G.P. Putnam, 1953.

Brownlow, Kevin. *Hollywood: The Pioneers.* New York: Alfred A. Knopf, 1979.

———. *The Parade's Gone By.* New York: University of California Press, 1968.

Cassara, Bill. *Edgar Kennedy, Master of the Slow Burn.* Boalsburg, Pa.: Bear Manor Media, 2005.

Chaplin, Charles. *My Autobiography.* London: Bodley Head, 1964.

———. *My Life in Pictures.* London: Bodley Head, 1974.

D'Agostino, Annette M. *Filmmakers in the Moving Picture World.* Jefferson, N.C.: McFarland, 1997.

Doyle, Billy. *The Ultimate Directory of Silent and Sound Era Performers.* Metuchen, N.J.: Scarecrow, 1999.

Durgnat, Raymond. *The Crazy Mirror: Hollywood Comedy and the American Image.* New York: Horizon, 1969.

Fowler, Gene. *Father Goose: The Story of Mack Sennett.* New York: Covici, Friede, 1934.

Fussell, Betty Harper. *Mabel.* New York: Ticknor and Fields, 1982.

Geduld, Harry M. *Chapliniana Vol. 1: The Keystone Films.* Bloomington: University of Indiana Press, 1987.

Gifford, Denis. *Chaplin.* London: Macmillan, 1974.

Goldwyn, Samuel. *Behind the Screen.* New York: Doran, 1923.

Huff, Theodore. *Charlie Chaplin.* New York: Henry Shuman, 1951.

Jacobs, Lewis. *The Rise of the American Film.* New York: Harcourt, Brace, 1939.

Kerr, Walter. *The Silent Clowns*. New York: Alfred A. Knopf, 1975.

Kiehn, David. *Broncho Billy and the Essanay Company*. Berkeley, Calif.: Farwell, 2003.

Lahue, Karlton. *Mack Sennett's Keystone*. New York: A.S. Barnes, 1971.

———. *The World of Laughter: The Motion Picture Comedy Short 1910–1930*. Norman: University of Oklahoma Press, 1966.

Lahue, Karlton, and Terry Brewer. *Kops and Custards: The Legend of the Keystone Films*. Norman: University of Oklahoma Press, 1968.

Lahue, Karlton, and Samuel Gill. *Clown Princes and Court Jesters*. New York: A.S. Barnes, 1970.

Louvish, Simon. *Keystone: The Life and Clowns of Mack Sennett*. London: Faber and Faber, 2004.

Maltin, Leonard. *The Great Movie Comedians*. New York: Harmony, 1978.

Manvell, Roger. *Chaplin*. Boston: Little, Brown, 1974.

Mast, Gerald. *The Comic Mind: Comedy and the Movies*. Indianapolis: Bobbs-Merrill, 1973.

———. *A Short History of the Movies*. New York: Bobbs-Merrill, 1971.

McCabe, John. *Charlie Chaplin*. Garden City, N.Y.: Doubleday, 1978.

McCaffrey, Donald. *Four Great Comedians: Chaplin, Lloyd, Keaton, Langdon*. New York: A.S. Barnes, 1968.

McDonald, Gerald D., Michael Conaway, and Mark Ricci. *The Films of Charlie Chaplin*. New York: Citadel, 1965.

Minus, Johnny, and William S. Hale. *Film Superlist: 20,000 Motion Pictures in the Public Domain*. Hollywood, Calif.: Seven Arts, 1973.

Mitchell, Glenn. *A–Z of Silent Film Comedy*. London: Batsford, 1998.

———. *The Chaplin Encyclopedia*. London: B.T. Batsford, 1997.

Neibaur, James L. *Movie Comedians: The Complete Guide*. Jefferson, N.C.: McFarland, 1986.

———. *Chaplin at Essanay*. Jefferson, N.C.: McFarland, 2008.

Niver, Kemp. *Early Motion Pictures: The Paper Print Collection of the Library of Congress*. Washington, D.C.: Library of Congress, 1985.

Oderman, Stuart. *Roscoe "Fatty" Arbuckle: A Biography of the Silent Film Comedian, 1887–1933*. Jefferson, N.C.: McFarland, 1994.

Okuda, Ted, and David Maska. *Charlie Chaplin at Keystone and Essanay*. Lincoln, Neb.: iUniverse, 2005.

Quigley, Isabel. *Charlie Chaplin: Early Comedies*. London: Studio Vista, 1968.

Reeves, May, and Claire Goll. *The Intimate Charlie Chaplin*. Translated, edited, and introduction by Constance Brown Kuriyama. Jefferson, N.C.: McFarland, 2001.

Robinson, David. *Chaplin: His Life and Art*. New York: McGraw-Hill, 1985.

Sennett, Mack. *King of Comedy*. Garden City, N.Y.: Doubleday, 1954.

Sherk, Warren M., compiler and editor. *The Films of Mack Sennett: Credit Documentation from the Mack Sennett Collection at the Margaret Herrick Library*. Lanham, Md.: Scarecrow, 1998.

Slide, Anthony. *The American Film Industry*. Westport, Conn.: Greenwood, 1986.

———. *Silent Players: A Biographical and Autobiographical Study of 100 Silent Film Actors and Actresses*. Lexington: University Press of Kentucky, 2002.

Stewart, William T., Arthur McClure, and Ken D. Jones. *International Film Necrology*. New York: Garland, 1981.

Tyler, Parker. *Chaplin: Last of the Clowns*. New York: Vanguard, 1947.

Vance, Jeffrey. *Chaplin: Genius of the Cinema*. New York: Harry N. Abrams, 2003.

Vazzana, Eugene. *The Silent Film Necrology*. Jefferson, N.C.: McFarland, 2001.

Walker, Brent. *Mack Sennett's Fun Factory*. Jefferson, N.C.: McFarland, 2010.

White, Wendy Warwick. *Ford Sterling: The Life and Films*. Jefferson, N.C.: McFarland, 2007.

Woollcott, Alexander. *While Rome Burns*. New York: Viking, 1934.

# Articles

"As a Dramatic Critic Sees Us." *Moving Picture World*, November 13, 1915.

"Chaplin Leaves Keystone." *New York Daily Mirror*, December 23, 1914.

"Chaplin's Unique Career." *Washington Post*, October 3, 1915.

"Charlie Chaplin in a Serious Mood." *Motography*, January 16, 1915.

"Charlie Chaplin's Story." *Photoplay Magazine*, July 1915.

# Internet Sources

Internet Movie Database, www.imdb.com

www.silentcomedians.com

alt.movies.comedy.charlie-chaplin usenet discussion group

alt.movies.silent usenet discussion group

# Index

# About the Author

**James L. Neibaur** is a film historian and professional educator. He has written hundreds of articles, including reviews and feature stories. He has more than forty entries in the *Encyclopedia Britannica* on subjects as diverse as Catherine Deneuve, Steve Martin, and film noir. His books include *Chaplin at Essanay: A Film Artist in Transition* (2008) and *The Fall of Buster Keaton* (2010, Scarecrow).